1,000,000 Books

are available to read at

Forgotten Books

www.ForgottenBooks.com

Read online
Download PDF
Purchase in print

ISBN 978-1-334-71202-9
PIBN 10602928

This book is a reproduction of an important historical work. Forgotten Books uses state-of-the-art technology to digitally reconstruct the work, preserving the original format whilst repairing imperfections present in the aged copy. In rare cases, an imperfection in the original, such as a blemish or missing page, may be replicated in our edition. We do, however, repair the vast majority of imperfections successfully; any imperfections that remain are intentionally left to preserve the state of such historical works.

Forgotten Books is a registered trademark of FB &c Ltd.
Copyright © 2018 FB &c Ltd.
FB &c Ltd, Dalton House, 60 Windsor Avenue, London, SW19 2RR.
Company number 08720141. Registered in England and Wales.

For support please visit www.forgottenbooks.com

1 MONTH OF FREE READING

at

www.ForgottenBooks.com

By purchasing this book you are eligible for one month membership to ForgottenBooks.com, giving you unlimited access to our entire collection of over 1,000,000 titles via our web site and mobile apps.

To claim your free month visit:

www.forgottenbooks.com/free602928

* Offer is valid for 45 days from date of purchase. Terms and conditions apply.

English
Français
Deutsche
Italiano
Español
Português

www.forgottenbooks.com

Mythology Photography **Fiction**
Fishing Christianity **Art** Cooking
Essays Buddhism Freemasonry
Medicine **Biology** Music **Ancient Egypt** Evolution Carpentry Physics
Dance Geology **Mathematics** Fitness
Shakespeare **Folklore** Yoga Marketing
Confidence Immortality Biographies
Poetry **Psychology** Witchcraft
Electronics Chemistry History **Law**
Accounting **Philosophy** Anthropology
Alchemy Drama Quantum Mechanics
Atheism Sexual Health **Ancient History**
Entrepreneurship Languages Sport
Paleontology Needlework Islam
Metaphysics Investment Archaeology
Parenting Statistics Criminology
Motivational

JOHN HARRISON, SURGEON,
FOUNDER OF THE LONDON HOSPITAL

A HISTORY OF
THE LONDON HOSPITAL

BY

E. W. MORRIS

SECRETARY OF THE LONDON HOSPITAL

ILLUSTRATED

SECOND EDITION

LONDON
EDWARD ARNOLD
1910

[All rights reserved]

A HISTORY OF
THE LONDON HOSPITAL

BY

E. W. MORRIS

SECRETARY OF THE LONDON HOSPITAL

ILLUSTRATED

SECOND EDITION

LONDON

EDWARD ARNOLD

1910

[*All rights reserved*]

PREFACE

A PREFACE is often an excuse. If an excuse is necessary for writing this book, I have none to offer except that my love for the old place led me to spend a good deal of time in reading up the minutes of its life, and I then felt that it was a pity that there should be no more accessible history of the Hospital than is obtainable from these voluminous minutes.

But I must also take the opportunity of a Preface for saying that I am alone responsible for every word here written. From the fact that I have been compelled, in writing of the Hospital, to refer to my Chiefs, it was impossible that—beyond obtaining leave to write this History—I could consult anybody about what I should say or how I should say it. I am anxious to make this as clear as possible. I alone am responsible for any sin of omission and of commission.

I wish to express my thanks to three of my fellow-workers at "The London" for their invaluable help—Mr. Arthur G. Elliott, Mr. Walter Richardson, and

Miss Ethel Willis. In the hunting up of faded and dusty records, and in classifying and preparing my own rough notes, these helpers have, I am afraid burned more midnight oil than they have chosen to tell me of. I should like those who may honour me by reading this little book to know of my indebtedness to my three friends.

E. W. M.

LONDON HOSPITAL.

TO THE SECOND EDITION

In response to the request of many friends, a chronology has been added to this Edition. I am indebted to many readers for pointing out certain errors and omissions, which have been corrected.

E. W. M.

CONTENTS

CHAPTER I
A GLANCE AT THE LONDON HOSPITAL TO-DAY	PAGE 1

CHAPTER II
THE SICK POOR AT THE TIME OF THE HOSPITAL'S FOUNDATION	25

CHAPTER III
MEDICINE AND SURGERY AT THE TIME OF THE HOSPITAL'S FOUNDATION	37

CHAPTER IV
EARLY DAYS. PRESCOTT STREET	47

CHAPTER V
THE NEW SITE, WHITECHAPEL	73

CHAPTER VI
SOME CURIOUS POINTS IN HOSPITAL MANAGEMENT	96

CHAPTER VII
QUARTERLY COURTS OF GOVERNORS—HISTORY OF THE JEWISH WARDS	114

CHAPTER VIII
RELATIONS BETWEEN HOUSE COMMITTEE AND STAFF	136

CONTENTS

CHAPTER IX
BREAK OF DAY - - - - - - - 155

CHAPTER X
SUNDRY INCIDENTS AND EVENTS - - 172

CHAPTER XI
THE MEDICAL SCHOOL - - - - - 186

CHAPTER XII
THE NURSING OF THE SICK POOR - - - - 204

CHAPTER XIII
THE LAST TWENTY YEARS - - - 215

CHAPTER XIV
THE ADMINISTRATION OF A MODERN HOSPITAL - - 235

CHAPTER XV
THE FUTURE OF VOLUNTARY HOSPITALS - - - 269

CONCLUSION - - - 286

CHRONOLOGY - - - .. - - - 293

INDEX - - - - - - 315

LIST OF ILLUSTRATIONS

JOHN HARRISON, SURGEON : FOUNDER OF THE LONDON HOSPITAL		*Frontispiece*
THE WAITING-HALL, OUT-PATIENT DEPARTMENT	*facing page*	10
THE FINSEN LIGHT ROOM	,,	14
IN ONE OF THE CHILDREN'S SURGICAL WARDS	,,	20
PATIENTS' ADMISSION TICKET, 1747	,,	66
HOGARTH'S ORIGINAL DESIGN FOR BACK OF ADMISSION TICKET	,,	66
THE LONDON HOSPITAL IN 1759	,,	80
WILLIAM BLIZARD, F.R.S.	,,	146
A MODERN OPERATING THEATRE	,,	162
THE LONDON HOSPITAL FROM THE BACK	,,	182
THE PRESENT MEDICAL SCHOOL	,,	188
THE LIBRARY IN THE MEDICAL COLLEGE	,,	202
ONE OF THE NURSES' SITTING-ROOMS, NURSES' HOME	,,	210
THE HON. SYDNEY HOLLAND, CHAIRMAN	,,	224
THE BOARD-ROOM	,,	224
BALCONY OF MARIE CELESTE MATERNITY DEPARTMENT	,,	230
LABOUR-ROOM OF MARIE CELESTE MATERNITY DEPARTMENT	,,	230
THE LONDON HOSPITAL FROM WHITECHAPEL ROAD	,,	234
A SUMMER DAY IN THE GROUNDS	,,	268

PLANS OF THE LONDON HOSPITAL

	PAGE
PLAN I.—MARCH 26, 1752	86
PLAN II.—1759	89
PLAN III.—1840	91
PLAN IV.—1886	93
PLAN V.—MODERN TIMES	95

A HISTORY OF THE LONDON HOSPITAL

CHAPTER I

A GLANCE AT THE LONDON HOSPITAL TO-DAY

PROBABLY until recent years the London Hospital was little more than a name to most people who dwelt north, or south, or west of the City. They had heard that there existed a huge hospital somewhere in the East End, but its address, Whitechapel, was not an attractive one. The very name of Whitechapel conjured up in the mind thoughts of dangerous slums, of foreigners of the lowest type wandering from the adjacent docks, of pickpockets, of highway robbery with violence, of murders, and of all kinds of crime.

Recently the Hospital has become better known to the dweller in the West End. He has found that Whitechapel is a place quite easily reached, that he has to pass through no slums to get there; nor, as he comes eastward from the Bank, is he likely to see anything which will shock him. On the contrary, he will see much to arouse his interest and curiosity.

But to the dweller east of Aldgate Pump the London Hospital is to-day a landmark as familiar—probably more so—than is Westminster Abbey or the Marble Arch to the West End inhabitant. He has passed the long ugly building (and whatever boasts "The London" may make, it has never boasted of being good-looking) which faces the Whitechapel Road on his way to and from his work for years. It is the end of the penny bus-fare from the Bank. He invariably glances up, as he passes, at the long lines of windows, with a never-ending curiosity as to what is going on inside. He knows which are the windows of the great operating theatres. He is sure to take notice if they are lighted up or not; if they are, he will probably mention the fact when he gets home, for he looks upon these operating theatres as the very battle-ground between life and death. His father did this before him, his grandfather before that.

But the resident within a one-mile radius of the Hospital—an area which contains a greater population to-day than the whole of London contained when the Hospital was founded—by no means regards the Hospital simply as a landmark. It enters into his life, and is part of it. He has never seen those great front-gates closed, and he never will. Hardly a house within that area but at some time or other has lent a patient to the Hospital, to be coaxed back to health and happiness; not a family but has had father or mother, brother or sister or child, lying within its walls. These people do not simply notice the Hospital: they love it. They understand and appreciate its work. And the love these poor people bear is often mingled with a tenderness most touching; for there, in spite of all that skill and care could do, some loved child or parent passed away. In more than one instance a few flowers are sent year by year to the ward on that sad anniversary. There is no more pathetic proof of this feeling than the way in which hundreds and thousands of the poorest of London's poor will, from year's end to year's end, give a penny a week of their earnings for the help of " the 'Orspital."

A visit to-day is well worth making, and visitors may be assured of a welcome ; and before turning to the ancient history of the Hospital, it may be of interest to follow such a visitor round the building. Having done this, the steady growth of to-day's splendid institution from its very small beginning may be better appreciated.

On leaving Whitechapel Station, which is on the District Railway, and exactly opposite the Hospital, one enters the main gates and walks up the slope to the main entrance. The visitor may be surprised to notice that his arrival at the main entrance is expected. The main entrance and the main gates are in telephonic communication, so that when a " case " enters the main gates, porters with stretchers are in readiness to receive it at the main entrance, to convey it to the Receiving-room. The saving of time is all-important on such occasions. It is to be hoped that the visitor will not make his first entrance to the Hospital as a " case," but his convenience may be served by the system in vogue, and he will not be kept long waiting for a guide.

He will enter first of all the main hall, and on his right is the Receiving-room. This is the great sieve of the Hospital, through which every patient must pass before he can be relieved, either as an in- or out-patient. It is never closed throughout the twenty-four hours, and the seven officers in charge work here in turns day and night. Their duty (they are all senior and highly qualified men) is to find out, not *all* that may be the matter with each patient, but whether the case is a slight one, a serious one, or one which comes between these two extremes, and they must decide what is to become of it. One of three things will happen to the patient, depending on whether his injury or illness is slight, more serious, or very serious. If a slight injury or illness, the patient will be given advice and one supply of medicine or dressing, and sent away. Such cases number seven or eight hundred a day. If more serious, and the patient requires watching and longer treatment, he will be transferred to the Out-patient Department. If it is a matter of life or death, he is taken into the wards at once.

It is interesting to watch these men at work for a few minutes. Half a dozen cases are being examined one after the other quickly; they are all trivial complaints, perhaps—trivial to the Hospital, but not trivial to the man, and may interfere with his work—cut fingers, slight sprains, sore throats, a tooth abscess, and so on. The seventh case to a layman appears to be no worse than the others, but some symptom has necessitated a more thorough examination; some sound in heart or lung has called the special attention of the officer, and he asks: "How long have you had this? Why did you not come before?" Instructions are given for such a patient to attend in the Out-patient Department of the Hospital, in order that he may be thoroughly examined by one or other of the specialists who visit every afternoon, and a course of treatment decided on. It may be that by weekly advice and weekly medicine the wage-earner is enabled to keep at work through the dreaded winter months.

The next case may be more serious still : arrangements must be made for the patient's immediate admission to a bed. The list, showing at that particular minute where the empty beds are, is consulted, and the house physician or house surgeon on "full duty" sent for. Even while this is being arranged there is a stir at the door; a Pickford's van has driven up the slope, and into a private room has been carried a figure on a stretcher. These very serious accidents —"smash-ups"—are not brought into the main Receiving-room, but into a separate room, to avoid alarming the other patients. The officer we have been watching immediately leaves the less urgent cases and passes into the room to examine this serious one. It is a case, perhaps, from the docks—a man has fallen down a ship's hold ; or it is a "run-over," or the result of some explosion, or an attempt at suicide. On one occasion a fully-laden bus dashed up to the main entrance at a gallop. The front passenger on top had attempted suicide by cutting his throat, and the driver, with great presence of mind, had driven full speed through the back streets from the Commercial Road to the Hospital, to the great astonishment of the inside passengers, who did not know what had happened outside. The patient, a Swede, was pulseless on admission, but was immediately attended to in the Receiving-room, and ultimately recovered, undoubtedly saved by the prompt action of the driver. A serious accident arrives at the Hospital's doors almost every five minutes. I shall never forget one scene in this Receiving-room. A man came rushing in, carrying in his arms a little girl; he carried her by the waist, and had evidently been running. Her head and her legs were hanging limp, and I thought she was dead. Her fair hair was like that of a little friend of mine, and it was this that first drew my attention to her. I went up. "Run over?" I asked. "No; she has swallowed something, and it has choked her." The little mite had quite lost consciousness. Receiving-room Officer, Dr. A., ran up. "You'll 'trachey,' I suppose?" I said. "I should like to watch you, if I may." But Dr. A. was a gentleman and a sportsman, and could "pass the ball." "Dr. B. happens to be here," he said; "he is quicker than I am." In twenty seconds Dr. B., who was not on duty, had slipped off his coat. Everybody did something. The Sister was ready with swabs. The tracheotomy set of instruments was at hand. The little limp body was slid along on the table until the head lolled back over the end and the throat was tight. In ten seconds the knife had passed into the windpipe and the tracheotomy tube slipped in. Then came the delightful sound of the air whistling through the tube into the lungs. "Jolly smart," said Dr. A. "I congratulate you; that was fine," I said. But Dr. B. was the coolest man on the house at the time—just washed his hands, put on his coat, and strolled off to lunch.

"Pretty near thing" was all he was heard to say. Within five minutes of coming in the child was in warm blankets in bed. The actual obstruction, a collar-stud, was removed later. The child did well, and is alive now.

Work exactly like this will be going on in the Receiving-room throughout the twenty-four hours from January 1 to December 31.

The examination of the patients here has to be carried out with great despatch; on an average not more than thirty seconds can be given to each. It is astonishing how expert the officers become, and how rarely their diagnosis is set aside when the more thorough examination is made later. Time was when a Receiving-room Officer would enter the room and call out: "All with coughs stand up"; "Now all with stomach-ache stand up"; but that day is long since passed. It might be thought that the work would become monotonous, but if an officer has the saving grace of humour, he will not be dull, and will have great opportunities of studying human nature. A dear old soul—an old woman—enters; obviously she has never been in a Hospital before. After glancing nervously round the crowded room, she appeals anxiously to the Sister-in-Charge, to know, "Where do yer sit for tumours?" Then a man enters who has evidently just emerged from a strenuous street row, and eye and cheek are cut and damaged. "Been fighting?" says the Receiving-room Officer. "Yass!" "'Fraid you've had the worst of it," says the sympathetic officer. "Garn!" says the patient, "the other bloke will be here in a minute; they're bringing him along in a cart."

Here, too, happened what has long since become an old story, and has got into *Punch*. A woman entered with a badly bitten cheek. "A dog, I suppose?" said the Sister. "No," said the woman; "another lidy!" Another patient calls to ask if it is advisable for her to eat vegetables, as she has been told that she has got "haricot" veins in the legs! A woman enters with a black eye, and tells the officer that her husband had done it. "Does he often treat you like this?" asks the officer sympathetically. "No, sir; that's the curious thing about it. He's been more like a pal to me than a husband."

As a rule patients are extremely grateful for any advice and attention given. Recently a coster entered to have a cut stitched, and whispered as he left: "Doctor, where can I leave yer a couple of nice fine 'addicks. I've got a barrer outside, and I shan't miss 'em." Tipping is not allowed at "The London," however. Other patients take everything as a right, and are apparently under the impression that the Hospital is supported by the rates; and only recently one of them addressed the tired and harassed doctor: "It's the likes o' me that keeps the likes o' you, and if it wasn't for us being ill, where would you be?" Needless to say, the Receiving-room Officers are unpaid, the only return being the experience they gain.

The poor in the East End believe that the Hospital can do anything to help them. A Receiving-room Officer was confidentially asked to "take baby into the Hospital for a week, 'cos we're moving, and mother's busy." Many patients, either through visits paid to other Hospitals or from previous visits to this particular one, get very knowing and important about their own ailments. Such patients are a perpetual embarrassment to the Receiving-room Officer. It is certainly surprising to hear a tattered tramp say that he has " a severe pain in the region of the pancreas," or that " my heart drops a beat."

Many patients begin their report on themselves to the officer by the remark, " I am an *inward* case." This is evidently intended to put the doctor on his mettle. One of the commonest of cases which come up to the Receiving-room is that of the young child emaciated and collapsed from wrong feeding. The doctor naturally inquires what the child is being fed on, and we get the oft-quoted and constantly-made reply, " Why, just the same as we 'as ourselves," which in the East End invariably includes beer, pickles, and tea.

Home pets, dogs and cats, are often brought up to the Receiving-room for treatment, and are never turned away. I remember a coster bringing in a dog which he had just seen run over—a dog he had never seen before. He considered it a perfectly natural thing to bring it into the Hospital, which, to his mind, kept its gates open for the relief of all suffering.

The visitor may now pass to another part of the Hospital, the Out-patient Department already referred to, and which is a hundred yards from the main building. Every case he sees here has come through the Receiving-room, as I have already explained. The patients in this Out-patient Department are too ill to send away with one treatment only in the Receiving-room, and yet not sufficiently ill, at their first visit at any rate, to be admitted as in-patients, for into the wards only the very worst cases can go. It is not the question of urgency alone, but of *comparative* urgency, which has to be considered, and therefore there is always a list of several hundred cases waiting to be written for as soon as room can be found.

Every patient who enters the Out-patient Hall must pass the Inquiry Officer, whose duty it is to discover that the patient is a proper person to receive free medical relief. Satisfactory replies must be given to such questions as, "How much are you earning ? How many are dependent on you ? Are you in regular work ? What is your rent ?" and so on. This is necessary for the protection of the private practitioner, and for fairness to the subscribers to the Hospital. Obviously a patient might be a suitable Hospital case if suffering from one disease, but unsuitable if suffering from another. And therefore the Receiving-room Officer, in sending the case to the Out-patient Department, always states on the patient's card what he considers to be the diagnosis. The Inquiry Officer might "pass" the case for phthisis, but refuse it for some trivial ailment.

It may be easily imagined that the greatest tact and sympathy are required on the part of the Inquiry Officer. The dress of the patient is no guide, for many a poverty-stricken girl will actually hire clothes for the day so as to come to the Hospital respectable.

After passing this officer, the patient waits in the Main Hall until called into one of the many rooms to see the surgeon or physician; and after seeing the doctor, and having received advice and treatment,

THE WAITING-HALL, OUT-PATIENT DEPARTMENT

the patient may be referred to one of the Lady Almoners.

A few words concerning the work of these ladies may be necessary. The day has gone by when a Hospital can exist all alone as a unit of charity. Its forces are wasted if it overlaps with other charities, or does not sufficiently avail itself of their help. The Hospital must be a link in a chain. The Lady Almoners link up the Hospital's work with that of other charities. These ladies are trained by the Lady Almoners' Association, and are in touch with various organizations which may be of assistance to the Hospital in its work—Emigration Societies, Labour Bureaux, Sick-room Aid Societies, Societies for Prevention of Cruelty to Children, Convalescent Homes, Associations for the Prevention of Phthisis, Apprenticeship Societies, and so on. When a case comes before a physician—such a case, for instance, as that of some poor girl who spends her time in a garret stitching buttonholes or blouses ("The Song of the Shirt" may still be heard), and who turns out to be suffering from incipient phthisis—the physician would naturally order all sorts of extra diet—meat, cream, and milk, more fresh air, and all the expensive extras a phthisical patient requires. Having done so—and he might just as well have ordered champagne—and given his advice, his strict duty as a Hospital physician ends. He is not in a position to see that his advice is followed, and if it is not, all his care is wasted. He sends, therefore, such a case to the Lady Almoner, who, by her training, can make arrangements for the patient to be provided with the extra food, gets her away to a Convalescent Home or

Sanatorium, and communicates with the Sick-room Aid Society and Health Visitors, or the Jubilee Nursing Association, who instruct the family in order that the disease may not spread. As a matter of fact, before the days of Lady Almoners many a physician helped his patients by dipping into his own pocket. How often have I heard one of them say: "You do not want medicine; you want a steak. Go and get it." Kind as this was, no permanent good was gained. A man must have food every day, not only when he meets a generous sympathizer.

The Out-patient Department contains sub-departments, where specialists attend to treat every disease that flesh is heir to—of the throat, ears, eyes, skin, teeth—as well as the departments for general surgery and medicine. It also contains the now famous Finsen Light Department, which was inaugurated by the Queen, the President of the Hospital, who presented the first lamp, and really introduced into England the cure of lupus by this light. Lupus is a disease which attacks the skin, usually in exposed parts, and is due to the tubercle bacillus—the same bacillus which, when it attacks the lungs, produces ordinary pulmonary consumption.

Finsen found that by focussing intensely powerful light on the part by means of lenses—Finsen at first used sunlight—the bacillus to which the disease was due was destroyed. Two of the members of the staff and two Sisters from the London Hospital went to Copenhagen to study the details of the treatment under Finsen himself. On their return the Light Department was opened, and the tradition of what

THE HOSPITAL TO-DAY 13

they learned has been faithfully handed on from Sister to Sister. When it was known that a cure had been discovered for this fearful disease, poor people from all parts of the world appealed to the Hospital, begging for treatment. They came from New Zealand and South Africa, Canada and South America, as well as from every county in the British Isles. One would hardly have believed that the disease was so common. But those who suffered usually, by reason of the fearful disfigurement, kept themselves hidden away. Now hope, long since abandoned, led them to creep out of their hiding-places. The department was on one day a seething crowd of sufferers. There were cheap excursions from all parts of England for the final Football Cup-tie at the Crystal Palace, and these poor people in hundreds had availed themselves of this cheap trip to come up and be cured. How bitterly disappointed they were I can never forget. Within a month or two of the opening of the department, the lamps were booked forward for two years, and no more patients could be treated. Oh, that awful time, when every post brought letters begging "that my child may be treated before too late," all of which letters had to be answered in the same dreadful way. Some of these letters haunt one still. Speaking of this department, I remember a man walking into the Secretary's office. His face was fearfully disfigured—so much so that it was difficult to look on him and not show the horror one felt, and that is the first duty that everyone who walks in a Hospital must learn. He was a Boer, and spoke broken English. He had come all the way from Johannesburg to the London Hospital to be cured. He had been saving every penny for three years; his friends had helped him a little, too, and he had partly worked his passage. He had landed at the docks with seven shillings left, and walked to the Hospital. He was in a state of great excitement naturally. At last he had reached the place where they could make his flesh become " as the flesh of a little child." He was examined. Two minutes were sufficient. It was not lupus at all. The lamps were powerless. It was another awful disease. That day he was admitted to Whitechapel Infirmary. I saw him some weeks after, and I am convinced that even then it had not clearly entered his mind that he could not have been helped by " The London."

Close by are the Electrical and Röntgen Ray Departments. These departments are always of interest to the lay visitor. In some of the rooms X-ray treatment is given for ringworm, rodent ulcer, and malignant tumour; in another room is the apparatus necessary for taking radiographs. Round the walls are prints of some of the more curious of the cases which have been radiographed—chiefly of articles swallowed by children: pins, penknife blades, nails, watch-keys, safety-pins, little tin soldiers, etc., and in one case a toy bicycle. There is also an interesting photograph of a bullet lodged in a burglar's neck. It was fired by his " pal " because he refused to " shell out " half the proceeds.

It will be noticed that some of the operators in the X-Ray Department have terribly damaged hands. The danger of the X rays was not known until two or

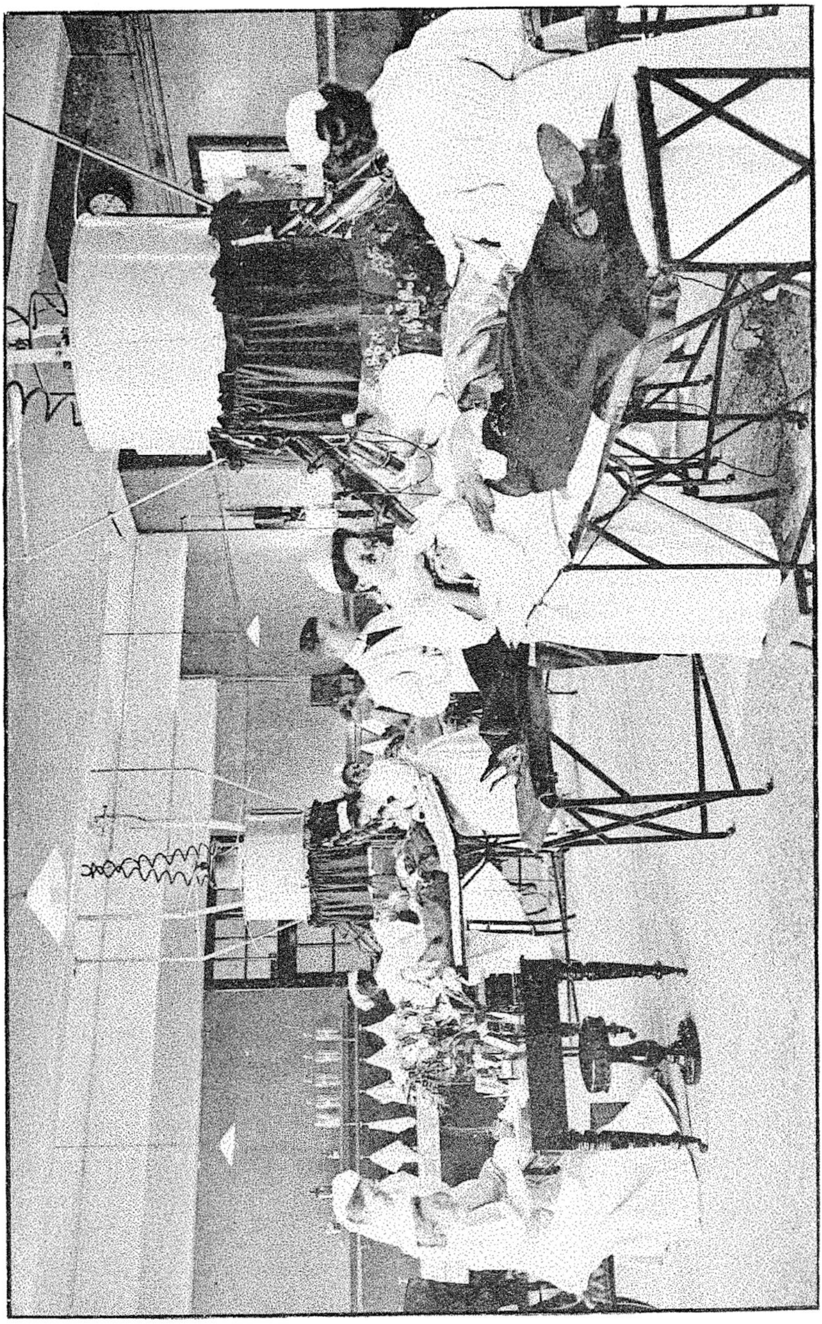

three years after their discovery; then all those who were in the habit of working with them complained that they were beginning to suffer from an extremely painful form of skin inflammation. The original workers all have damaged hands; joint after joint has had to be amputated, and nothing so far has been found which has had any effect in curing the malady. Modern workers run no risk. When the danger of long-continued exposure to X rays became known, a means of lessening—indeed, of removing—the danger was soon discovered. A glass which contains in its composition a certain percentage of lead, added when the glass is in a molten state, entirely prevents the passage of the rays, and the screens which the visitor notices around each X-ray tube are made of this lead-glass. At "The London" a further precaution is taken: it is impossible for the operator even to switch on the current for the X-ray tube except from the inside of a cabinet which is lead-lined.

The "Tyrnauer Baths," for the treatment of rheumatism by hot air, are situated in the Out-patient Building, and are worth a visit. They are the invention of Dr. Tyrnauer, of Carlsbad, who kindly came over and saw them properly installed. There are eight separate baths, cleverly adapted to apply great heat to the various parts of the body—legs, arms, hands, back, neck. The heat is dry, and therefore patients are able to bear a very high temperature—far higher than that of boiling water. Hundreds of patients have been relieved from the pain of rheumatism and rheumatoid arthritis by these baths since they were given to the Hospital by Princess Hatzfeldt at the beginning of

1909. Rheumatism is the curse of the East End poor.

The Pharmacy must also be seen. It is a medicine manufactory rather than a chemist's shop. The department is fully equipped with machinery for making lozenges, tabloids, pills, ointments, tinctures, spirits, ice, and mineral waters, thereby saving expense and insuring purity and accuracy. Here is made a certain magical cough lozenge which is used to the amount of three tons a year. I have heard that they have been seen on certain hawkers' barrows in Middlesex Street on a Sunday being sold at four a penny. But that is nonsense. Patients to whom they are given would not part with them at any price.

At the eight windows of the Dispensary stand long lines of patients, like the queue outside a theatre pit entrance, waiting for their medicines, after having paid their visit to the physician or surgeon.

Every patient who can afford it pays threepence towards the cost of his week's medicine. Children are exempt, so are those who are unemployed or very poor, and also those sent up to the Hospital by an outside private practitioner for a consultant's opinion. The threepence does not pay for the medicine received. I have known a patient tc take away twenty-three shillings' worth of drugs for threepence. There is no cutting down of the cost of medicine at the Hospital; no prescription is tampered with in any way in the Dispensary; what is ordered is given, whatever the cost. The ignorance of the poor as to the nature of medicine may be noted. Patients may sometimes be seen exchanging sips from each other's bottles. The idea seems to be that medicine which has done a patient good is good medicine—a sort of charm—and will do every patient good who is privileged to share it.

Before leaving the Out-patient Department, a visit must be made to the Department for Cripples—the Orthopædic. In no part of the Hospital is more important work done than here, although quite unobtrusively. Crippled children are transformed into ablebodied men and women. Thousands of children are treated here annually, for " The London " has a name for this work, and children are brought from all parts of the country. There ought not to be any cripples, and if there were some powerful organization to relieve crippled children in the very early days there would be none, or, at any rate, none who could not be rendered fit to earn a living. The children are always brought too late.

Having visited the more important parts of the Outpatient Department, where a quarter of a million new patients are seen and treated annually, the visitor will be taken to some of the wards and to other departments. It would be impossible to visit *all* the wards, but those visited may be taken as types of the rest. The walls of many of them are covered with glass tiles, and all have a strikingly cheerful appearance : they are gay with flowers, and laughter is heard more often than groans. Some of the wards are allotted to surgical cases, some to medical, others to children under seven years of age, and some to lying-in cases. It is a mistake to think that a visit to a hospital ward is a sad experience. The majority of the patients are getting well, and are full of hope.

At "The London," and at every good hospital, no patient is simply a case; it is always remembered that "the case" is also a man or a woman or a child. One of the wisest physicians the Hospital ever had was going through the wards with his class, and was questioning one of the students about a case—What did he think was the matter? What should be the treatment and the diet? The student answered correctly as to the complaint, and gave the strictly theoretical treatment, which was a severe one. The physician approved. "Yes, that is quite right for the *case*, but for the *man* I think we will prescribe a little ale with his lunch and a pipe in the garden in a wheel-chair every afternoon."

About the poverty of most of the cases there can be no doubt whatever. The incident has often been told of the starving little child admitted to one of the children's wards, and on being given a cup of warm milk, according to custom, asked that pathetic question, "How far down may I drink, please, Sister?" A cup of milk had to go far at home. The poverty at home can be easily guessed, too, by the remark a little toddler of eight was heard to make to his mother one visiting-day: "Don't let Willie wear out my trousers while I'm in here."

In going round the wards nothing is more touching than the kindly lies which are constantly told, by the wife, for instance, on visiting her sick husband. It is quite obvious that the husband's cure is being delayed by his anxiety as to what was going on at home—Were they starving? Was the rent being paid? Were the children well ? Judging from the replies of these poor women, the entrance of the husband into the Hospital is the sign for the entrance of a fairy godmother into the patient's home. Nothing is more astonishing than the love which the poor bear towards each other, deep and strong, in spite of bad language and sometimes of unkind behaviour. Sir Frederick Treves told me of a poor woman who was brought into the Receiving-room, shockingly burnt. She reported that her husband in a passion of temper had thrown a lighted paraffin lamp at her, and then a second. Obviously she could not live more than an hour, and she was at once removed to one of Sir Frederick's beds, and a magistrate sent for to take her dying depositions. The magistrate arrived and sat by her bedside, but the patient did not speak. The surgeon, knowing that time was short, urged her to say what she had already said to him. At last the patient struggled up, cried, "Why, *I told yer:* it was a pure accident," and fell back dead. It was not what she had told him, however, but it was a splendid lie !

The kindly encouragement which one patient who has been in for some time will give to a newcomer is sometimes amusing. A boy had been in for some time with stricture of the œsophagus, brought on by swallowing in mistake some caustic potash. One of the surgeons saw him daily, and had to keep the œsophagus open by passing sounds. When the patient had been in for some months, another boy was admitted with precisely the same trouble, though from some other cause. The first patient immediately took upon himself to comfort the newcomer. " You'll be all right in 'ere," he said, " Mr. —— will be your surgeon ; he looks after me and the King !"

The Children's Wards are always cheerful, especially the Surgical Wards, and the comments of the children, used all their lives to the squalor of a Whitechapel home, are often entertaining. "What are them?" said one of the children. "Snowdrops," said the Sister. "Well, they're a bit droopified, ain't they?" Another little mite who had been listening to Sister's description of heaven remarked plainly " that *she* did not want to go to heaven, sitting on the marble in her little nightie a-blowin' a trumpet." To dance round a piano-organ was a higher heaven to her.

Many of the cases in these Children's Surgical Wards are accidents from the neighbourhood, and due to the life the poor have to live. If the mother has to leave home all day charing, it is not surprising that the children find their way to the Hospital, and they come in hundreds—run over, scalded, burnt, fallen from windows. One little child came to the Receiving-room and said she felt ill and " did not want to die in mother's bed !"

The most pathetic patients in the Children's Wards are the hip-disease cases. There they lie flat on their backs, week in, week out, and it seems that these little hip children never murmur. Everyone has noticed this. After months in Hospital, they are sent to some Convalescent Home, and eventually return to their homes well—it is to be feared merely to relapse within six months as the result of ignorance, poverty, and dirt. It would be so much more encouraging coaxing these children back to home and health if the homes were

IN ONE OF THE CHILDREN'S SURGICAL WARDS

but worth the going back to and life for them worth the living. Children are splendid patients.

The visitor would perhaps now be shown the Operating Theatres. There are twelve of these for in-patients and four for out-patients. They are perfectly equipped, and are one of the finest suites of theatres in England.

The methods adopted to carry out the principles of aseptic surgery will be more fully described in a later chapter. The Anæsthetic Rooms are distinct from the theatres, so that no patient may see the theatre. Recently (since writing this the tale has been published) a little patient—a boy of ten—in one of these Anæsthetic Rooms, just as he was about to be anæsthetized, was found to be clutching something in his fist. This turned out to be a brass button from the tunic of his father, who was a soldier, and the little chap had grasped this talisman to give him courage in his ordeal. The poor little chap died, however, but bravely.

Then the Kitchens might be visited, where from 1,000 to 1,200 dinners are cooked daily. The methods adopted to deliver these dinners hot and punctual to the minute over a building which covers eight acres would probably interest the visitor.

Then the Jewish Wards would be shown, and a visitor could not but be struck at the very minute arrangements made in order to observe the rites of the Jewish people. These wards have, of course, their separate kitchens and separate food-supplies. The Mazuza on the lintel of the doors should be noticed.

The "Marie Celeste" Lying-In Wards would be shown. These wards are endowed by the liberality of

Mr. James Hora, a Vice-President of the Hospital, in memory of his wife. The good done in this department for the very poor mothers within a mile radius of the Hospital can hardly be overestimated. The London Hospital Maternity Nurses may be seen in every lane and alley at every hour of the day or night. Their uniform passes them safely in the small hours of the morning in slums where a policeman would hardly venture alone in daytime. There has never been an instance of a nurse receiving the slightest insult, although her work lies in a district marked black on Mr. Charles Booth's Map of London.

Every mother confined in the Hospital or in the district attended by our Maternity Nurses is provided with what is known as a "Derby Bundle," owing to the Dowager Countess of Derby's generous gift. These bundles contain warm clothing of the most useful kind.

The clergy and various charitable associations assist the Hospital in making inquiries as to the recipients of this part of the Hospital charity, and every care is taken that the charity is not abused.

This department is one of the registered training centres for the examination of the Central Midwives Board, and forty-eight nurses are trained every year to become midwives.

Then the visitor would be taken to the Nurses' Homes, with accommodation for over 700 nurses. The homes contain Lecture Halls for teaching anatomy, physiology, and sick-room cookery; there are also beautifully fitted recreation-rooms—sitting, reading, and writing. Adjoining one of the Homes is the

Nurses' Garden (usually known as the "Garden of Eden"). The last Nurses' Home erected is called the "Lückes Home." On entering, the following inscription will be noticed :

THE EVA LÜCKES NURSES' HOME,
OPENED 1905.

"By the unanimous vote of the House Committee it was resolved to associate the name of the Matron with this 'Home,' and thereby to commemorate her loyal and devoted service to the London Hospital, and to the improvement of Nursing. This vote was passed in the hope that Miss Eva Lückes' name and work may be gratefully remembered, and in the belief that the high standard which she has established will ever remain as a tradition and example to the Nursing Staff of the London Hospital."

Then the Isolation Block would be pointed out, with wards for infectious cases—measles, diphtheria, erysipelas, scarlet fever, etc.

The Laundry, too, might be visited, with machinery and staff sufficient to wash 10,000 "pieces" daily.

Then a call would be made at the Medical School, and here the Lecture Theatres, Demonstration Rooms, Museums, and Laboratories would be shown.

When the visitor has finished his round he will probably be tired. He will have walked some miles, and will have been astounded at the enormous amount of work carried out in such an institution in the course of a single day. He will be astonished at the smoothness and quietness with which the whole work goes on. Every man has his post, and is at his post ; every man knows his duty, and does it.

The work would, indeed, be overwhelming were it not that it is the growth of years.

Everything which the visitor has seen to-day, and which will be referred to in more detail later, is the result of a little meeting of seven men which took place in the bar-parlour of the Feathers Tavern, Cheapside, in the evening of September 23, 1740, "when," as the old minute quaintly words it, " a motion was made—whether with the sum already subscribed (100 guineas) it would be proper to begin the said Charity. And unanimously agreed it was." A hundred guineas !—that sum would to-day "run" the Hospital from breakfast to dinner time !

But that was a great gathering in the Feathers Tavern, Cheapside.

CHAPTER II

THE SICK POOR AT THE TIME OF THE HOSPITAL'S FOUNDATION

THE names of those who attended this important meeting at the Feathers Tavern on September 23, 1740, should be recorded. They were Mr. John Snee, senr., Mr. Sclater, Mr. Fotherley Baker, Mr. G. Potter, Mr. John Harrison, Mr. Josiah Cole, and Mr. Shute Adams. Evidently there had been previous meetings, for at this one " Mr. Harrison delivered in the lease of the house taken for the *intended* Infirmary, which was approved." They met again on that day week in the same place. At this meeting a man and a woman were engaged to look after the house for £20 a year between them. Mr. John Harrison and Mr. Potter were commissioned to provide furniture "for the doctor's, surgeon's, apothecary's, managers', and patients' rooms for a sum not exceeding £15, and that the Treasurer do pay the bills for the same." The treasurer, doctor, surgeon, and apothecary had not yet been appointed, however. Another meeting was held in the following week, this time at the Baptist Head Tavern in Aldermanbury. Seven persons were again present, three of whom were candidates for the post of surgeon, physician, and apothecary respectively.

Mr. Fotherley Baker was chosen first treasurer, Mr. John Harrison the first surgeon, Dr. Andrée first physician, and Mr. Josiah Cole first apothecary.

The house taken was in Featherstone Street, "near the Dog Bar, for £16 per annum, with liberty to quit the same at six months' notice." It was decided to open this "the intended Infirmary" on the first Monday in November, 1740.

The newly elected apothecary was asked to draw up a list of his wants in "medicines, plaisters, and ointments," and he was to refer such a list to those subscribers "who were of the physical profession." Two thousand letters were to be printed "on a half-quarto paper on the cheapest terms"; these were to publish abroad the news of the birth of this charity. Then there came the first check—furniture had been bought, the house taken, the staff appointed, and the Infirmary was to open in a fortnight, but the treasurer reported financial difficulties—"there be only one shilling in the Bank."

While the treasurer is settling his difficulties with the committee and staff, we may seize the opportunity of making some inquiry into the condition of the sick poor in London at the time the charity was founded.

Up to this time there existed in London but two great hospitals—St. Bartholomew's and St. Thomas's; these had existed for over 500 years.

But within a few years all the following hospitals were founded: the Westminster, in 1720; Guy's, in 1724; St. George's, in 1733; "The London," in 1740; Middlesex, in 1745; Queen Charlotte's, in 1752; and many others.

Why, after 500 years of apparent neglect, this sudden awakening to the needs of the sick poor ? Was there some sudden advance in medicine and surgery in the benefits of which the rich considered the poor should have their share ? Was there some great wave of public philanthropy ? Was it a time of great sickness and of great poverty ? Or were the hospitals founded for reasons which must be described as selfish ? Were the sick poor herded together because it was better for the sick poor, or because it was much better for the non-sick rich ?

Perhaps a reference to the history of the two royal and ancient hospitals already mentioned may help us.

St. Bartholomew's was founded by Rahere in 1123. Rahere is usually believed to have been the jester of Henry I., the Conqueror's son. Mr. Wheatley says that there is no authority for this, although Rahere was known to have been a frequenter of the Palace and Court.

Every schoolboy remembers that Henry I. was the gentleman who never smiled again after the death of his only son by drowning. Such an inflexible determination to see nothing funny in Rahere's jests, whether he was the official jester or unofficial one, seems to have had a depressing effect upon the humorist. He gave up the follies of his career, became pious, and made a pilgrimage to Rome. Here he appears to have been seized with some severe illness. His past life, which must have been a wicked one, as well as a merry, rose up before him, and impressed him profoundly; in his extremity he made a vow that if health were given him and he were allowed to return to his native land, "he would make an hospital in recreation of poor men, and to them so there gathered necessaries minister after his power."

Rahere returned to London, and his old master the King gave him a site in the Smoothfields—now Smithfield—in the western suburbs of the City. The actual place was a marsh at the time, and had to be drained. Rahere collected the money to build the priory and hospital, and became the first prior. He died after having been a prior for over twenty years.

Mr. Wheatley points out that the hospital was from the first a hospital for the sick, and not a mere almshouse.

The hospital, no doubt, had times of good and evil fortune until the time of the Reformation, and the dissolution of the religious houses under Henry VIII. This, so far as St. Bartholomew's was concerned, came as a terrible blow to the citizens of London. To quote from Sir Henry Burdett's "Hospitals and Asylums of the World":

"The poor were deprived of the charitable relief which had been bequeathed to them by the piety of former ages. This was specially the case in London, where the indigent had to be supported by the private charity of the citizens, who were not only called upon to relieve their own poor, but many others, still more wretched, who, tempted by its great reputation for wealth, flocked into the City. By the dissolution of the Religious Houses, not only was much misery caused, but disorder and confusion were increased to such an extent that the administration of justice, sanguinary as it was in those days, could not entirely subdue them. The poverty and misery in the City of London at length reached such a height that in 1538 the Mayor and Commonalty of the City of London prayed that they might from henceforth have ' the order, rule, government, and disposition of the hospitals or spitals—commonly called St. Mary's Spital (Bethlem), St. Bartholomew's Spital, St. Thomas's Spital—and the New Abbey at Tower Hill, with the rents and revenues appertaining to the same, for the annual relief of the poor, needy, and sick persons.' Nor did the Worshipful Body, in any of their supplications, attempt to conceal from the King the real state of the poor in the City of London, for they reminded him that the three great spitals named were ' fownded of good devocon by auncyent fathers, and endowed w^t great possessions and rents, onely for the relyeff comforte and ayde of the poore and indygent people not beyng hable to help theymselffs, and not to the maynten'nce of preestes chanons and monks carnally lyvyng as they of late have doon, nothyng regardyng the myserable people lyeing in the streete, offendyng every clene person passyng by the way w^t theyre fylthye and nastye savors : Wherefore it may please yor mercyfull goodness, ever enclyned to pytie and compassyon for the relyef of Crystes very images, creatyed to hys owne symlytude, to order and establyshe by graunte or otherwise, by yor most vertuous and sage dyscrecon that the Mayre and hys brethren of yor cytye of London or suche other as shall stande w^t yor most gracyous favor shall and may from hensfurth have the order rule dysposicon and governance of all the sayd hospytalls and abbey.'

"The prayer of the Corporation was granted, and the above-named hospitals were placed under their management, but six years elapsed before any direct system of administration was organized. The first spital handed over to the civic authorities was that of

St. Bartholomew's, which was for ever to be styled 'The House of the Poor in West Smithfield in the suburbs of the City of London, of King Henry the Eighth's foundation,' in order, as Stow states, that 'there might be comfort to the prisoners, visitation to the sick, food to the hungry, drink to the thirsty, clothes to the sick, and sepulture to the dead.'"

St. Thomas's was founded in the reign of William Rufus by a woman, " pious, robust, and unmarried," who amassed a fortune by running a ferry across the Thames near the site of the present London Bridge. With this she built and endowed a convent and hospital near her residence in Southwark. She was canonized under the title of St. Mary Overie (Mary over river).

This hospital, like St. Bartholomew's, had varying fortunes, and also, like St. Bartholomew's, it fell, in 1538, into the hands of Henry VIII. A charter was not given until 1553, in the reign of Edward VI., and it was dedicated to St. Thomas *the Apostle*. It had previously been dedicated to St. Thomas à Becket.

These two hospitals, it would seem, although originally founded as an act of piety, were re-founded in the time of Henry VIII. and Edward VI., not entirely as an act of piety, but rather for the convenience of the healthy citizens. To have diseased and often infectious mendicants lying, and often dying, on their doorsteps was a nuisance ; Dives objected to Lazarus : " the myserable people lyeing in the streete, offendyng every clene person passyng by the way w[t] theyre fylthye and nastye savors." And selfishness *may* have been a reason for the foundation of the group of hospitals in the middle of the eighteenth century. But I think there were other reasons.

Was there any special amount of sickness and poverty about this time or before ? In attempting to answer this question, I must acknowledge my great indebtedness to Dr. Charles Creighton, from whose exhaustive and deeply interesting work, "The History of Epidemics in Great Britain," I quote freely.

The Eastern bubonic plague entered Britain in 1348, and was known as the Black Death. It appeared from time to time (in the fifteenth, sixteenth, and seventeenth centuries, several times in each) for the long period of 300 years. There are no trustworthy statistics of the earlier plague epidemics, but of those of 1603, 1625, and 1665, Dr. Creighton gives the following particulars for London :

Year.	Estimated Population.	Total Deaths.	Plague Deaths.	Highest Mortality in a Week.	Worst Week.
1603	250,000	42,940	33,347	3,385	Aug. 25 to Sept. 1
1625	320,000	63,001	41,313	5,205	August 11 to 18
1665*	460,000	97,306	68,596	8,297	Sept. 12 to 19

Dr. Creighton discusses at great length the reasons for this long-continued survival of this disease in Britain, while other exotic infections—*e.g.*, Asiatic cholera—have not become domesticated. He believed that the virus of the plague had its habitation in the soil, and that it depended for its continuance upon

* The year of *the* Plague of London.

the decomposition of human bodies. If he is correct, he says,

"then it is easy to understand that the immense mortalities caused by each epidemic would preserve the seeds of the disease ... in the soil. Buried plague-bodies would be the most obvious sources of future plagues."

Be this as it may, one cannot help feeling that this regular appearance of plague in London must have had a terrifying effect upon the citizens, culminating in absolute horror in the year of "*the* Plague." And for many years after 1665—indeed, right up to the time of the foundation of the London Infirmary, as the Hospital was first called —isolated cases of plague occurred which kept this terror alive; and an epidemic of plague in Marseilles created a panic in Western Europe (Wheatley).

But the bubonic plague was not the only epidemic which harassed the inhabitants of London. Creighton has shown that scarcity and want due to a run of bad harvests were always followed, or nearly always, by an epidemic of some kind. For instance, the opening years of the eighteenth century were years of abundant harvests; then in 1708 came the excessively severe winter—"one of the three memorable winters of the eighteenth century." This was followed by a deficient crop in 1709, and the price of wheat rose from 27s. 3d. per quarter at Lady Day, 1708, to 81s. 9d. at Lady day, 1710. *Then* began an epidemic of fever—the dreaded typhus. In 1710 the deaths from fever reached the highest total since 1694. Creighton says:

"The tremors, offensive sweats, and offensive breath are distinctive of a form of typhus that became common towards the middle of the century, and was called *putrid fever*."

Epidemics of typhus, and smallpox too, continued to come periodically, and, to quote again from "Epidemics in Britain":

"The eighteenth century, even the most prosperous part of it, from the accession of George I. to the beginning of the Industrial Revolution in the last quarter of it, was none the less a most unwholesome period in the history of England. *The health of London was never worse than in those years*, and the vital statistics of some other towns, such as Norwich, are little more satisfactory. This was the time which gave us the saying that God made the country, and man made the town."

Now we have come to the time and year when the seven men we have spoken of sat talking in the bar parlour of the Feathers Tavern.

"The harvest of 1739 had been an abundant one, and the export of grain had been large. At Lady Day the price of wheat had been 31s. 6d. per quarter, and it rose 10s. before Lady Day, 1740. An extremely severe winter had intervened, another of the three memorable winters of the eighteenth century. The autumn-sown wheat was destroyed by the prolonged and intense frost, and the price at Michaelmas, 1740, rose to 56s. per quarter, the exportation being at the same time prohibited, but not until every available bushel had been sold to the foreigners. The long cold of the winter of 1739-40 had produced much distress and want in London, Norwich, Edinburgh, and other towns. In London the mortality for 1740 rose to a very high figure—30,811—of which 4,003 *deaths were from fever and* 2,725 *from smallpox.* In mid-winter, 1739-40, coals rose to £3 10s. per chaldron, owing to the navigation of the Thames being closed by ice; the streets were impassable by snow, there was a 'frost-fair' on the Thames, and in other respects a repetition of the events preceding the London typhus of 1685-86. The *Gentleman's Magazine* of January, 1740, tells in verse how the poor were ' unable to sustain oppressive want and hunger's urgent pain,' and reproaches the rich—' colder their hearts than snow, and harder than the frost '; while in its prose columns it announces that ' the hearts of the rich have been opened in consideration of the hard fate of the poor.'

" The great epidemic of fever in 1741-42 was the climax of a series of years in London all marked by high fever mortalities. If there had not been something peculiarly favourable to contagious fever in the then state of the capital, it is not likely that a temporary distress caused by a hard winter and a deficient harvest following should have had such effects. This was the time when the population is supposed to have stood still or even declined in London.

" Drunkenness was so prevalent that the College of Physicians, on January 19, 1726, made a representation on it to the House of Commons through Dr. Freind, one of their Fellows and member for Launceston:

" ' We have with concern observed for some years past the fatal effects of the frequent use of several sorts of distilled spirituous liquor upon great numbers of both sexes, rendering them diseased, not fit for business, poor, a burthen to themselves and neighbours, and too often the cause of weak, feeble, and distempered children, who must be, instead of an advantage and strength, a charge to their country.'

" ' This state of things,' said the College, ' doth every year increase.' Fielding guessed that a hundred thousand in London lived upon drink alone ; six gallons per head of the population per annum is an estimate for this period, against one gallon at present.

" *The mean annual deaths were never higher in London*, not even in plague times over a series of years, the fever deaths keeping pace with the mortality from all causes, and, in the great epidemic of typhus in 1741, making about a fourth part of the whole. The populace lived in a bad atmosphere, physical and moral."

We may take it, then, that there was *special* poverty and *special* distress ; and here is one of the causes. Arbuthnot said, in 1733, " that the very first consideration in building of cities is to make them open, airy, and well perflated," on which Creighton comments as follows :

" In the growth of London from a medieval walled city of some forty or sixty thousand inhabitants to the ' great wen ' of Cobbett's time, these considerations had been little attended to so far as concerned the quarters of the populace. The Liberties of the City and the out-parishes were covered with aggregates of houses all on the same plan, or rather want of plan. In the medieval period the extramural population built rude shelters against the town walls, or in the fosse, if it were dry, or along the side of the ditch. The same process of squatting at length extended farther afield, with more regular building along the sides of the highways leading from the gates. . . . The out-parishes were covered with houses and tenements of all kinds, to which access was got by an endless maze of narrow passages or alleys; regular streets were few in them, and it would appear from the account given by John Stow in 1598 of the parish of Whitechapel that even the old country highway, one of the great roads into Essex and the Eastern Counties, had been 'pestered.'"

And Creighton says later :

" But that which helped most of all to make a foul atmosphere in which the contagion of fever could thrive was the window-tax. It is hardly possible that those who devised it can have foreseen how detrimental it would be to the public health ; it took nearly a century to realize the simple truth that it was in effect a tax upon light and air."

It was high time some properly equipped organization was created to meet and fight this army of distress, disease, and death !

And what of the medical profession at this time ?

CHAPTER III

MEDICINE AND SURGERY AT THE TIME OF THE HOSPITAL'S FOUNDATION

At the time of Rahere the clergy were the doctors, and the healing art in England remained in their hands for some centuries after Rahere's day—at any rate so far as medicine was concerned. By an edict of 1163 the clergy were forbidden to perform operations which involved the shedding of blood. Surgery, therefore, passed out of their hands—into the hands of the barbers!

It was not good for medicine that it should be left in the hands of the monks. The Church wished to maintain "a superstitious atmosphere by its own system of miraculous healing," and there could be no growth in true knowledge in such an atmosphere. Writing in "System of Medicine," Dr. Payne says, although speaking of an earlier date:

"The Church, while it condemned the Oriental magic, without doubting its power, as being of Satanic origin, maintained a superstitious atmosphere by its own system of miraculous healing. For the impious charms and magical rites of the heathen were substituted invocations of saints, pilgrimages to sacred shrines, and the like. To put trust in these methods was held to be more pious as well as more efficacious than to have recourse to secular medicine. Miraculous cures happened every day."

In the same article he points out that there was one branch of the ancient medicine which never entirely died out—the knowledge of medicinal herbs:

"Among the late Latin medical writings we find herbals. . . . These books were the manuals of the Benedictine monks, who, while cherishing some remains of the old medical lore, were never without a herb garden to provide their simple remedies, which were ever at the service of the poor. The herbal medicine steadily held its ground, and was one of the foundations on which this low reconstruction of medical science was based."

Chaucer's description of the doctor was a fairly accurate description for some hundreds of years after the "Tales" were written:

> "With us ther was a Doctour of Phisik,
> In all this world ne was ther noon hym lik,
> To speke of phisik and surgerye;
> For he was grounded in astronomye.
> He kepte his pacient a ful greet deel
> In houres, by his magyk natureel.
> Wel koude he fortunen the ascendent
> Of his ymages for his pacient.
> He knew the cause of everich maladye,
> Were it of hoot or cold, or moyste or drye,
> And where they engendred and of what humour;
> He was a verray parfit practisour.
> The cause y-knowe and of his harm the roote,
> Anon he yaf the sike man his boote.
> Ful redy hadde he his apothecaries
> To sende him drogges and his letuaries,
> For ech of hem made oother for to wynne.
>   * * * * *
> Of his diete mesurable was he,
> For it was of no superfluitee,
> But of greet norissyng and digestible.
> His studie was but litel on the Bible."

"There was little advance until the beginning of the seventeenth century. The doctor was influenced, not by reason and research, but by superstition and theory ; not by facts observed, but by an appeal to authority and dogma.

"The method of advancing knowledge was by dialectical reasoning. And whatever may have been the case in philosophy, there can be no doubt that in physical science and medicine the syllogism was not only an ineffectual instrument, but actually a hindrance to progress."

A remedy blessed by the patronage of royalty was deemed to be most efficacious. Henry VIII. devised plasters and decoctions. Here are some :

"The Kinges Majesties owne plastre, a black plastre devised by the Kinges Hieghness, a plastre devised by the Kinges Majestie at Grenewich and made at Westminstre to take awaye inflammacions and cease payne and heale excoriations, a decoccioun devised by the Kinges Majestie, a cataplasme made ungtment-lyke of the Kinges Majesties devise made at Westminster" (Wheatley).

Charles I. treated 10,000 patients for "glands of neck" by the royal touch, and Charles II., although somewhat sceptical, continued to " treat " patients in this way.

Dr. Creighton notices that, although during the various epidemics which from time to time swept the country the doctors made more or less desultory notes on the cases, all interest appeared to cease when the epidemic was over. Nothing seems to have been learned by experience ; scientific search for causes from observed effects was lacking.

But in the beginning of the seventeenth century

some notable advances were made. Harvey discovered the circulation of the blood in 1621. Francis Bacon lived, and " his influence on the progress of medicine, though indirect, was considerable."

Gradually the spirit of investigation and inquiry was spreading; superstition was dying out.

The greatest physician of the seventeenth century was Sydenham, and his method of studying disease illustrates well the change which was coming—indeed, had come, since the days of Henry's wonderful plasters. He held that—

" First, diseases are objects of natural history which have to be studied by observation alone, without trying to ascertain their remote causes and without framing hypotheses. The description of a disease must be complete, including all its features, mere narrations of individual cases being insufficient and unimportant. Diseases have their own natural laws, their own course, their times and seasons. In acute diseases there is a rise or climax and a spontaneous decline. Secondly, Nature is the true healer of disease; the physician has to imitate her processes of cure, to aid them if they appear weak, and to moderate them if they are too violent. A disease is, in fact, an effort of Nature to expel the morbific matter. In therapeutics experience is the only test of what is right. Whatever does good is best."

But as yet there was no regular clinical teaching in England, although medical schools and organized medical study had sprung up on the Continent.

In the eighteenth century, from the middle of which the London Hospital dates, and which has been called " the century of enlightenment," the most important

TREATMENT IN EARLY DAYS

factors of advance were the organization of medical teaching all over Europe, the rise of morbid anatomy to the position of a science, and the elucidation of a number of special diseases due to these improvements (Payne). And we shall see that soon after the Hospital's foundation a medical school attached to the Hospital was inaugurated, now one of the oldest in London, and the first in which a complete course of medical education was established.

It has been pointed out that, when the clergy were forbidden to perform operations which necessitated bloodshed, the barbers became the surgeons. So early as 1310 barbers were appointed " to keep strict watch at the City gates so that no lepers should enter the city," although one would have thought that this was more the duty of the physician than the barber.

If it can be said that the monks fostered superstition, the belief in miracles, voices, appearances, incubation (or temple sleeping), for the good of the Church and the benefit of their own Order in particular, it must also be said that the barbers worked on the credulity of the public, not for the good of the Church, but entirely for the good of their own pockets. The textbooks of the masters took less care to teach the disciples how to cure the patient than to teach them how to extract fees.

Arderne, one of the first writers on English surgery, teaches his pupils " to beware of scarse askings," states what he should charge " a worthy man and a great," and also " a lesse man." The fees he suggests are preposterous. Concerning him Mr. Wheatley writes :

" He counsels doctors to be careful in estimating the length of time of a cure—in fact, to suggest double the time they expect. If the patient wonders at the rapidity of cure, and asks, 'Why that he putte hym so long a tyme of curyng, sithe that he helyd hym by the halfe? Answere he, that it was for that the pacient was stonyherted and suffred wele sharpe thingis, and that he was of gode complexion, and hadde able fleshe to hale, and feyne he other causes pleasable to the pacient for pacientez of syche wordez are proude and delited.' Arderne's instructions for the guidance of doctors are very sensible, and they help to form us a correct estimate of the manners of the public who were patients."

Dr. Poore, after giving an analysis of the surgeon's work, writes:

"It is evident that John of Arderne was a consummate man of the world, and knew all the tricks of his trade. His fees seem to have been enormous, and, indeed, he is only one of many examples among our early professional forerunners who made very large professional incomes."

I am indebted for the following notes on the barber-surgeons to an article in the *London Hospital Gazette* of May, 1894, by Mr. Jonathan Hutchinson.

The red lamp now seen over the doctor's door was originally a bottle of blood, but in the fourteenth century the custom of putting blood in the window was forbidden, and the barber "who was so bold or so hardy as to put blood in his window was fined two shillings." A Guild of Barbers was founded in 1308. A Guild of Surgeons also existed from very early times in London; they appear to have been a very select and exclusive body, superior to the common barbers—consultants, perhaps. Mr. D'Arcy Power says:

"The Guild of Surgeons was always a small body, probably never more than twenty in number, and sometimes dwindling to less than a dozen."

The Guild of Barbers and the Guild of Surgeons were constantly quarrelling. The barbers were jealous because certain of the surgeons, aldermen of the Surgeon's Guild, were sworn before the Lord Mayor, as master surgeons, that

"they would well and faithfully serve the people, in undertaking their cures, would take reasonably from them, would faithfully follow their calling, and would present to the said Mayor and Aldermen the defaults of others undertaking cures, so often as should be necessary; and that they would be ready at all times, when they should be warned, to attend the maimed or wounded, and other persons; and would give truthful information to the officers of the city aforesaid, as to such maimed, wounded and others, whether they be in peril of death or not. And also to do all things touching their calling."

On which Mr. D'Arcy Power comments:

"It is certain that they took so wide a view of their duties as to harass the members of the Barbers' Guild who meddled with surgery. Thus in 1410 certain 'good and honest folk, barbers of the city, appeared by their counsel in the private chamber of the aldermen and sheriffs, and demanded that they should for ever peaceably enjoy their privileges, without scrutiny of any person of other craft or trade than barbers, and this neither in shaving, cupping, bleeding, nor any other thing in any way pertaining to barbery, or to such practice of surgery as is now used, or in future to be used, within the craft of the said barbers.'"

The rival guilds combined in 1493, or, rather, "entered into a composition" (the composition recognizing the independence of the two fellowships) which lasted until 1745.

In 1745 the surgeons seceded and formed the Surgeons' Company, which came to an end in 1796. In 1800 the Royal College of Surgeons was established.

The old surgeon-barbers had very little legitimate opportunity of becoming skilled anatomists, or of teaching anatomy to their apprentices. They were provided with four bodies annually of those who had been executed. The beadle of the company used to attend public executions and select suitable subjects, the hangman being entitled to the clothes. The beadle was frequently attacked by the mob.

"In 1740 a remarkable event occurred. A criminal named Duell had been hung at Tyburn, and his body duly removed for dissection. He had not been five minutes on the table when, to the consternation of everyone present, he showed signs of returning to life. He was bled, and other restoratives applied, with the result that after some hours he could be safely wrapped in a blanket and removed to Newgate, being subsequently transported for life" (Mr. Jonathan Hutchinson).

Surely this may have been one of the topics discussed by our friends in the Feathers Tavern on that September evening in 1740.

The laws relating to the apprentices of the barber-surgeons were strange and interesting.

"No barber or surgeon was to teach any but his apprentice, and no decrepit, diseased, or deformed apprentice was to be retained. . . . The apprentice corresponded to the modern medical student; he was not allowed to wear a beard of more than fifteen days' growth under a penalty of half a mark, to be paid by the master. . . . Attendance at the four public dissections was compulsory, but the enforcement of the order must have been difficult. One Hugh Ward was summoned before the Court for his absence from lectures; he then used opprobrious language and defied the Court, and was committed to the Compter; but when the officer attempted to seize Mr. Ward, he 'drewe his knife and swore he would sheathe it in his guttes and soe he made his escape from the officer.'"

It is easy for us in 1910 to indulge in a cheap sneer at these worthies of the past groping about in the dark. After all, it is by their groping that we are in the light, or, at any rate, can see signs of the dawn. Perhaps some hospital official writing a hundred years hence will smile that we should have thought we were in the light. We hope he will judge us as we try to judge these men of long ago. We forgive their ignorance; we admire their patience. What little material they had! Chemistry, as understood to-day, was as yet unborn; even oxygen had not been discovered. Cell structure was unknown. The presence of micro-organisms was unsuspected. The microscope as an agent for detecting disease was undiscovered. The functions of most of the organs was understood but partially, or wholly misunderstood. The need of antiseptics was not appreciated; indeed, the need of ordinary cleanliness was hardly considered of moment. The investigations of the modern pathologists were not dreamed of. Anæsthetics were unknown. Even the homely stethoscope was not used until 1815.

The physician to-day enters the ward and proceeds to examine a case newly admitted—an obscure case. Behind him stand the physiologist, the bacteriologist, the chemist, the anæsthetist, the pathologist, the psychologist, and still others.

Let us remember that Dr. Andrée walked into his wards alone.

CHAPTER IV

EARLY DAYS. PRESCOTT STREET

LET us return to the little company of men and their embarrassed treasurer whom we left wondering how the "intended Infirmary" was to be opened with only "one shilling in the Bank." They talked long, but as little good was to be done in this difficulty by talking, and as the Infirmary was not to be opened for a fortnight yet, they left it to Mr. Harrison to consider what should be done, and to report at the next meeting; and then they immediately set to work to draw up some rules for the management of the new Charity. Their difficulty and their determination "to do the thing that's nearest" has been repeated a thousand times since in the history of the old place. Hopeless times have followed each other over and over again, and hopeful times have followed these, and the hopeless have always been turned into hopeful by the strong action and bright, unquenchable cheeriness of one man, and "The London" is what it is to-day because of the line of these men, apostolic successors to "John Harrison, Surgeon." One is reminded of the well-known lines:

" One who never turned his back, but marched breast-forward,
  Never doubted clouds would break,
  Never dreamed though right were worsted, wrong would triumph.
  Held, we fall to rise, are baffled to fight better,
  Sleep to wake."

"John Harrison, Surgeon" (that is how he is generally referred to in the old, faded minutes) would have been very much surprised to hear such words applied to him. There was nothing sentimental about him. He simply marched into the next little meeting of his friends, this time at the Black Swan Tavern, Bartholomew Lane, and said that he had managed to get ten guineas, and that he had called on the Duke of Richmond, made him interested in the movement, and obtained from him a promise to become an annual subscriber.

The little house in Featherstone Street was opened as the "London Infirmary" on November 3, 1740. It was agreed that the Staff—the physician, surgeon, and apothecary—should attend the house daily from eight to ten on summer mornings, and from nine to eleven in winter. No medical man was resident, nor were nurses considered necessary. The man and wife who had been engaged were evidently thought competent to carry out all that was necessary between the visits of the Staff.

Mr. Cole, the apothecary, agreed to attend on one afternoon a week "for the practice of midwifery and the distempers incident thereto."

Subscribers agreed to meet at one of the taverns every Tuesday week at 7 p.m. to discuss details of administration, and *all* subscribers could attend these meetings. From among the subscribers a committee was chosen to meet at the Infirmary itself every Thursday in the morning, "to inspect and examine into the management of it." This weekly committee of the subscribers seems to have been the origin of the present weekly meetings of the House Committee. A Mr. Josso was elected the first chairman at one of these weekly inspection meetings. He must have had some glimmerings as to the honour of the post he held, the first of a long list of fine chairmen, because "Mr Josso paid for one bottle of wine on his being chosen Chairman of the Committee," a custom no longer existing. It may be noted that the elected Staff were themselves subscribers to the Charity, and served on the committee.

I have not been able to discover what was the number of beds for patients in this house. There could not have been many, however, as it will be remembered that the rent was only £16 a year.

By January, 1741, the Infirmary had got well to work. Week by week a list of subscribers, all of five guineas, was read out. These subscribers were called managers or governors.

A secretary, Mr. Richard Neil, was chosen. I am not impressed with the business ability of Mr. Neil. He never discovered, for instance, that a new year had begun before April or May had arrived, and this error in the date occurs in the minutes continually during the time he was secretary. The committee found him lax, too, or they would never have passed a minute to the effect that he must write up his minutes after a meeting "before he left the room"—necessary, perhaps, as the meetings always took place in a tavern. But what could the committee hope for? They paid him ten guineas a year, and this is what he was expected to do for his ten guineas:

"To reside near the Infirmary; to write all letters to noblemen and others; to attend all courts and committees; to attend the House Visitors twice a week from 11 to 1, and not to be absent without leave from the Chairman; to collect subscriptions; to keep a register of patients' names; to keep the accounts; to make out all summons; and to perform all other work usually performed by secretaries."

No wonder he applied for (and obtained) a " rise " to £25 per annum. Three years after his salary was raised to £40, " on condition that he act as Attorney or Solicitor to the Charity in all such business in law or equity as this Charity may require." At last he came to a sad end so far as the Hospital was concerned. He embezzled £400 of the Charity's money. There must have been some strange and endearing quality about this happy-go-lucky, though hard-working, under-paid secretary, because " nine gentlemen guaranteed to replace the £400 within two years, with interest, out of compassion for the unfortunate secretary, his wife and children, and the Court *unanimously* decided that he continue secretary." His disgrace, however, overwhelmed him, and he insisted upon resigning.

Everything was managed with the greatest care and economy. Evidently every penny was counted; for instance, it " was agreed that a sum not exceeding £3 2s. 11d. be spent for converting the wash-house into a kitchen "—not three guineas, be it observed, but one penny less.

An account was now opened with Mr. Thomas Miners, banker, of Lombard Street.

Within three months of opening the house in Featherstone Street the work had so increased that it became necessary to consider a change of abode, and the treasurer was asked to make inquiries. He reported that he had found a house a little east of Aldgate, which appeared to be suitable. It was in Prescott Street, Goodman's Fields. The street still bears the same name, and is a turning out of Leman Street, to the left before one comes to the railway arch. The treasurer was asked to send his servant to call on all subscribers to collect outstanding subscriptions before "so extraordinary an expense" could be undertaken as a change of abode. The servant must have had a pleasant manner ; at any rate, he managed to collect the necessary subscriptions, and the house in Prescott Street was taken on a three years' lease at £25 per annum, "in the name of Mr. John Harrison, Surgeon." The move was made in May, 1741, the first house having been occupied for five months.

The materia medica of that time were limited. A few drugs only were in use—roots, leaves, and barks—but to have bought up an apothecary's shop, lock, stock, and barrel, for the benefit of the new Infirmary, for £14 10s., "according to the inventory delivered," speaks well for the business ability of the governors. Perhaps "Mr. Harris in Aylott Street in Goodman's Fields," who sold the shop, let his charms, nostrums, and formulæ go at sale prices. The day was near when they would indeed be a drug on the market.

Soon after the opening, in 1742, was made the first organized appeal for public help, which is interesting as showing what the founders wished to be the aim of the Charity. It was agreed—

"That papers be printed with the following preamble on a half-sheet—viz. : 'There being an infirmary set on foot by subscriptions in Goodman's Fields for charitably relieving poor manufacturers, sailors in the merchant service, their wives and children, with medicine and advice in case of sickness or accident—for the assistance and promoting of so laudable a design, we do subscribe the sumes opposite our respective names.'"

During this year (1742) a rule was made that certain diseases which were considered "unclean" should "not be taken under the care of the Infirmary." It was agreed, however, that such cases might be *treated*, but not admitted. The interesting point about this is, that the arrangement may be considered to be the origin of the modern Out-patient Department. Of course, in time, all kinds of cases came to be treated as out-patients, and what led up to this will be seen later.

A committee was now appointed from among the governors (subscribers of £5 5s.) to draw up a set of rules for the Infirmary. This committee communicated with St. George's Hospital, which had been founded seven years earlier, and had safely passed the critical period of infancy, and from the governors of that charity they received much assistance. They recommended the appointment of a " Grand or House Committee " of twelve subscribers of five guineas (governors) for directing and transacting all affairs relating to the Infirmary. This committee was to be elected by all the governors at a " Court " every three months, and was to sit weekly, electing its chairman at its first meeting. The recommendations were carried out, and the committee invariably met at a tavern ; and " the Crown Tavern, behind the Royal

Exchange, and the Angel and Crown Tavern, Whitechapel Bars," appear to have been the favourite houses. The House Committee soon made a rule of appointing two of their members to be, in turn, "House Visitors."

The meetings always took place at seven in the evening, and it was wisely resolved that no business be done after 10.30. The meetings at these taverns seem to have been lacking somewhat in dignity. Once, after sitting too long, and possibly patronizing the house too well, a noble resolve was made not to hold these meetings at taverns any more, "it being represented that it was improper."

A kind offer, made by the Master of the Haberdashers' Company, to lend a room in Haberdashers' Hall to the governors for their meetings was accepted, and for many years all the meetings of the governors were held at Haberdashers' Hall.

As illustrating a fact which has often been noticed and urged as one of the greatest boons in the voluntary hospital system—viz., the long-continued and hereditary interest of well-known families with one or other hospital—it may be noted that on one of these committees which sat within a year of the Charity's foundation (1741) there was a Mr. John Buxton, and from that day to this the committee has rarely been without a Buxton. Mr. Thomas Fowell Buxton, who died in the year 1908, was chairman from 1857 to 1867, and treasurer from 1868 to 1878. His son, Mr. John Henry Buxton, has worked for the Hospital with as much zeal as did his father. He was chairman from 1877 to 1884, and treasurer from 1884 to 1903. A son of

Mr. John Henry Buxton now serves on the House Committee.

Many other names, household words in the Hospital 100 or 150 years ago, are still found on the committee to-day, or are connected with the Hospital in other ways—the Charringtons, the Hanburys, the Paulins, the Barclays, the Wigrams, and others.

One of the first things which the first committee did was to introduce a book in which to insert names of donors of gifts in kind, and such a book stands on the table to-day at every Board Meeting. One looks up the first entry in the hope that some beautiful and romantic gift might have been entered, a worthy forerunner to the hundreds of gifts which have been made to the Hospital later; the entry, however, is an unfortunate one: "Mr. Gascoigne presented a waterbutt"—a useful gift, doubtless, but not romantic.

Certain of the governors recommended the appointment of all sorts of subcommittees—of accounts, of drugs, of contracts, etc. The House Committee was jealous of its honour, and would have none of them:

"It is the opinion of this Committee that the weekly Board of this Infirmary is capable of transacting all the current business of auditing accounts, admitting and dismissing patients, and doing all the business usually done by Committees in other hospitals, without appointing any other Committees or any part of the same."

And they certainly seem to have given the most minute attention to details. Nothing escaped their notice; for instance: "Agreed that 2s. 6d. be paid for a cap and strap to the pestle"; "Agreed that the messenger bespeak 2 dozen candles "; " Agreed that an ink standish be bought for the dispensary." And everything was to be paid for within a week of purchase; no running accounts were allowed.

An interesting note occurs in the minutes about this time (May, 1741). It has already been stated that there were no medical schools attached to the hospitals in London. A man became a surgeon by being apprenticed to a surgeon. Mr. Harrison asked that one of his apprentices might be allowed to study at the Hospital.

"Mr. Harrison, the surgeon to this Infirmary, desiring to enter Mr. Godfrey Webb as a pupil of surgery within the said Infirmary for the space of one year, it was ordered that the said Mr. Godfrey Webb be so entered on the books for one year from this day, and that if he be constantly attendant on the practice of this Infirmary, he shall have a certificate signifying this attendance, and for what space of time, from the weekly Committee of this Infirmary."

In November, Mr. Cole, the apothecary, retired, and this same Mr. Godfrey Webb, who had only entered the previous May, was appointed apothecary in his place. Bearing in mind what could have been the extent of Mr. Webb's experience after only six months in the Hospital, one cannot but feel that it was hardly fair to place such important duties on his young shoulders. He was not to practise out of the house—the committee were kinder to the outside public than to their own patients—he was to keep a proper stock of medicines in the dispensary (probably the pharmacopœia was not large); he was to keep accurate account of his drugs; he was to give full instructions to patients as to their medicine; he was not to " lye abroad " nor be out after ten at night; he was to bring no wife or child into the house; he was to take no pupil. For all of which he was to receive £30 a year,

" with a room, coal, and candles, and shall be permitted to have his food drest at the Infirmary, but shall board himself, furnish his room, and provide his own washing."

About this time it was felt by the committee that some person should be engaged to look after the patients other than the man and his wife who were the caretakers of the house. It was beginning to dawn on the governors that patients needed nursing as well as the attention of the physician, surgeon, and apothecary. When one considers, however, the type of woman they chose for this important work, one is filled with curiosity as to what they expected such a woman to do. I believe as a class they did much more harm than good, certainly for the first fifty years, and the great Blizard's strong denunciation of them, years after the time we are now speaking of, cannot but make one feel that they were a hindrance to the surgeon rather than a blessing.

The first nurse ever appointed at the London Hospital was called " Squire," simply " Squire." She is not even honoured with " Mrs. " or " Miss." She certainly was not " Miss," for nurses then were invariably broken-down and drunken old widows. " Squire " was paid 5s. a week, and lived out! The committee also engaged a night nurse at a rather lower salary—3s. 6d. per week. The night nurses were acknowledged at the time to be of even a lower grade than the nurses. They were called " watches," and, if good, might hope to work up to the position of " nurse " some day. It was strange that the least experienced woman was on duty at a time when help could least easily be obtained. The first minute referring to this honourable society of topers—they were confessed to be inclined " to drink," at a time when everyone drank—was as follows :

" Squire was reported to have taken money from patients ; she was not dismissed, however, as it was not in the rules that she should *not* do so. She promised not to do so again."

From this date (1742) there is hardly a meeting of the committee but some nurse or watch was dismissed for drunkenness, although they were repeatedly forgiven. The type of woman thought good enough may be inferred from the fact that the head nurse, who was called matron, was the wife of the hall-door porter !

" It was agreed that the matron and the messenger be allowed their diet from this day at the rate of a 2d. loaf per day, and double the quantity of cheese or butter allowed to patients."

The matron's salary was £15 per annum. It is evident that the type of woman engaged was not above extorting various gifts from patients whom they were nursing, and who were completely at their mercy. A system of blackmail existed. The committee found that a nurse had refused to bring the most ordinary necessities to patients without promise of a " tip."

The first matron (Mrs. Elizabeth Gilbert) was paid 6d. a day by the committee for each patient, with which she was to provide food. It was found that she had practically starved the patients, and the little she had supplied them with had been given at the expense of local tradesmen, with whom she had run up accounts and then decamped. After this the committee decided to do their own catering, and asked for tenders.

It was decided in 1743 to make the nurses and watches resident, and their salaries were £6 per annum for a nurse and £4 for a watch. This salary could even then hardly be expected to attract superior women, physically, mentally, or morally. Sarah Spencer was engaged, but Sarah Spencer was discharged within a week because she was found to be "lame in her arm." Two others saw no harm in petitioning the committee, "praying for some cordials." The committee discharged one of them, as she was under the influence of cordials when she appeared before them. They forgave the other, however, "on her submission." I think the committee were beginning to be doubtful whether nurses and watches were a success, because they advertised "for a sober, *grave* person who is capable of acting as a nurse." One of the ladies engaged as the result of this advertisement was very soon dismissed, for reasons that are not fully explained, although hinted at, and to have described herself as either "sober" or "grave" could, under the distressing circumstances, hardly have been strictly accurate. The committee raised the salary to £7 for nurses and £5 for watches as an attraction, but there was no improvement. Perhaps the accommodation was not good, for the House Visitors report "that the nurses receive their friends in the room in which the watches sleep, to the disturbance of their rest," and it was ordered that in the future nurses " should receive their acquaintances in the kitchen!" What could the committee expect? They certainly got what they deserved.

I shall speak of the birth and growth of the profession of sick-nursing in another chapter.

Mr. Harrison, partly from ill health and partly because of the increasing amount of work in the Infirmary, asked in 1743 that he might have an assistant for helping in the work. This was quite a different thing from the appointment of an assistant-surgeon to the Infirmary. Nowadays a surgeon who is appointed on the staff is called assistant-surgeon for seven years, and afterwards a surgeon. But Mr. Harrison wanted permission for someone to assist him in his work and obey his orders. The request was granted, and such a man was appointed for one year. Evidently the experiment was satisfactory in every way, for next year the committee recommended the *permanent* appointment of an assistant-surgeon " upon the same foot as they are at St. Bartholomew's."

It is interesting to note that Harrison, who knew nothing about micro-organisms or of sepsis, found that the result of his operations varied under different conditions, and it is significant that he should have had observation enough to urge the committee to remove all paper from the walls of his wards, and have the walls varnished instead, "so that they can be washed down." We line the walls of our operating theatres to-day with glass tiles for that very reason.

His zeal aroused jealousy, and his detractors reported

to the committee that he was full of fads, incompetent, neglectful, and unkind to his patients. The charge was even brought that he was dishonest, and appropriated medicine from the dispensary for his own use. A subcommittee was appointed to look into this, and here is its report :

"We find Mr. Harrison attends every day from about 11 to 1, except in summer-time, when he is out of town ; he used to get the apothecary to see his accidental cases, but some misunderstanding having lately arisen between them, Mr. Harrison has directed your beadle to send for him on any emergency ; failing Mr. Harrison, to go for the assistant-surgeon ; failing him, for the surgeon-extraordinary ; failing him, *for any surgeon who is a Governor.* If all of these were out of the way, then such accidental patients have been dressed by Mr. Harrison's pupils. With regard to the complaint as to William Burridge, a patient, it was reported to the subcommittee that this patient was brought in as an accident, being a compound fracture of the leg ; that he was brought in at 3 p.m., and is stated not to have been seen till next morning ; the leg was then so swelled that it could not be set ; that no surgeon had attended him, or was sent for, pupils taking such care of him as they could, or thought proper, and that he was so much neglected that his groans disturbed the patient in the next bed. Your Committee, on examination of these statements, found the facts to be as follows : The patient was brought in at 3 ; Mr. Harrison was out of town ; Mr. Wood (a pupil), who had served almost a year in the Hospital, besides a previous apprenticeship to a surgeon, went to Mr. Jones, surgeon-extraordinary, who was not at home ; then to a governor who was a surgeon, and he was out of town too ; so Mr. Wood undertook the patient himself, with the assistance of the other pupils, as he apprehended himself capable of it, and accordingly set his leg. Mr. Harrison saw the case next day and approved; the patient did well for ten days, at the end of which he complained of his bowels and of a shivering, and that upon opening some abscesses which were found gathering in his leg, the discharge was so great that he lost his appetite and sank under it. The warmth of the weather was supposed to contribute not a little. Mr. Harrison had ordered him fish, chicken, or anything else he could eat, and large nosegays to prevent his being affected by the stench of his leg, and that the man was thankful, and particularly so on the day of his death."

We need not go into other complaints, although they are interesting reading enough. It is sufficient to quote that

" Mr. Harrison, the surgeon-in-ordinary, hath acquitted himself to the satisfaction of this Court in point of practice and attendance on the patient, and hath discharged his duty in every respect."

Nothing, however, could affect Harrison's popularity as a teacher, and every week or two he asked the committee's permission to introduce another and another pupil to the Infirmary for a year. They came from all parts of the country; one, I noticed, was a Mr. Geoffrey Lang of Newton Abbot, in Devonshire. He was more popular as a teacher than was Dr. Andrée the physician.

Each pupil had to come before the committee and receive a printed charge, which was as follows:

" Sir, you are recommended by our Physician (or Surgeon) to be entered on our books as a pupil under him for one year. At the same time as we receive you as such I am to acquaint you that humanity to the patients and a conformity with the laws of this Charity, and a decent behaviour, is what the Governors expect from you, and which will intittle (*sic*) you to our friendship, and a certificate from the Board of your attendance and good conduct when your term shall be expired."

The spiritual welfare of the patients was not neglected. The Rev. Matthew Audley, from the year of the Infirmary's foundation, had volunteered his services. He had read prayers twice a week, and had preached a sermon every fortnight, which the committee always attended. He did not conduct services on Sundays, however, as he had his own church to attend to. For his kindly work, which was not noticed, apparently, for a long time, he was presented by the Court with—a surplice. Later he was made an honorary life governor, but it was many years before the Court gave him " an annual present of Thirty Guineas." The Bishop of Oxford was much exercised that there was no service on Sundays, and repeatedly wrote to the committee about it. The committee replied that they could not see their way to spend anything but on the health of the patients.

They distinguished, evidently, between " an annual present " and a fixed salary to a chaplain. At last, however, on account of the frequent appeals of the Bishop of Oxford, persisted in during several years, Mr. Audley was appointed Chaplain to the Infirmary at £100 a year, and had to give his whole time to his duties, which, of course, included preaching on Sundays.

He gave up a good living to do so, but the Hospital work was near his heart. He held the post until his death in 1790, a noble and self-sacrificing record of fifty years. He was a quiet, unobtrusive man. In looking up the records for this little history I have become very familiar with his name; it appears week by week in the faded, musty old minute-books, and when his name dropped out I felt I had lost an old friend. How many despairing and despondent sufferers did this good old man encourage and cheer during his fifty years of faithful service! There is never reference to him but shows that he was loved and respected by all—a silent saint.

There were many other silent workers in those early days of the Infirmary. One loves to picture them. Who was Mr. William Myre? He certainly added a brick or two in the building of the great palace of healing we see to-day, for the committee passed a minute saying that "the success and happiness of this establishment is owing in a great measure to the indefatigable zeal and industry of Mr. Myre," and asked him to accept a life governorship, "it being the only means we have of acknowledging the many services he has done." And there were others, too, too poor, perhaps, to give large donations, but who gave what labour they could. For instance, a Mr. Meares, who was poor, but would make trusses for the patients gratuitously, and who, so the minute says, "treated all patients sent to him in a compassionate and tender manner." The love which men had for the place was wonderful; for instance, Sir James Lowther, a member of the committee who, lying ill—he had a leg amputated—received a deputation of sympathy from the committee, and sent a message to the committee in reply " that he wished the greatest prosperity to this Charity, and that living or dying he would never tire of showing his regard to it."

I cannot imagine that those dignified old merchants and bankers who considered their " friendship " sufficient reward for good conduct could have had a sense of humour, and yet there are symptoms of it in the minutes, as when a benefactor sent twelve bound books to the committee entitled " The Knowledge and Practice of Christianity *Made Easy to the Meanest Capacities.*" There were at the time twelve members of the committee, but they evidently did not think themselves of the " meanest capacity," so they ordered a copy to be chained in each ward " for the benefit of the miserable objects."

When the Infirmary had been one year in its new home in Prescott Street its vigorous growth necessitated enlargement. As a baby it had soon outgrown its cradle, now as an infant its cot proved too confined for its rapidly increasing vigour. It had made a fine circle of friends. Every Bishop in England was on its subscription list, and every honoured name we know in contemporary history. Mr. Harrison, as usual, was the one who urged immediate extension. His sympathies were moved towards those unfortunate outcasts whom the governors decided ought not to be treated, and it was he who led the way in preaching that the duty of the Hospital was to ask three questions of its patients—" Are you poor ?" " Are you ill ?" " Can we help you ?" and that it was not part of the

Hospital's duty to ask a fourth question—" Are you moral ?" So an extra house was taken and opened—a house always spoken of as the " Lock," a name which seems to be derived from " Loke," a house for lepers in Southwark.

When the Infirmary had been opened one year a report of its work was published. One hundred and twenty-seven in-patients had been treated, of whom 105 were said to have been cured, 12 were incurable, and there had been 10 deaths, a death-rate of 8 per cent. The total income for the year was £298 14s. 6d., and the expenditure £206 5s. 6d. The following are some of the items of the expenditure :

Furniture, £29 5s. 4d. ; candles, £1 3s. 4d. ; firing, £11 8s. ; house-rent and taxes, £19 10s. ; salaries and wages, £27 15s. 5d. ; provisions, £27 11s. 6d. ; dispensary, £63 3s. 1d. ; turnery, £1 3s. 5d. ; repairs, £15 0s. 3d. ; stationery, £9 15s. 11d. ; and soap, 10s. 6d.

Soap 10s. 6d. ! And yet a death-rate of only 8 per cent. The figures do not seem to commend the gospel of cleanliness.

One cannot resist comparing these figures with those in the report of the London Hospital for 1908, although it almost seems " bad form " to boast of ourselves when talking of the pioneer work of these men.

The in-patients treated numbered 14,781 ; the death-rate was 10·17 per cent. ; the total income was £149,735 ; the total expenditure was £111,799 ; and on the altar of cleanliness were placed the following gifts : Expenses of laundry, £6,100 ; cleaning and chandlery, £1,356 ; water, £296 ; and annual cleaning (*i.e.*, spring cleaning), £2,924.

The " abuse of hospitals," of which one hears so much to-day, is nothing new, evidently, for in 1744 we find :

" Relief is administered to persons capable of paying for their cure, under the specious pretence and cloak of poverty, and your Committee think it a duty incumbent upon them, as immediate trustees of this Charity, to seek a remedy for this growing evil."

As patients were only treated on the recommendation of a subscriber, a letter was sent to all subscribers begging them to take particular care to recommend only proper cases. The habit of subscribers sending cases up from the country for in-patient treatment, without first ascertaining that a bed was vacant, was as great a difficulty then as now :

" Diverse persons from town and country having been sent by the Governors of this Charity to be admitted as In-patients at a time when the house was full, which must be attended with charge to the patients for their conveyance, this [*i.e.*, advertisement] to desire every gentleman who may have In-patients to recommend that they would inform themselves of the steward or matron if there be room, that they may not meet with disappointment ; should there be no room in the house, patients will be treated as out-patients until there is a vacancy."

And this last seems to have been the chief use of the Out-patient Department and the chief cause of its growth. It was for patients waiting for a bed. There is still a " waiting-list " to-day which numbers nearly 500 names. I see that the committee were sometimes at expense in sending patients back to the country when sent up in this way.

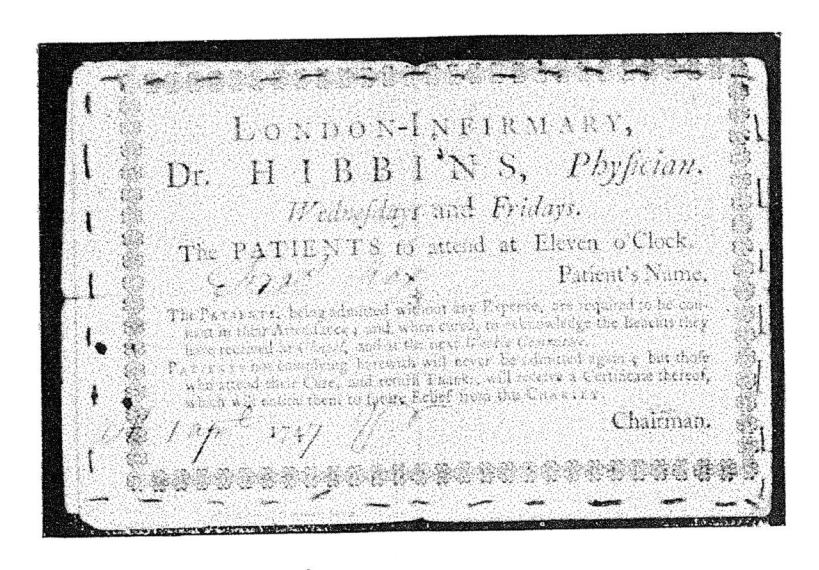

PATIENT'S ADMISSION TICKET, 1747

HOGARTH'S ORIGINAL DESIGN FOR BACK OF ADMISSION TICKET

The Hospital authorities soon learned the value of advertisement. All patients had to return thanks for their cure before the committee, and the governors were much hurt because some neglected to do so—"whereby the Charity appears less extensive in its good effects than it actually is." On the admission-card of each patient was the following, and the steward was to draw each patient's attention to the rule at the time of his admission:

"The patients, being admitted without any expense [this was not quite true; each patient was charged one shilling "for the use of utensils"], are required to be constant in their attendance, and, when cured, to acknowledge the benefits they have received at chapel and at the next weekly committee. Patients not complying herewith will never be admitted again; but those who attend their cure *and return thanks* will receive a certificate thereof, which will entitle them to future relief from this Charity."

And when a patient had returned thanks "in the chapel and before the Committee," there was still more to be done; a card was given him to give to the officiating clergyman of his own parish church, to be read out in the "Thanksgiving" on the Sunday following the patient's discharge:

"A person having lately received great mercies from Almighty God by a cure at the LONDON HOSPITAL, desires to return humble and hearty thanks for the same."

This custom made the Hospital well known, and the idea, not having been patented, is offered without fee or reward to all whom it may concern.

In-patients who were convalescent were allowed to leave the Hospital during the day if they wished, returning to sleep at night. Patients with such leave constantly disappeared; the sights they saw in hospital were evidently too much for them. The horrors of a hospital before the days of anæsthetics can easily be imagined. Such runaway patients had their names entered in a "black list," and were forbidden all further treatment. One, however, was forgiven, and the reason is curious: "On confessing his error, and it appearing he had lately lost a leg in the service of his country, he was pardoned."

Smallpox was, of course, much commoner then than now, and much trouble was caused by these smallpox patients attending the Hospital and mixing with other patients.

"Your Committee being informed that among the objects recommended to this Charity [patients were always spoken of as "objects" or "miserable objects"] many appear to have the smallpox, which being contagious, they cannot, according to the rules of the house, be received, and such patients being thereby exposed to great danger, it was moved that application be made to the smallpox hospital to know on what terms they would receive these objects; and Mr. Harrison having, at the request of your Committee, waited on Sir Samuel Gower, the Treasurer of that *Charity*, reported that they had agreed to receive such poor under that complaint as shall be recommended by this Charity. It was decided, therefore, to subscribe ten guineas in the names of Dr. Andrée and Mr. Harrison." (From the quarterly report of the House Committee to the General Court.)

I find about this time the first dietary scale referred to. Breakfast always consisted of " milk pottige " or " water gruel " only ; for dinner, boiled meat (always boiled) was given on alternate days, and boiled or baked pudding alone on alternate days ; for supper there was broth or " milk pottige." There was no selection of diets which could be used according to the patient's disease ; it was to be this or nothing—" it was agreed that no other diet be expected or allowed on any account whatever."

The Infirmary now consisted of the original house and the one added known as the Lock. On account of the rapid increase in the work, it was proposed to take three more houses adjoining, in Prescott Street. After due consideration, this was done ; the extra houses were taken on a twenty-one years' lease at £15 a year each ; £300 was spent in alterations, one of which was that " the shed at the bottom of the garden be fitted up as a place for out-patients to wait in, so that they may be protected from the inclemency of the weather." Hitherto they had waited in the garden or street.

One of the five houses soon came to be known as " The Jews' House " (1745), but there is no reference in the minutes to any special accommodation or diet prepared for them as yet. In the alterations there was little regard to hygiene, and the drainage was of the simplest. " As the frequent filling and emptying of the cesspool is a great expense, it is decided to let it drain into the other cesspool *under the arbour.*" A neighbour complained that the overflow from the Hospital's cesspool ran over his garden, as his ground lay lower than that of the Hospital. The committee ended his complaint, but not the cause of it, by taking his garden at 40s. per annum. It was decided to build a dead-house (a room for post-mortems was built over this next year), a place for drying herbs, and a cold bath. A cold bath! There was accommodation for sixty-eight patients besides the servants.

Nothing was more noticeable in these years than the absolute disregard of all cleanliness, and one wonders how wounds healed at all. One pair of sheets only was allowed to each bed. How often could they have been washed, for beds were never empty? To make a patient sleep in sheets in which his predecessor had died seems too horrible, but I am afraid it is true. The committee did seem to have some slight qualms about this; at all events, the more fastidious of them expressed some slight fear lest beds in which patients died "might have retained part of the indignity of their distemper."

An increase of the medical or surgical staff of this Hospital, or any hospital, nowadays is a matter of the most serious deliberation. The Staff is not paid, but the honour of belonging to the staff of a great hospital is so great that it is most jealously guarded. Certainly such an honour is not to be had for the asking. It is usually the result of many years of hard and gratuitous work for the Hospital. It does not seem to have been so in the days of which I am writing; for instance:

"The Chairman reported to the Committee that Dr. Cunningham had offered to attend as Physician Extraordinary to this Infirmary, which, being moved and seconded, it was resolved that Dr. Cunningham be desired to attend as Physician Extraordinary, and the thanks of the Court were returned to him for favouring the Hospital with his advice and attendance."

Dr. James Hibbins, about the same time, also offered his services as Physician Extraordinary. Apparently Dr. James Hibbins was not quite up to the standard, for he was elected Assistant Physician.

Dr. Cunningham died three years after (1749), and by this time the post of Physician to the London Infirmary appears to have come to be considered a desirable honour, for there were many candidates. At the Court to elect a successor 363 governors were present. Dr. John Sylvester headed the poll with 242 votes, the other votes being distributed amongst the other candidates. He was called upon to make a speech, but his feelings at his success appear to have been too much for him, and all he was able to say, in returning thanks for his election, with reference to his future work, was "that he hoped to be able to acquaint the apothecary with a remedy for killing bugs," which shows, at any rate, that Dr. Sylvester was a very practical man.

One of the committee's greatest worries was with the coroner, who constantly refused bodies to be buried "without sitting on them." As the committee had to pay his fee, which was thirteen shillings, they very naturally objected to so much of this "sitting." For instance, the committee reported to the Court of Governors :

"Your Committee having received into the Infirmary a Swiss soldier who had been dangerously wounded, were afterwards informed of his death, and that the Parish refused to bury him without the Coroner's warrant ; the Steward applied to Mr. King [the Coroner] for that purpose, who refused to sit upon the body without his fee, notwithstanding there were no assets ; whereupon the Corps becoming obnoxious, the Committee wrote him the following letter : ' Sir, the Governors of this Charity have ordered me to acquaint you that they were in hopes you would have granted an order for the burial of a Swiss soldier (who is become a prodigious nuisance) without putting them to any expense, as they have nothing but the benefactions of charitable people, but they still hope you will be so good as to send it by the bearer, who has orders to satisfy you if you are not inclined to save this Charity that expense.' But he still refusing his warrant, the steward, pursuant with their letter, paid him his demand of 13s."

The five houses in Prescott Street by 1746 were costing so much in upkeep and repairs (they were very old houses) that the committee began seriously to consider whether it would not be better to buy a site somewhere in a convenient neighbourhood, and build an infirmary of their own. This project will be considered in the next chapter.

CHAPTER V

THE NEW SITE, WHITECHAPEL

Soon after the foundation of the Infirmary in 1740 there was instituted the custom of having an annual festival.

At this festival a sermon was preached at one of the City churches in the morning, and then the whole congregation marched in procession to the Hall of one of the City companies or to one of the taverns, and dined. At the dinner the praises of the Infirmary were sung and donations collected.

At many hospitals this custom of an annual festival still survives, although the sermon is dispensed with; but it has ceased to be an annual function at the London Hospital for many years.

In early days, however, the annual festival of the London Hospital was a very great event, and everybody who was anybody attended, from Royalty downwards. As some of these festivals had an important bearing on the Hospital's career, it may be of interest to describe the function in more detail.

The " annual festival " was instituted in 1742 at the suggestion of " Mr. Harrison, Surgeon," and the arrangements made by him for the first festival were but very slightly altered after. The President of the

Infirmary (who at this time was the Duke of Richmond and Lennox) was asked to fix a date suitable for him to attend. Then one of the Bishops was applied to, and asked to preach the annual sermon on the appointed day. On going through the records, one notices that the Hospital has been beholden to every Bishopric in England. The sermon was usually preached at Bow Church, in Cheapside. The first preacher was Dr. Maddock, then Bishop of St. Asaph, and afterwards Bishop of Worcester.

After the sermon the whole company formed up in procession, and marched through the City amid pealing of church bells to the place chosen for dinner. The Halls of the Mercers', the Haberdashers', and the Drapers' Companies were favourite places, and so was the London Tavern. The procession itself was quite an imposing one, and, if it did no more, served to remind the City of the Hospital's existence. The procession was drawn up by the City Marshal, and included, in groups, the President and Vice-Presidents of the Hospital, the House Committee, the Physicians and Surgeons, the Lay Staff (including the Hospital beadles, who were always presented with new uniforms for the festival), and the guests. A band accompanied them, and as one of the items of expenditure at these festivals was invariably " 72 yards of Garter blue ribbon from Mrs. Davenport in Whitechapel for favours and two dozen white wands for the Committee," the procession must have given a gay and festive appearance to the City. In order, however, that there should be no undue levity on the part of City urchins, it marched under the protection of a large body of City Constables.

The outburst of bell-ringing was not quite so spontaneous, I fear, as the onlookers thought, or why do we find in an old notebook belonging to the Secretary, " For the bells of St. Botolph's, to commence at 10.30, two guineas; for St. Michael's bells, as the procession passes, one guinea," and so on ?

The dinner itself was always the gift of the " festival stewards " of the year. It was an expensive honour for them, and usually cost each of them from twenty to twenty-five guineas. The diners paid for their tickets, and this was a clear profit to the Hospital, as the stewards had provided the dinner.

The ponderous meal began at five o'clock, but the stewards " were not expected to pay for wines drunk after midnight." Up to midnight, however, all were welcome and were expected to drink heartily, and it is recorded that " the Stewards decided to cover the tables with Port Wines; that Madeira and Sherry be distributed discretionally, but Claret be only at the upper table." Strong beer was provided *ad libitum*. Two " careful persons " were to be procured " to take care of the wine, one in the dinner-room to receive it, and one at the door to prevent its being carried away." This precaution was probably necessary, because the guests brought their own servants to wait on them, and these were provided with a dinner and one pint of wine each. At the later festivals this custom was put an end to on account of the expense to the stewards, who themselves found servants to do the waiting. It had been found that many persons joined the procession on its march through the City, and got into the dinner on the plea of being somebody's servant.

Musicians were usually engaged, and were allowed a dinner and a bottle of wine each. The "publick professional singers" were not always present, however, the stewards sometimes deciding to be "satisfied with the volunteer songs of the company at large." Can one imagine it ? The Bishop who had preached the sermon, the Princes of Royal blood at the upper table, Members of Parliament and leaders in the army (I see both Pitt's and Wellington's name among the guests), sitting at a dinner which lasted from five until twelve, and "satisfied with the volunteer songs of the company at large"! And what toasts! No less than sixteen toasts are found on the list for one of these dinners. They included, after the Loyal Toasts, among others :

> Prosperity to the London Infirmary.
> Health to the Bishops of England.
> Health to the Nobility of England.
> Health of the Lord Mayor.
> Health of the House Committee of the London Infirmary.
> Health of the Stewards for providing this excellent entertainment.
> Prosperity to the City of London.
> Success to all other Charitable Institutions.
> Prosperity to Trade and Navigation.

No wonder the stewards had to "cover the tables with port wines"! From the very first a separate table was provided "for gentlemen of the Hebrew Nation," the food being cooked by a Hebrew cook.

At the first dinner £36 14s. 6d. was collected ; at

the second, £82; and these collections grew year by year until they amounted to thousands of pounds. At the record Festival Dinner of 1856 £26,000 was promised and given.

In all references to the Charity in the minutes up to the year 1747 it is called the "London Infirmary." After that date it is "The London Hospital." The reason for the change was some remarks made in the after-dinner speech of the Duke of Richmond at the Festival Dinner of 1748:

"The Duke was pleased publickly to drink to the success of this Charity under the title of the London *Hospital*, being pleased to declare that from the great encouragement now given it, and the extensiveness of its benefits to the poor, it deserved that appolation " (*sic*).

The sermon preached by the Bishop of Worcester seems to have been particularly eloquent and successful in raising funds. During the three months following his appeal no less a sum than £650 was received in new subscriptions, traceable to the wide circulation of the Bishop's sermon. Copies had been sent to the Lords of the Admiralty, Lord Mayor and Court of Aldermen, the Trinity Masters, the Lieutenant of the Tower Hamlets, and to all the hospitals which had been founded about the same time. The success of the Bishop's sermon seems to have been due to its plain common sense; there was nothing emotional or Utopian about it. It urged strongly that in view of the decrepit condition and costly upkeep of the five houses in Prescott Street, it was the clear duty of the governors to found a special fund, with the object of buying a site and building a hospital of their own. He gave emphasis to his remarks by himself inaugurating the fund by sending "a draught on his goldsmith for £20." The governors were filled with enthusiasm at the Bishop's suggestion, and the following letter was circulated to all the nobility throughout the country :

"The Lord Bishop of Worcester, out of his great regard to this Infirmary, has opened a subscription for raising a fund to erect a new building by the time the leases of the present premises shall expire, which will then be too old and ruinous to continue in longer. But this building will not be attempted until a sum sufficient be given for that purpose ; and in the meantime the money accruing will be laid out at interest, and none be applied but for the particular use for which it was directed."

The fund increased rapidly, and all donations were carefully invested. Three trustees were appointed, and within a year the Capital Fund had reached to over £5,000. (It was also called the Building Fund, the Benefaction Fund, the Bishop of Worcester's Fund.)

Within two years there is the following report from the House Committee to the Quarterly Court :

"Your Committee, having had it represented to them, and having considered that the design of the Bishop of Worcester's sermon was to inculcate the necessity of providing early for a building to the use of this Charity, and as the expenses attending the tenements at present occupied for that purpose leave no room to doubt they will be incapable of further use at or before the expiration of the present lease, apprehend we cannot too early secure a proper piece of ground for the same. And the more so as there are at this time convenient places for that purpose to be had, which may not offer should there be any delay. And as there is money enough vested in Trustees for that particular end, which being purchased, a proper plan and estimate of such intended building may be layed before this Court for their approbation, to be then engraved on a copper plate and copies thereof dispersed amongst the Governors of this Charity, and others inclinable to promote it, and at the same time convince the world that there is nothing ostentatious, sumptuous, or unnecessary intended . . . which, we conceive, will greatly tend to hasten the execution and completion of the same. To which purpose it is further humbly submitted that certain gentlemen be appointed to take upon them to examine into and procure such piece of land in the cheapest and best manner they can by a full authority from this Court, as a purchase of this kind will require great management, secrecy, and expedition."

A subcommittee was at once formed to look for a suitable site, and in reading the various reports of this subcommittee one sees by how small a chance the London Hospital is where it is to-day. A site in Lower East Smithfield was examined and reported on, and disregarded because it was thought to be too small. A site on the north side of Whitechapel Road, "a little to the eastward of Whitechapel Church," was also considered. Then negotiations were entered into with regard to a piece of land "situated near that part of Tower Hill commonly known as the Ditch Side," but these, too, fell through. Sites were advertised for, inspected, reported on, and declined during a period of six months. In June, 1748, Mr. Robert Mainwaring, an architect and member of the committee, was asked to look for a suitable piece of ground, and he reported " that the only thing he had met with suitable for the occasion is situated near Whitechapel Road, commonly known by the description of the Mount Field and Whitechapel Mount." Mr. Mainwaring further discovered that the premises were now possessed by Mr. Samuel Worrall, " a bilder," under a lease from the City for sixty-one years from midsummer, 1740. This lease would expire, therefore, in 1801. Mr. Worrall paid to the City a yearly rent of £26. The City, so Mr. Mainwaring reported, were not the freeholders, but had the same on lease from Lady Wentworth for 500 years, of which he believed about 440 were yet to come. He had interviewed Mr. Worrall, who would be willing to assign his interest therein for £750, he having at this time (1748) fifty-three years to come in his lease from the city.

Mr. Mainwaring's report was not favoured by the committee. There were strong objections to the site. What was the good of a hospital standing out in the fields all by itself ? How could patients be expected to come to so lonely a spot ? Was it fair to ask the physicians and surgeons to come, especially at night, for Whitechapel Road was one of the great roads out of London, the main artery to the Eastern Counties, and was infested by highwaymen, footpads, and riffraff of all kinds, ready to rob unprotected wayfarers coming in to or leaving London ? Moreover, the com-

THE LONDON HOSPITAL IN 1759

THE NEW SITE, WHITECHAPEL

mittee thought Mr. Worrall's price unreasonable altogether. Mr. Mainwaring's suggestion for a site was not approved, and the committee continued their search for another six months. At Christmas Mr. Worrall offered to sell his interest in the piece of land at Whitechapel Mount for £500 (instead of £750), but " this was unanimously rejected as unreasonable."

A year after this—viz., September, 1750—the committee were still advertising and still unsuccessful.

At last, 1751, the committee, in despair, again opened negotiations with Mr. Worrall, and were inclined to take his piece of land. They could find no other at all suitable. The chief attraction was the fact that this site had land behind it right to the river, which was offered to the committee, and which was likely to become of value as a building estate. After much delay we find the following :

" The Committee recommend that Mr. Samuel Worrall be given £800 for his term of the piece of ground and improvements thereon which he holds of the City of London, situate at and near the Whitechapel Mount, subject to the rent of £26 a year paid by him to the City for the same, provided that the City should, after the expiration of the term granted to Mr. Worrall, grant to this Charity the remainder of their term in the said premises."

The Court agreed that this was the best that could be done, and it was arranged that a deputation from the Hospital should attend the Committee of City Lands to lay the proposal before them, which was done. The deputation was well and kindly received, and the Committee of City Lands promised to put the matter before the Court of Aldermen and Common Counsel, urging that the request of the Hospital authorities be granted :

Within a month is the following minute :

" The Court of the Lord Mayor, Aldermen, and Common Counsel concur with their Committee of City Lands to grant to this Charity their reversionary term of the premises which lye eastward of Whitechapel Mount, after the expiration of Mr. Worrall's term therein, subject to the rent of £15 a year for the same."

The governors had to contract " that the site should be used for the building of an Infirmary, and not for any other purpose," and it was one of the conditions in the lease—and this seems to have been overlooked—" that the arms of the City be set up on all future Buildings."

The City's reversionary term was granted to lessees " which are named and accepted, as no agreement could be made with the President and other Governors of this Charity, not being incorporated."

The names of the lessees are given, and among them, of course, is " Mr. John Harrison, Surgeon." It may be noted in passing that the inconvenience caused in this transaction on account of the Charity not being incorporated drew Mr. Harrison's attention to the necessity of a charter.

So to-day the greater part of the ground on which the Hospital is built is leased from the City. It is that portion, consisting of the whole frontage, extending from Turner Street on the west to East Mount Street on the east, and back to about a line drawn between these streets running through Queen Alexandra's statue. The lease ends, it may interest readers to know, on September 26 in the year 2166. What

THE NEW SITE, WHITECHAPEL

will the Hospital do then ? The City will not be able to renew the lease, because the City's lease from Lady Wentworth ends five years later. Our successors will have to note that it is in the lease that, when the property returns to the City, "the bolts and locks are to be in good order."

The governors, having now obtained the site, lost no time in getting to work on the building. A new Building Committee was appointed, on which, by-the-by, sat the Archbishop of Canterbury.

Very definite instructions were given to this Building Committee by the Court. No contract exceeding £100 was to be entered into unless at least thirteen of the Building Committee were present; no plan for the new building was to be accepted until laid before a General Court, nor was any expenditure exceeding £500 to be incurred without the permission of the Court, which the committee were empowered to summon at any time. No business at all was to be undertaken by the Building Committee unless seven members were present.

The Building Committee were fortunate in being able to let the houses in Prescott Street for the unexpired part of the lease, through Mr. Mainwaring, who was now appointed Surveyor to the Hospital.

On September 25, 1751, the Building Committee reported as follows :

"That after having unanimously resolved that a building ought to be erected for the use of this Charity, they had desired Boulton Mainwaring, Esq., your Surveyor, to prepare a plan or plans of a building for the reception of patients, with proper offices, who accordingly laid before your Committee at their last meeting five several plans, two of which, one for the reception of 396 patients, and the other for the reception of 366 patients, each with proper offices, were approved of; and Mr. Mainwaring was desired to make some calculation what the expense of erecting each plan might amount to. Who accordingly at the next meeting informed your Committee. But they being of opinion that the expense was more than the Charity ought in its present circumstance to engage in with prudence, and that a building without ornaments, not so large, and to contain accommodation for a smaller number of patients, might be sufficient for the present, desired Mr. Mainwaring to prepare a plan as near as he could conformable as to convenience and elevation with that for the reception of 396 patients, but not so large, and which should be capable of further extension and enlargement if at any future time there should be occasion for it, and to give a calculation of the expense. The said gentleman was also desired to take the opinion of your physicians and surgeons, and to make the rooms no higher than they should think necessary for the health of the patients."

After submitting several plans, one was at last accepted both by the Committee and the Court. It provided accommodation for 350 beds. Nearly all the wards had a south aspect (the wards were in the main building, facing south—*i.e.*, over the present quadrangle; the wards in the present wings face almost due east and west). The wards would be well away from the dust "of one of the most frequented roads," and sheltered from the cold winds; the building would be continuous, so that "the physician, surgeon, and apothecary might at all times attend the patients in all parts of it without danger, to which they might be

THE NEW SITE, WHITECHAPEL 85

exposed by their attendance in different detached parts, as proposed by the former plan "; the front was to be parallel with the highroad, "with an area of above 20 feet between for the coaches and chariots of the Governors." An engraving of this approved plan was to be prepared and circulated amongst the governors and to all guests at the ensuing feast. It was decided that the building was to be erected "under the immediate care and supervision of Mr. Mainwaring." He was asked to examine the site as to its suitability for building. He did so, and reported that it would be necessary to go down 18 feet for a foundation.

The method adopted for the erection of a large building in those days strikes us as peculiar. Now an architect would be asked to prepare a set of plans; specifications would be drawn up, and tenders invited, and one contractor would erect the whole building. This was not how they arranged matters then. Inquiries were first made as to what amount there was in the Building Fund available. It was agreed that there was sufficient to dig the foundations and raise the shell of the building to the first floor. An advertisement was inserted asking bricklayers to tender for their work, carpenters for theirs, and later, plumbers, masons, and painters. Each tradesman was to be paid for his own work, and all to work under the direction of the Hospital surveyor. The Building Committee were empowered to draw from the Building Fund, " but care must be taken that the contracts do not exceed the whole of the money appropriated for the building." When the money was spent, the building was to be stopped until more funds

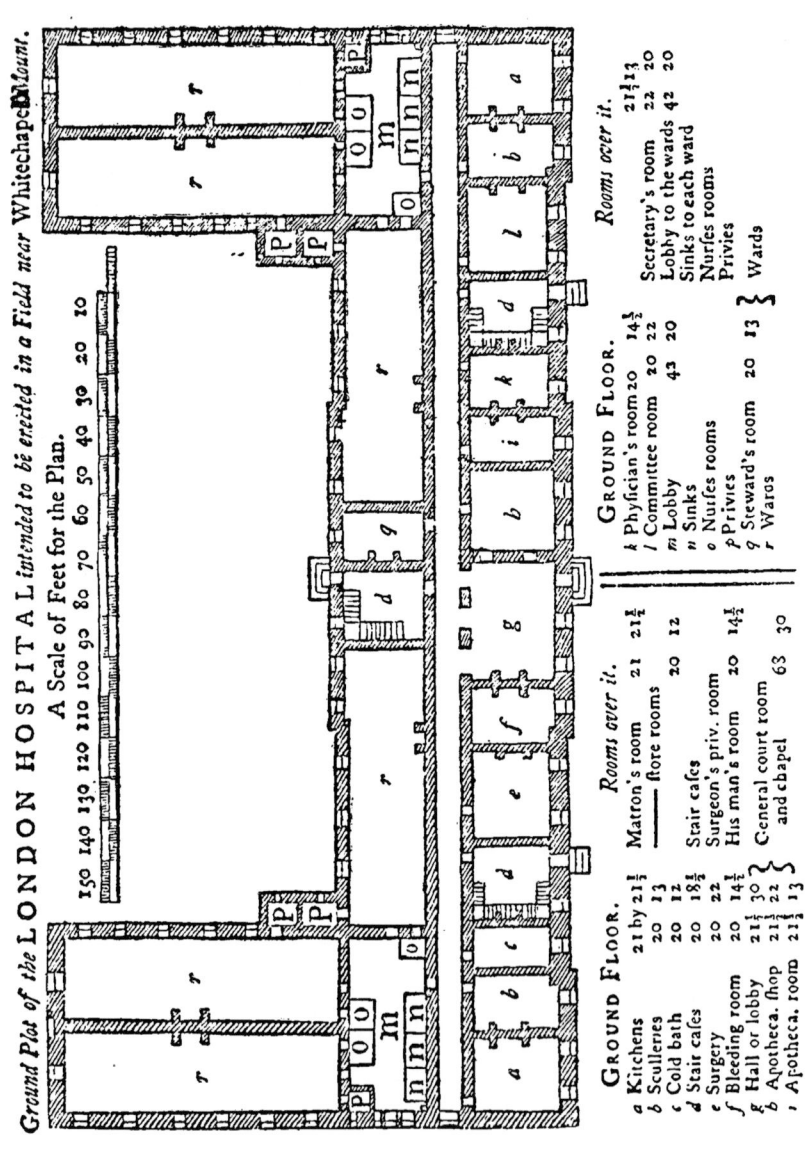

Ground Plot of the LONDON HOSPITAL *intended to be erected in a Field near Whitechapel Mount.*

A Scale of Feet for the Plan.

GROUND FLOOR.			Rooms over it.			GROUND FLOOR.			Rooms over it.		
a Kitchens	21 by	21¾	Matron's room	21	21¾	k Phyſician's room	20	14½	Secretary's room	21¼	20
b Sculleries	20	13	— ſtore rooms		12	l Committee room	20	22	Lobby to the wards	22	20
c Cold bath	20	12	Stair caſes	20	18½	m Lobby	43	20	Sinks to each ward	42	20
d Stair caſes	20	18½	Surgeon's priv. room	20	22	n Sinks			Nurſes rooms		
e Surgery	20	22	His man's room	20	14½	o Privies			Privies		
f Bleeding room	20	14½	General court room	63	30	p Privies			Wards		
g Hall or lobby	21¼	30	and chapel			q Steward's room	20	13			
h Apotheca. ſhop	21¼	22				r Wards					
i Apotheca. room	21¼	13									

PLAN I.—*March 26, 1752.*

were raised. At last, as the Building Committee reported, "the foundation of the Hospital began on the 11th day of June, 1752, being His Majesties accession to the throne." (That is, of course, the anniversary of it.) The foundation-stone was laid by Sir Peter Warren, Bart., K.B., Admiral of the Fleet, on October 15, 1752. The building was finished in 1759. The long time taken in building was due to the repeated stoppage of the work from lack of funds. The general funds of the Hospital were never drawn upon, and more than once the treasurer advanced money out of his own pocket to pay the workmen, because no money was left in the Building Fund—on one occasion as much as £350. He never charged interest.

When the Hospital opened its doors to patients, which it did in September, 1757—two years before the building was finished—it consisted simply of the central block facing Whitechapel Road. The long corridor as seen from the main entrance, east and west, shows the length of the original building. The foundations of the east and west wings were laid (half their present length—*i.e.*, as far as to the present lobbies between the wards), but the wings were not erected for more than ten years after. The Alexandra Wing, where the Committee-room is, and the Grocers' Wing, where Yarrow Ward is, are quite modern.

When the Hospital opened it had accommodation for 161 beds. The approved plan showed 350 beds, but the wings had not been built on account of lack of funds. It has now nearly 1,000 beds. The additions from 1759 to the present time are shown on the accompanying four plans.

PLAN II.—1759.

This is from Mainwaring's original plan. At this date the two short wings shown were not built, but their foundations were laid. They were not built until ten to twelve years after completion of the main building. The small building on the left was the Post-mortem-room and Store-rooms. It will be noticed that Turner Street was not made, and that the Mount came right up to the Hospital boundary. Although shown in the plan, as a matter of fact the New Road did not open into Whitechapel Road until 1761, and the small section of the Hospital estate necessary to make this opening was purchased by the Trustees of the New Road for £50. Oxford Street was not made. The Hospital stood in fields, and in a map of this district, slightly before this date, New Road is shown as a footpath leading from Whitechapel Road to the river. The plan shows that part of the Hospital grounds which are leased from the City of London. The building attached to the Hospital on the right is the shed for the "Chariots of the Governors."

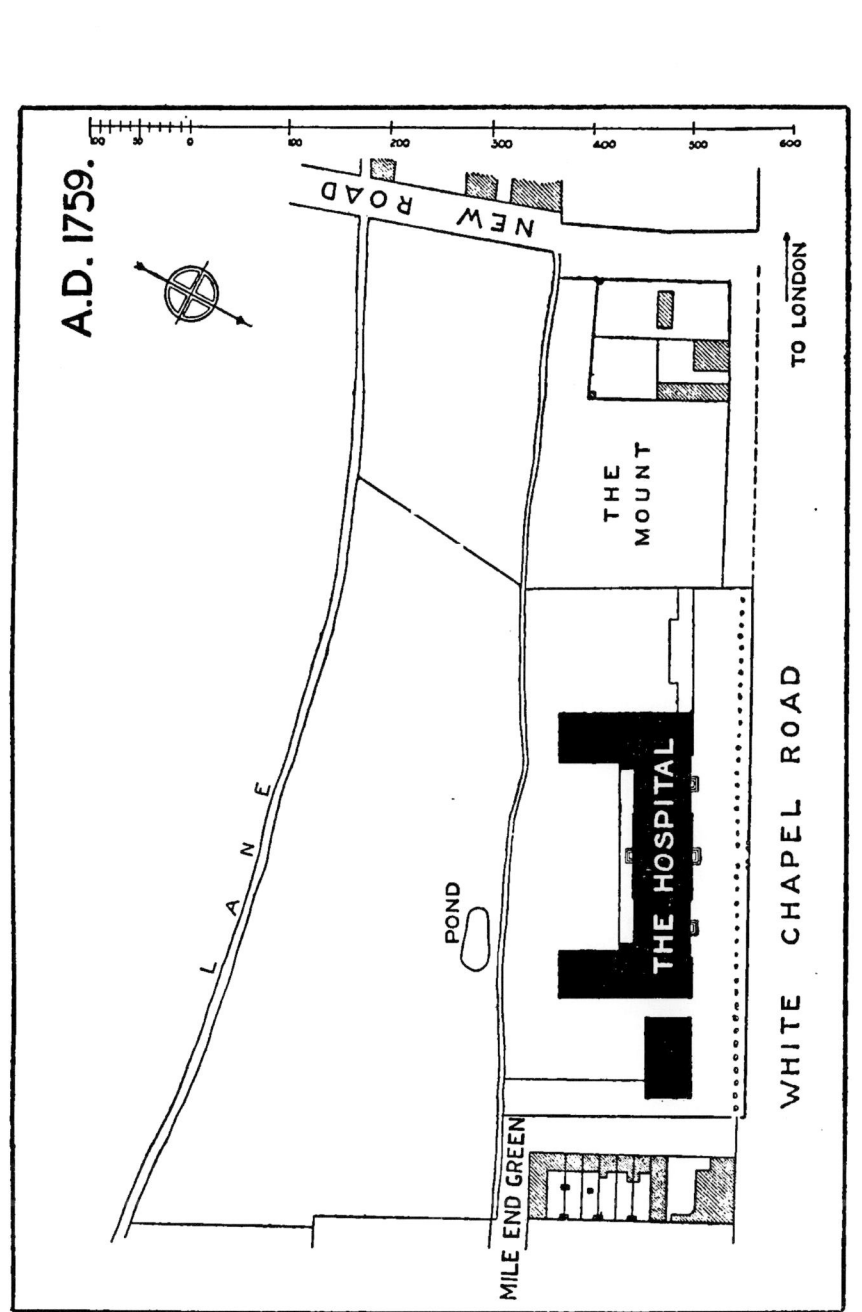

PLAN II.

PLAN III.—1840.

It will be noticed that the east and west wings have now been extended to the present length. On the east side there is now a Medical School, with Post-mortem-room, and rooms for the Pathologists. Note also that that part of the ground now known as "The Field" was the burial-ground for patients who died in the Hospital. This space was let out for grazing sheep until a comparatively recent date. Turner Street has now been made, and the Hospital estate behind has been mapped out into streets and blocks of buildings. At this time the water was pumped up from the Hospital's own wells by means of a horse-pump.

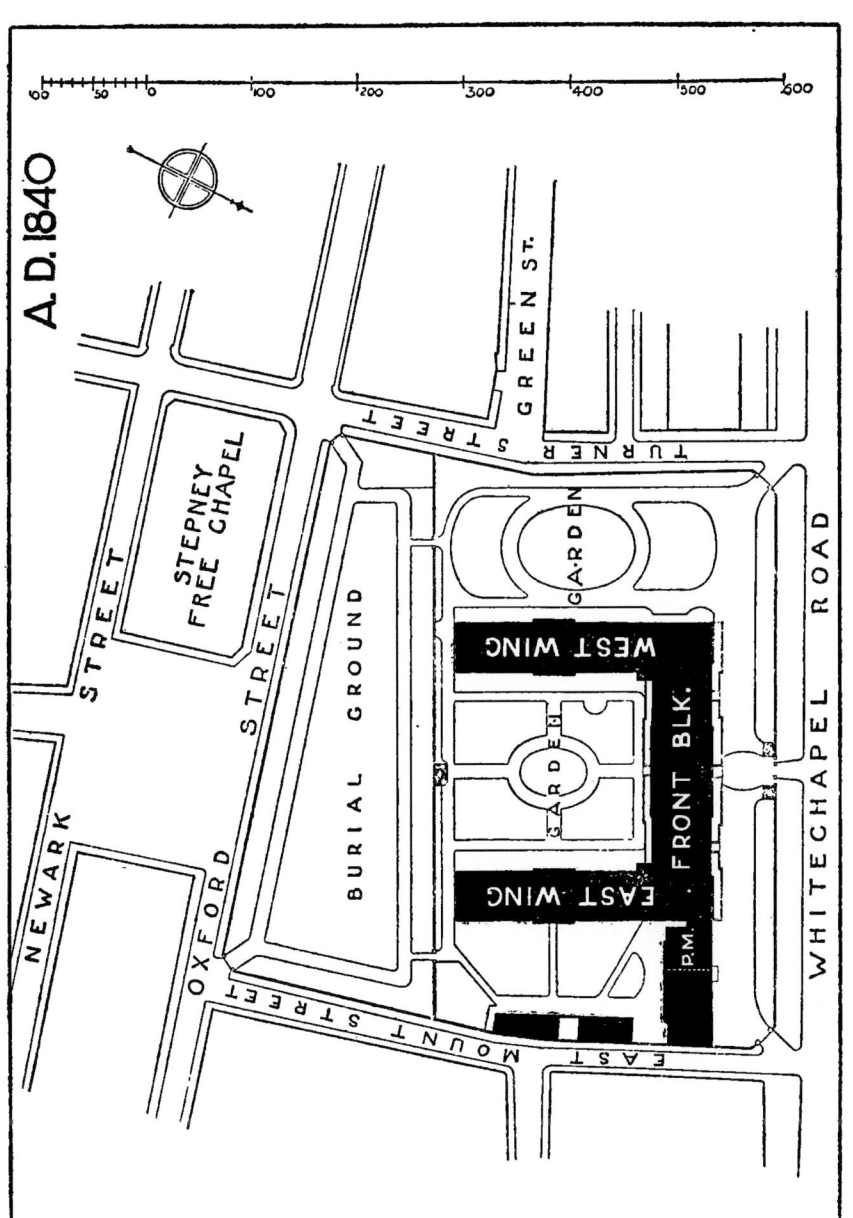

Plan III.

PLAN IV.—1886.

It will be noticed that the Medical College has been removed to its present site in the south-west corner of the grounds. The Alexandra Wing has been built. The Grocers' Wing has been built, and at the end of the east wing the first of the three present Nurses' Homes has been built; the Chaplain's house also, and workshops.

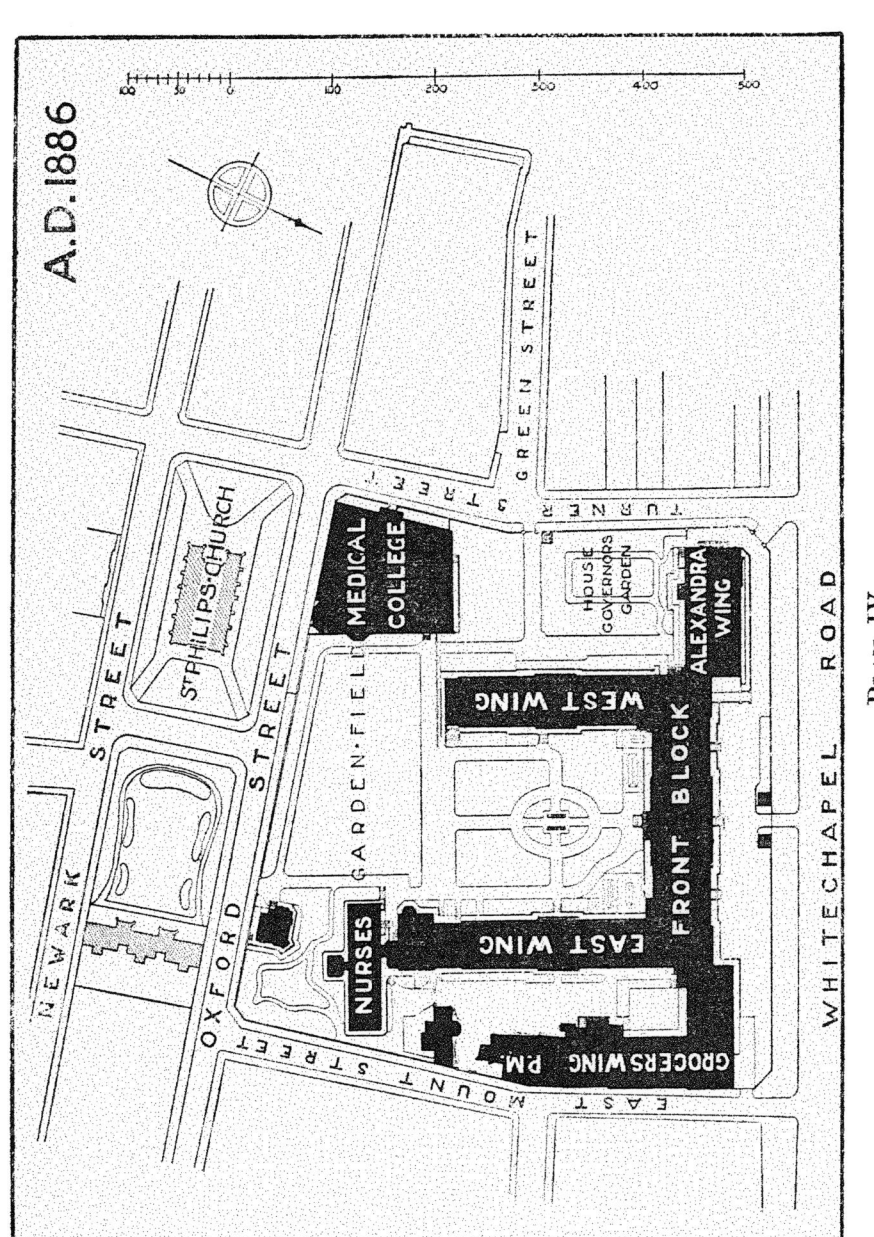

PLAN IV.

PLAN V.—MODERN TIMES.

The second and third Nurses' Homes have been built, and the main entrance of the Hospital added. There was no porch at the main entrance until 1897. The Isolation block has been erected. The College has been considerably enlarged. The Out-patient Department has been built. The Grocers' Wing has been entirely changed, and near this wing has been built one of the finest Pathological Departments in England. A laundry has been built, and extensive workshops. The alterations are considerably more than can be shown on a plan, as nearly the whole of the Hospital has been raised one floor, in some parts two floors, and there is hardly one part of the vast building which has not been altered and improved to perfect it for doing its work. These alterations, with the necessary equipment, have cost no less than £500,000.

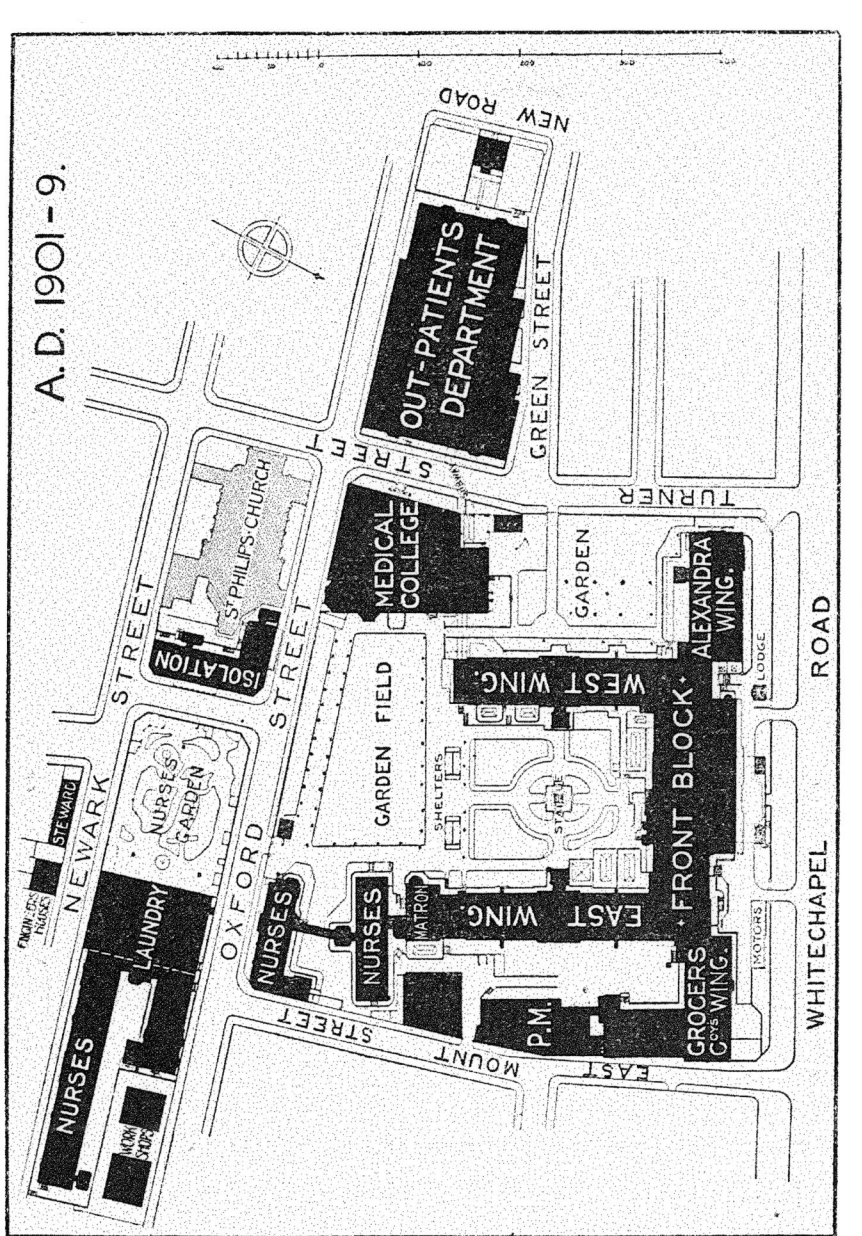

PLAN V.

CHAPTER VI

SOME CURIOUS POINTS IN HOSPITAL MANAGEMENT

WHEN the Hospital was founded, everyone who subscribed five guineas a year, whether lady or gentleman, was a " governor " or " manager " so long as he continued to subscribe, and in 1743 it was agreed that donors of thirty guineas became life governors. All governors were concerned in the management and the affairs of the Charity. As the number of governors increased, it became impossible to conduct the business of the Hospital on such lines. Meetings attended sometimes by as many as 500 governors were not likely to do much to further the interests of the Charity, and consequently this cumbersome form of management was discarded quite early in the Hospital's history. It was decided instead to elect from among the governors certain representatives who should meet every week, and who should report once a quarter to the full Court of Governors on all that had been done during the preceding weeks, and receive the Court's approval. With some not very important modification, the Hospital is to-day managed in this way.

At first the House Committee consisted of thirteen

members; there are now thirty. For many years the House Committee was elected quarterly by the Court; now it is elected annually by the Court which sits in December.

It is not easy to imagine what it could have been like to manage a hospital in those days (1740-1800). No telegraph, no telephone, no railways! The secretary was to summon the committee for 10 a.m., and business was to commence at 11. All who were not there when the clock struck eleven had to put a shilling into the poor-box. The decision that all committeemen should pay this fine was solemnly passed every three months. So these dear old gentlemen used to turn up at ten, and, apparently, gossip until eleven. There was time to gossip then. There was always time, too, to be courteous, and one finds many instances of this throughout the minutes. Letters sent to unimportant people on unimportant matters receive long and careful consideration as to the wording. Telegram letters were not used. I am sorry, however, to find the following minute:

" Resolved that this Committee for the future do adjourn to the Angel and Crown Tavern, Whitechapel, at 4 o'clock, for the better transacting the business of the Infirmary."

And they had begun business at 11 a.m.! The secretary and the beadle were also to adjourn with them. That the secretary should attend one can understand. But why the beadle? Dare one suggest that the beadle assisted some of these worthy gentlemen home after they had wearied themselves—overwearied themselves—in transacting the business of the Infirmary ? Perhaps it is not surprising that the following occurs a few months after :

" Resolved that all business to be done by this Committee *when held by adjournment to any other place* be read over the next Committee Day for confirmation."

They had time, too, to pay compliments. One sometimes wishes there was time for more resolutions to be passed now, such as the following. A similar graceful acknowledgment of service rendered is to be found at the end of every report of the House Committee to the Quarterly Court :

" Your Committee have now laid before you the principal transactions and occurrences of this Quarter, and hope the steps they have taken for promoting the Charity will meet with your consent and approbation. But they cannot on this occasion omit expressing with the utmost pleasure and satisfaction how wonderfully the hand of Providence has showed itself in setting on foot, increasing, and establishing in so short a time a work of such publick benefit and utility. It is true several gentlemen have distinguished their extraordinary zeal in this good cause by using their interest for the increase of its supporters, and that with so much success that it is hoped, besides the private satisfaction it must give them, their names and services will always be most gratefully remembered, and that it will be an incitement to others to follow their laudable example with equal prosperity and advantage. A further but necessary duty of this Committee is to acknowledge the constancy of Mr. Peck, our Chairman, in the execution of that office, who has during six months past never failed in the most punctual attendance, not only on Committee days, but whenever any affair of importance was directed by the Committee, by whose ability and application several disorders and inconveniences have been either prevented or removed, and some of the most desirable advantages obtained. We therefore unanimously join in recommending to the Court that he may have their publick thanks, as he has unfeignedly those of this whole Committee."

The minutes do not say what were the special services rendered by these excellent men, but that does not belittle them at all. Minutes may tell of " desirable advantages obtained "; they do not always draw attention to " disorders and inconveniences prevented." Perhaps they were somewhat more easily pleased than we are. For instance, in a previous chapter reference was made to a neighbour who, when the Infirmary was still in Prescott Street (1745), complained that the overflow from the Infirmary cesspool ran over his garden, which was lower. This was certainly no small fault, and one can imagine how an epidemic of typhoid would run riot under such conditions. At the very Court before which the complaint of this fastidious neighbour was brought, the committee concluded its report in the following words :

" The Committee congratulate the Court with joy that the Infirmary is now established on such a basis, and governed by such laws and regulations, *as not to admit of any innovations.*"

It would be a bold House Committee who could pass such a minute to-day !

In 1786 the committee was in a state of panic on account of funds, and, as usual with people in panic, they did some very strange and unwise things. They actually made a rule that the annual expenditure was not to exceed £2,500. I have heard of somewhat similar rules being made to-day in hospital management. Of course, the principle is a perfectly right one, that you must make expenditure suit income, and the principle may be applied in every walk of life. But in an institution like a hospital the rule cannot be invariably adhered to. Is a hospital to stand doing nothing when an epidemic chooses to arrive at the end of a hospital's financial year, and it had spent the sum allotted? Is a hospital to let some scourge like cancer or consumption continue to slay its thousands, after the discovery of a remedy, because the hospital had spent its cash in hand when the discovery was made? Is all research to stop on a certain day in October because funds are not in hand to carry on the work to December? Can a hospital discharge a skilled staff one day and re-engage it another? These dear old men had not yet discovered—how could they?—that whereas usually expenditure must follow income, in a voluntary hospital income follows efficiency. So they passed a solemn resolution that "the first object of the Hospital is the stability of it." There appears to have been no one present to tell them that "the first object of the Hospital is the usefulness of it." The stability of a useless hospital is of no account whatever. So a great many weak and foolish rules were made which deserved to bring the Charity into ridicule. One of such foolish rules was that not more than twenty in-patients were to be treated in any week. So the twenty-first was to be turned away, not because the patient was in less need, but because he was the twenty-first. The Hospital now admits about 270 new in-patients a week. But the growth in its usefulness was never stimulated by such policy as this of 1786. John Harrison strongly opposed such a policy, and after a time these dark and hopeless days passed. They have returned from time to time, but the light has followed, and there has always been a man who has " greatly dared " to show the way.

It was in this year (1786) that the House Committee was first elected for the year, instead of for the three months, as hitherto. At the same time the number of members was increased to thirty.

The House Committee from the first appointed two of its members to be House Visitors for a fortnight at a time. These House Visitors were instructed by their orders to make the following inquiries :

First, whether any of the patients or servants have been guilty of cursing, swearing, drinking, abusive language, or any other disorderly behaviour ?

Secondly, whether the patients have been duly attended by the physicians and surgeons, apothecary, matron, nurses, watches, and other servants ?

Thirdly, whether the provisions have been duly distributed ?

Fourthly, whether any offence hath been committed against the rules of the Hospital ?

I have come across an old book in which the House Visitors used to report, and perhaps some of these reports may be interesting enough to quote, and they will certainly give some idea of the way the work was carried on.

"1768, *February* 28*th*.—Visied the patientes of this house & had complaints of James Dye, this day whent out with out Live & of is Bad Beaver in the ward cauled Geo ward. I tasted the Bear & Fund it very ordney.—JNO COBB."

John Cobb's spelling was imperfect, but his meaning is clear. Did he write his report immediately after tasting the "smoll bear"?

"1768, *May* 19*th*.—Visited the house. No complaints from ye patients. In old John's ward nurse complained that William Crookshanks behaved very bad and swore and cursed; he whent out yesterday without leave and is not returned.—JAMES PEPWELL. P.S.—A part of the ditch behind the hospital is fell in, which ought to be put to rights."

The ditch referred to was an open sewer!

"1769, *January* 2*nd*.—No complaints, only there was but 17 patients at chapel to-day. The nurses complain of the minister coming late. Last night Sarah Trigg was delivered of a boy she being admitted under the care of Dr. Leeds by the complaint of obstructions.—WILLIAM TWEDALE."

Mr. Twedale makes this note because of the rule that pregnant women were not to be admitted to the Hospital.

"1769, *Thursday evening*, 7 *o'clock*.—Visited the house. Found ye nurses and patients agreeable except in Sarah's ward. Elizabeth Hutton's behaveour, a bad woman and no thanks to your charity. Please

CURIOUS POINTS IN MANAGEMENT   103

to call her to acct for ye Benefitt of ye charity. Great complaints against ye mutton and with great reason for I saw it myself and thought it very indifferent and the deception in ye legs of mutton was repeated. Complaint against one patient in Richmond's ward, John Patten, who had leave to go out yesterday, and half a guinea from a brother patient to buy him two shirts but has not yet returned.—J. W. BATSON."

The habit of patients to run away before treatment has been referred to. It was the duty of the apothecary to give leave of absence to patients. Mr. Batson, who made the above report, we know well. To this day, as a result of the " Batson gift," certain account-books must be brought before the committee for inspection every April and October.

And I recognize Mr. Jno. Cobb again. His spelling has not improved, and I am afraid it was an injustice to have suggested that his orthography was due to his conscientious care that the patients' " smoll bear " was of proper quality.

" 1770, *Feb. 26th.*—Vissited the House & had Greate Complaintes in ould Jno' Ward met [meat ?] being bad, & the a Loueces very smoll as they say. had sad complant of the Pepell [pupil ?] for St. Jno's Ward. One George Nesbitt in old George's Ward Got Drunk on Sunday and abused the Nurse and swear, Cursed, and used much abuseful Language. Complaints against Sophia Preston for abusing the Nurse & saying she gives Better Vituals to her dog. Order her out of the House Directly. Sophia preston is in Mary Ward. The nurses in New George acquaint me that they have had no water for several days past, pump being as they say out of repair. Ashes has not been cleared away this 2 months which the Cooks say blows in at the windows the top of the dust hill being raised above the levle of the windows. The beadle told me that the surplis of the minister is stowle a way. Please take it in consideration. Had complentes of smoll Bear but I find it mended when tasted it.—JNO COBB. (the surplis is found)."

A very good morning's work. I think somebody must have teased Mr. Cobb about his spelling, for from now on his reports, always practical, are " writ fair " by the secretary, and then follows the big sprawling signature, " Jno. Cobb."

The shortage of water and the stoppage of sinks were sometimes reported for six or seven consecutive weeks before anyone thought of doing anything. No wonder that one visitor reported, " The house very offensive, so much so that I could not Bare the smell " ! One of the visitors certainly felt that a little more cleanliness would be better for the patients, for he wrote :

" 1789.—I make an observation that there are no towels allowed in any of the women's wards, nor soap for the hands, etc., of any of the patients."— J. HOWARD."

I do not think the secretary in 1782 could have been very popular, or why did the Rev. Dr. Mayo write—

" Visited all the wards, heard no complaints. 194 patients. The Apothecary and his assistant, the steward, and the matron were in the house, but the secretary, that son of ——, was at the Gun.—HERBERT MAYO " ?

CURIOUS POINTS IN MANAGEMENT 105

Two of the committee for several years focussed their attention on the number of people who attended Divine service in the Hospital. The two gentlemen were the Rev. Dr. Mayo and a Mr. Thomas Blunt. This is the sort of thing which is written over and over again :

" 1790, *Dec.* 12.—Attended divine service. The chaplain gave a very suitable good discourse. Present —the steward, apothecary, 4 nurses, and 35 patients. All behaved very well and were very attentive."

" Visited the house in which were 156 patients, 15 of whom attended chapel. Heard of no complaint except some of the patients who were well enough to attend chapel went with great reluctance.—THOMAS BLUNT. P.S.—It appears from Matron, for good reasons, there was no service in the chapel this day. Of course the number mentioned by the nurses is not true."

The nurses' reference, therefore, to the "reluctance" of the patients seems to have been " merely corroborative detail, intended to give artistic verisimilitude to a bald and unconvincing narrative."

In 1782 the acting-chaplain was a Rev. Mr. Churchill, Mr. Audley being away on sick-leave. Mr. Churchill resented so much reference to his department. The trouble began through a note in the Visitors' Book by Mr. Thomas Blunt :

" 1782, *Oct.* 28*th.*—The chaplain did not attend this morning. Watch of Sarah's Ward, notwithstanding no prayers were read in the chapel, said that five of her patients certainly attended chapel and heard prayers read. Would wish her reprimanded by the Committee for this.—THOMAS BLUNT."

To this Mr. Churchill replied in the Visitors' Book as follows:

"It has been asserted that prayers of the chapel were omitted on Monday last, and the omission imputed to the non-attendance of the clergyman. The assertion is true, but the imputation is false. I was at the hospital on that day, and waited some time, but no person could be found to ring the bell or open the chapel.—W. CHURCHILL."

Then Mr. Blunt, also in the Visitors' Book:

"Mr. Churchill is requested, when he makes minutes in future in the Visiting Book to be a little more decent in his expressions and imputes. What was inserted in that book of the 28th October against him was owing, as it appears from his own account, to a wrong information of those of whom B. inquired. Had Mr. Churchill done as is the duty of the chaplain, he would have waited more than 10 minutes before he departed the hospital, and then have made his complaint in writing in order that the committee might have been able to judge on whom the neglect lay.—THOMAS BLUNT."

Mr. Churchill has the last word:

"I esteem myself much obliged to Mr. Blunt for his kind information relative to the impropriety of my language, and shall certainly pay such attention to it as it deserves—*i.e.*, I shall not again be guilty of the like impropriety of language (as he thinks it) unless Mr. Blunt is guilty of the like impropriety of behaviour. If in future Mr. Blunt will take a little time to consider before he acts or writes, perhaps his conduct, as well as his orthography, will be less exceptionable."

This was a knock-down blow for Mr. Blunt, and the committee, like a modern editor, decided "that this correspondence must now cease."

Nothing irritated the committee more than that "the miserable objects" in the Hospital should show any reluctance at the treatment meted out to them. Any patient who was so absurd as to shirk an operation (and without an anæsthetic, be it remembered) was bundled out promptly in disgrace. Liptrap, who in 1785 was instrumental, with the great surgeon Blizard, in founding the Medical School, reported to the committee :

"In Gloucester Ward is William Shaw, a boy whose disorder appears to be more of idiotism than anything else, as he will not take his medicine, and a blister which was put on his head he immediately pulled off. He also disturbs the patients in the ward by singing ; therefore, in my opinion, a very improper object for this charity."

So the child was discharged because he very naturally objected to a blister on his head.

Some of the most interesting reports are those from gentlemen of "the physical profession." They were evidently proud of the term, and in their reports tried to impress the committee with their overwhelming wisdom. For instance :

"1785, *April* 15*th*.—Passing through some of the wards, I found several of the nurses and patients complaining of the bad quality of the milk ; this led me to examine particularly into the origin of the complaints, how far it was, or was not, to be considered as valid—*i.e.*, founded on absolute fact. The Officers (*i.e.*, the matron, house pupils, etc.) informed me that from Tuesday last to this day they had seen none but what was sour. The cook and some of the nurses asserted that it was in that state when *received*, and this assertion was confirmed by the declaration of all the patients. By entering into the composition of porridge, etc., milk constitutes an essential part, and, to some who are on that diet, the principal article, of their nourishment. If, then, by the addition even of a considerable quantity of *water*, it does not possess those qualities which milk in its *natural state* ought to be possessed of (which I have great reason to believe particularly in this house always to be the case), our end in giving it as a *Nutrient Substance* is perfectly defeated. But if at the time it be brought in it has already acquired acidity, so far from being followed by salutery, its *internal* exhibition or *external* application must be attended with hurtful effects to the patients. And inasmuch as they are made to pay for what (can be clearly proved) they do *not receive*, to the Governors also of the Hospital, so far with respect to quality. I have also some reason to think that if inquiries were properly directed, it would be found that more of this (if I may be allowed the expression) *Degenerated Milk* is paid for than is actually received, and more received than there is occasion for.—THOMAS THOMAS."

In considering the administration of the Hospital a hundred years ago, the rules for the admission of patients seem particularly strange. Governors had the right of having one patient in the Hospital at a time. The treasurer and chairman of the House Committee had power to order the admission of "serious accidents or extraordinary disorders." The Staff had no power whatever to admit cases; indeed, there were special

CURIOUS POINTS IN MANAGEMENT 109

regulations prohibiting them from doing so, as we shall see. And then, too, as has previously been stated, patients were only admitted on one day in the week—the day on which the committee sat. Each patient came before the committee with his recommendation from a governor, and the committee decided whether he should be admitted or not; and no case was considered unless the recommendation was delivered in before eleven.

Every time the committee sat the physicians and surgeons came before them with a long string of "miserable objects," and the Staff represented that these miserable objects had been cured by them (I counted a list of seventy-five introduced by one member of the staff on one committee day—a good week's work, and no small advertisement to the surgeon concerned). And all these poor objects were asked then and there to contribute to the poor-box kept in the committee-room for the purpose. No patient was allowed under any consideration to remain in the house longer than two months, except cases of "fracture." In 1756 a list of diseases was put up, and patients suffering from these were not to be admitted. The "prohibition list" included "ulcerated cases," women with child, children under seven (except for amputation or "cutting for stone"), patients suffering from fits, smallpox cases, cases of itch, distempers, consumptives, asthmatical cases, infectious cases, and all "disordered in their senses."

Patients were not allowed to leave the building except by permission of the apothecary; they were not to swear or curse in the wards, nor to play any kind of game, especially games of chance ; nor were they to "smoak" in the wards. And the men were not allowed in the women's wards, nor the women in the men's, except "by leave."

Pewter medals were made, the size of a crown piece, with the words "London Hospital" round the edge, the name of the ward in the centre, and a number corresponding to the number of the bed. All in-patients had to wear these medals "fixed to their clows," so that they might be readily distinguished. This custom was eventually given up because the medals were lost by the hundred. It appears that the patients stole them as mementoes of their visit (1790).

When a patient was about to be discharged from the Hospital, a printed notice to the following effect was given to him :

"Thro' the charitable assistance of the Governors of this hospital, you have in your late afflictions, without any expence, been provided with comfortable lodging and proper advice. By the blessing of Almighty God on their humane endeavours, you are now so much recovered that you will shortly be discharged. The Governors, in return, expect and require nothing from you but that you attend devoutly in the Chapel of the Hospital on Monday next at 10 o'clock in the forenoon, and also in your Parish Church or other usual place of worship on the Sunday after you are discharged, publickly to return your thanks to Almighty God for His great goodness to you. You will have a paper given you to be conveyed to the minister for that purpose. That you appear to return thanks before the Committee on Tuesday morning next at 11 o'clock, and that, if admitted by a recommendation, you by no means omit to show your gratitude, and give notice of the opportunity for some other distressed person to be relieved, by delivering the letter of thanks, which will be given you, to the Governor who recommended you. Should you fail in these, remember that you will show yourselves ungrateful both to God and Man, and wholly unworthy of the blessings and benefits which you have received, and you will be deservedly precluded from any future relief at this hospital. They hope and trust that during the hours of affliction and sickness your minds have been employed in religious meditation; that the good advice and instruction which you have received will be seriously attended to; that you will henceforth endeavour to live in the fear of God, who alone can protect you from disease and accidents and evils, and preserve to you that health to which you are now by His blessing restored."

This paper, strange though it may seem now, was given to every patient from 1793 until comparatively modern times.

About this date the Staff made serious complaint to the committee that the Out-patient Department was in a very unsatisfactory condition. The patients were said to be very irregular in their attendance, thereby wasting the time of the doctors and the medicine of the governors; that a great many of the patients seen could afford to pay, and were absolutely defrauding the Charity; that in this department patients were often cured, but refused to return thanks, "and this procedure lessens the credit of the Hospital." The committee agreed that there had been great abuse of the Charity. This was partly through ignorance, the public not understanding what were the aims and intentions of the Charity. In its infant state medicine and advice had been given to all who asked in the Out-patient Department. This would now be stopped. Governors should have, as hitherto, the right of recommending in-patients. Subscribers of less than five guineas should have the right of recommending out-patients, and no out-patient, except accidents, would be seen except by such recommendation, which would remain in force for two months.

Even these rules did not sufficiently reduce the numbers of the out-patients, and it was at last decided that not more than twenty new out-patients per week could be treated, and all subscribers were told of the new rule. Up to 1785 new out-patients were seen on one day a week only, the same day as in-patients were admitted, but in 1786 it was decided that out-patients might apply any working day.

Up to 1788 there was no division of patients into medical and surgical wards; all were nursed in all wards. In this year one of the physicians, Dr. Hamilton, proposed that the surgeon's and the physicians' patients should be in separate wards. The proposal was strongly opposed by the surgeons, and the Court refused to adopt Dr. Hamilton's proposal. Indeed, there seems to have been a very hazy notion as to what were the distinctive duties of physician and surgeon. The Staff quarrelled about it, and referred the matter to the House Committee, who appointed a subcommittee to consider and report. This subcommittee reported in due course as follows :

" In obedience to your order of reference, we proceeded to inquire into the practice of physick and surgery in the House, and after mature deliberation thereon, and a full hearing of the several parties concerned, we humbly propose the following rules as a proper plan for regulating the said practice and preventing all difference between the physicians and surgeons for the future. In the forming of which rules we have had the good of the poor patients and the improvement of the Charity principally in view. First, that the surgeon have liberty to order internals for his own patients in all cases merely chirurgical, with this restriction—that upon the appearance of apprehension of danger, he do apply to one or more of the physicians. Secondly, that all cutaneous eruptions which do not require external applications or operations shall fall under the care of the physicians. Thirdly, that the physicians and surgeons do regularly go round the house together every Thursday at eleven in the forenoon to consult in such cases belonging to them respectively as may require it; after which such of the out-patients as likewise require their mutual assistance or advice shall be called in for their opinion."

It would seem, therefore, that it was generally felt that the surgeon was to attend to external ailments, and the physician to internal!

CHAPTER VII

QUARTERLY COURTS OF GOVERNORS—HISTORY OF THE JEWISH WARDS

A VERY pleasant feature, repeatedly seen in looking back through the old minutes, is the jealous way in which the honour of the Institution was guarded. To the committee no trouble was too great in investigating and refuting any breath of slander. Complaints made by the public as to the treatment of a patient, sometimes quite trivial, received an amount of attention quite out of proportion to their importance. Frequently a deputation waited on the person concerned to lay the whole case before him, a subcommittee having previously sat to make inquiries. The following report to the Quarterly Court in 1744 is a good instance of this :

" Your Committee being informed that Mrs. Holden, a good benefactress to this Infirmary, was pleased to express some uneasiness relating to the usage of the patients belonging to the same, and that in particular an unhappy person whose leg was broke, and brought into the said Infirmary, was neglected for three days without any attendance given him, which coming to the knowledge of your Committee, who were then sitting at the Infirmary, they immediately made inquiry if any such treatment had ever been given to any poor patient then or at any time before, and upon the strictest examination of the affair could find no ground whatever for such complaint. Your Committee thought proper to depute some Gentlemen then present to wait on Mrs. Holden, to know how she came by the said information, and to express their great concern for such report, as likewise the ill consequences that might attend the Charity, not only in disobliging her in particular, but likewise all the other kind and charitable Benefactors to the said Infirmary. Accordingly, John Peck, Esq., Chairman, Sir John De Lange, and William Myre, Esq., waited on the abovesaid lady, who, upon their acquainting her with the purport of troubling her with such a visit, exprest a very great concern in giving them that trouble. However, she did say that such a report had been made to her, but so far from giving her any uneasiness, she had never thought of it since, nor could she then anyways recollect from whom, or how, she heard it. The aforesaid Gentlemen then took the liberty of explaining to her the nature of the management of the said Infirmary, which would now be tedious to insert here, but after having heard them, she said that she was fully convinced of the falsity of such report, and was pleased to say from what they had related to her she wished every Charity of the sort was as well conducted, and that Gentlemen who would give so much of their time as those of the Infirmary did ought to have the thanks of all who were well disposed for supporting so good a work; and upon them taking leave of her, wished them all success in their undertaking, and if anything of that nature should ever happen, as she had reason to hope never would, that for the future she would endeavour all that in her lay to satisfy any person who should attempt to put so uncharitable a construction on the management of the Infirmary, and that this she was the better able to do from her being so well acquainted and satisfied with the nature of the care and pains that was taken therein."

The committee must have wasted much time and energy in investigating complaints which were quite trivial or entirely imaginary, for a rule was at last made (1765) that patients who made any complaint after they left the Hospital, and had not done so before they left, would have their names entered in the Black Book. This meant refusal to help such patient ever afterwards.

It was doubtless due to the same anxiety that no word should ever be spoken against the fair name of the Charity that it was decided in 1750 "That no chaplain, physician, surgeon, or other officer or servant of this Charity who shall hereafter be elected shall act as a governor of this Charity during his continuance in office"; also that "no tradesman or artificer serving this Charity shall be of any committee."

The meetings of the Quarterly Court were by no means invariably meetings of dull formality. The governors seem to have had strong feelings on all subjects, and did not hesitate to express themselves forcibly, although always politely.

The quorum for the Court was fifteen, as it is now; but frequently the attendances reached some hundreds, especially when some election was to take place. The reports of the House Committee were read and re-read paragraph by paragraph, criticized, modified, referred back, but rarely unanimously adopted; nor did the House Committee on its first meeting after a Court hesitate to state what it thought of the Court's proceedings. For instance, at a Court in 1807 a Dr.

Buxton was elected a physician to the Hospital by a narrow majority, his success being due to a decision of the Court earlier in the proceedings of the day that minors had no right to vote. This infuriated the House Committee, who had recommended another candidate, and especially as some of the members of the House Committee had made their children governors on purpose to insure the success of their candidate. They protested at the Court itself—" we do hereby protest against the election of this day "—on account of what they considered the unfairness of the voting. They did more. At their first meeting they passed the following resolution :

" The House Committee, deeply impressed with a sense of the evil consequences that may result from a law that would deprive a considerable part of the governors of those rights and privileges they have hitherto exercised, and which have been repeatedly confirmed by the custom of the Hospital (and this Committee cannot but be mindful of the great benefits which have arisen, and they have good reason to hope will continue to the Hospital from old attachments, which, commencing in youth, gather in strength as they advance in age), resolved unanimously that the resolution of the Court of the 9th June denying the right of governors under age to vote at an election of a physician, not having been specified in the summons for holding such Court, was an act illegal in itself and mischievous in its tendency, and ought to be rescinded ; it is further resolved that the above resolution be inserted in the *Times* and ' Public Ledger.' "

The strong protest of the committee had an effect upon the Court, for at the next sitting the resolution as to the illegality of minors voting was rescinded. The harm had been done, however. Dr. Buxton had been elected—the only man I have ever found on the London Hospital Staff of whom I am ashamed. He came on to the staff by a trick, and when he resigned in 1822 the Court, in accepting his resignation, passed the following resolution :

" The Court cannot refrain from noticing a report that he has been negotiating to resign his situation as physician to the Hospital for a pecuniary consideration, and this Court is anxious to give Dr. Buxton an opportunity to exculpate himself from an imputation which it considers highly discreditable to his profession, and destructive of the best interests of this valuable Institution."

Dr. Buxton did not reply, and the Court minutes never refer to the matter again. His name seems to have been his only good asset. But I must not omit to say that he was in no way connected with the family of Buxtons who have done so much for the Hospital.

Voting at the Quarterly Courts was by ballot, and very definite rules were laid down as to the mode of procedure. When, for instance, a member of the Staff was to be elected, the names of all candidates were printed on slips of paper, the chairman received the ballot-papers in a glass, the secretary checked off each governor who dropped in a ballot-paper, the governor signed his paper, and if it was found he had dropped in two, both were cancelled. As many " fyles " were provided as there were candidates ; the chairman drew out the papers and stuck them on the corresponding " fyle " ; a governor acted as champion to each candidate, attending to his "fyle" and checking his votes. The ballot always opened at eleven and closed at two.

Peers of the realm and ladies were allowed to vote by proxy, but the vote was invalid unless the proxy was signed by the principal.

As appointments on to the Staff became more valuable it paid candidates to make governors (at five guineas each) who should attend the Court and vote. The governors, however, tried to put an end to this practice by not allowing anyone to vote whose subscription had not been paid seven days before the election took place. This seven days was extended in 1790 to one year. The following report of the House Committee on the subject may be of interest :

"The Committee conceive they cannot close their report more consistently with the proper dignity and real design of the Hospital than by their decided and unanimous proposal to the General Court to extend still further the approved principles of their late experimental motion made to prevent part of the inconvenience of admitting annual governors in contemplation of an election, some of them on the actual day of election and during the progress of the ballot, by which motion it was resolved 'that no annual governor shall vote at any election who has not been a governor seven days.' The Committee perceive with concern the disadvantage of admitting new voters even with this cautionary resolution, since the Charity has seldom retained these casual contributors beyond the period of their subscriptions, while it has lost through this influx of voters some able and ancient governors who had for a series of years been the tried friends of the House, and whose personal services and prompt supplies would infinitely have outweighed any advantage that has arisen from those temporary and transient aids. The Committee therefore, wishing to see the Institution elevated and honoured, to raise its revenue and exalt its rank, as well as to evince respect for constant benefactors and cordial friends, which alone can merit or maintain the continuance of their friendship and of their bounty, do respectfully recommend and earnestly exhort the General Court to carry their experimental decree into a positive decision, that no annual governor or governors admitted from this date shall vote at any election who has not been a governor or governess one year, the election day inclusive ; but that *perpetual* governors shall possess the privilege of voting from the instant of their admission as a just discrimination between those who are attached to the Charity for life, and such on whose connection no confident reliance can be placed beyond the duration of a single year. This immediate transfer to Life Governors of the right of voting is also sanctioned by the example of the Royal Hospitals of the City of London."

The above resolution was carried unanimously by the Court.

A good illustration of the necessity of such legislation and of the energy with which an election was conducted was shown on the election of Dr. Little to the Staff in 1839. I am indebted to an article in the *London Hospital Gazette* of February, 1895, for the following account of this contest : A vacancy had occurred by the death of a Dr. Davies. The House Committee recommended, according to custom, four candidates to the Court, each of whom was eligible to fill the vacancy. Two of these retired before the day of election, leaving Dr. Little and Dr. Fox to contest the appointment. Each of these employed a host of canvassers, who visited the governors daily, and worried them to support their candidate. Each candidate had committees meeting at his house, and some of the methods adopted by these committees to further the cause of their friend are worthy of a Parliamentary election a hundred years ago.

Dr. Fox's committee saw nothing very dishonest in publishing by advertisement in the public press a series of resolutions said to have been passed at a meeting of the governors in Dr. Fox's favour.

Dr. Little's committee retaliated by also publishing in the press a statement that not only were the statements made as to his rival's adoption by the governors fictitious, but no meeting whatever had taken place; and this statement of Dr. Little's committee was actually signed by four vice-presidents and eighteen members of the House Committee, including the chairman.

Dr. Fox objected to this interference as being " dictatorial, oppressive, and unjust."

Dr. Little's committee announced that on the day of the election they would sit at the London Tavern, " where carriages are in readiness for the convenience of Dr. Little's friends." Dr. Fox's committee made similar arrangements at a house in Billiter Street.

On the day before the election the following anonymous letter was circulated :

" The Committee of Dr. Little, in again thanking you for the very kind manner in which you have tendered him your support, viewing with regret the circumstances of their canvass, even at this late period have reluctantly determined not to proceed to the poll, as they are of opinion this step will be most conducive to his future prospects, and tend to make friends where a vexatious opposition might create enemies. They therefore respectfully release you from your attendance at the Hospital to-morrow on his behalf.

"10, FINSBURY SQUARE,
"*July 2nd*, 1839."

The trick was detected in time. Of course, Dr. Little had no intention of resigning from the contest. Handbills were distributed on the day of election by Dr. Little's committee, denouncing such a scandalous letter.

No doubt it was the Englishman's sense of fair play, so shamefully outraged, which helped to make Dr. Little's return the triumphant one it was.

After the election there was a good deal of bad feeling, Dr. Fox stating that his defeat was due to "crushing family influences."

The election cost Dr. Little over £500, and no less than thirteen people became life governors, paying thirty guineas each in order to be allowed to vote.

Dotted throughout the minutes one comes across report after report on "Economy."

The modern craze for economy in hospital management is no new thing, although a good deal more public attention has been drawn to it than formerly. The public to-day have got hold of a catch phrase—"the cost per bed"—of hospitals. I have known many instances of supporters withdrawing their subscription from one hospital because its "cost per bed" was more than that of another, to which, I presume, the subscription was transferred. This figure, "the cost per bed," is obtained by dividing the hospital's expenditure by the number of beds in occupation, and the hospital's management stands condemned or commended according to the amount of the quotient. If all the hospitals were doing the same kind of work, there might be reason in such a comparison. But they are not, and many questions need to be asked and answered before the figure is of the slightest value in comparing one hospital with another. To do so without asking such questions is as reasonable as to compare the cost per day of two ships, which have nothing in common except that they both float on the sea. The difference in the work of hospitals is as great as the difference in the work of a battleship, a private yacht, a Cunarder, and a cattle-ship.

These oft-repeated reports on "Economy" are interesting, however, from the fact that they give many a peep into the work of the time.

In 1748 such a report tells us that the cost per day of a patient was $6\frac{1}{2}$d.—

"which your committee apprehend to be very reasonable, and they do not think it possible to make any reduction unless it shall be thought proper to discontinue the gratuity of 2 guineas per annum to the banker's clerk."

The committee also suggested that an appeal might be made against the window tax, the Hospital being assessed at £5 11s. for window lights. It is gratifying to note that the appeal was successful. In the report of an "economy committee" in 1754 I note that the cost per bed in that year was £12 per annum. (In 1767 it had grown to £17 15s., and in 1822 to £26 9s. 4d. It is now about £90 per annum.) The people to-day who spend so much time in doing "cost per bed" sums would surely have admired the Hospital's work in 1754. No better illustration could be given of the danger of the modern worship of all that is cheap. One has nothing but admiration for those who use every endeavour to get efficient work performed at as little expenditure as possible, but there must be no "trimming" of one's idea of what is efficient. To-day a hospital bed costs nearly eight times as much as it did in 1754. It is doing eighty times the good. In 1754 the Hospital's duty was to cure John Smith of a disease. In 1910 its duty is to destroy disease, to stamp it out, so that every John Smith who lives need never enter the walls of any hospital. The modern hospital says:

"We have had a patient with a certain disease; we have found what has caused it; that patient need not have had it; no man, woman, or child henceforth need have it. And this, cost what it may, is to be done, in order that no one need suffer from it."

And so, one after the other, diseases are disappearing. Smallpox, typhus, hospital gangrene, diphtheria, malaria, Malta fever, consumption, are all going. All "germ" diseases are going. Length of life is extending. As many people died at forty in the reign of Elizabeth as now live to seventy.

But let us return to some of the decisions of the various "economy committees."

Some of their recommendations were thoroughly

good and sound. It was wise, for instance, to insist that complete inventories of the Hospital's "furniture, utensils, dispensary equipment, sheets, and linen" should be taken periodically; that all purchasing was to be by public tender; that "tips" to servants were to be abolished; that an efficient system of book-keeping should be inaugurated. All these recommendations were carried out before the year 1800, and most of them are in force to this day.

These dry economy reports always commenced with a pompous exordium and expression of pious opinion. For instance, in 1792:

"Attention to economy is essential whether we reflect on the effect of example as influencing the class of people admitted into this Hospital or refer it to the enhanced price of provisions and increased expenditure. A public charity, not very affluent in its revenue and resources, is under more immediate obligation to attend closely to economy, not only as dispensing public contributions seriously devoted to the relief of misery, but as every deviation from strict frugality abridges the power of doing good, and excludes many afflicted petitioners, who, in agony and indigence, throng about the gates with unavailing entreaties for that healing aid which cannot on the present scale of expense be afforded them, etc."

One of such reports was by no means complimentary to the House Committee and its management. The committee appointed had "attentively compared the expenditure of the London Hospital with that of other similar establishments, and they grieved to report an apparent extravagance highly reprehensible." They recommended that an expert, thoroughly conversant with the management of such establishments, be engaged to look into the whole matter and advise the committee as to economy. This was in 1807. So a Rev. Mr. Rudge was engaged to act as superintendent for one year. The experiment was eminently satisfactory. The minutes speak of greater comfort to the patients, greater cleanliness, and greater economy. When Mr. Rudge retired, in 1809, to attend a small living in the country, the committee voted him £650 as " a thank-offering for the zeal, talents, and exertion he has so constantly and successfully practised." We hear no more of Mr. Rudge, but doubtless his influence is felt to this day. When he left, the committee decided to make the appointment of superintendent a permanent one, and so advertised for " a man between the age of thirty and forty, single, and of an active and firm mind."

In 1818 this appointment, then known as that of House Governor, was merged with the duties of Chaplain in the person of the Rev. William Valentine. He was paid £250 a year, with board and residence.

One of the chief features of the Hospital to-day is the accommodation given to those of the Jewish faith. There are four wards exclusively reserved for Jews, in which all the religious rites of these people are very carefully observed. Separate contracts are entered into for Kosher meat. A separate kitchen is provided, which is under the charge of a Jewish cook. There is a Jewish mortuary for the dead. Every convenience is given for the observation of the great religious festivals—the Feast of the Passover, of Tabernacles, and for the rite of Circumcision. The ordinary visiting-day at the Hospital, when friends are enabled to see patients, is Sunday. For Jews it is Saturday, their Sabbath. One of the rules of the Hospital is that out-patients who can afford to do so should pay 3d. per week towards the cost of medicines or dressings. About half the patients who attend pay this small charge towards the expense of their cure. To the strict Jew the carrying of money on the Sabbath is forbidden. In order that there may be no suffering on the part of Jews, who would refuse to attend the Hospital on their Sabbath with such a rule in force, certain members of the House Committee have guaranteed to pay the 3d. for any Jews who conscientiously object to carry money on the Sabbath.

A district near where the Hospital is situated has been a dwelling-place for Jews for more than a hundred years. In 1747 their numbers were so great that they had thoughts of founding a hospital of their own, for we find a deputation visited the committee of the Hospital, led by a Dr. Castro Samento, " to desire the favour of being informed of the scheme upon which this Charity was first founded, the Jews having decided to found an Infirmary for their poor." The steward was directed to give all information possible. The information was given, evidently, for three months after we find that—

" Joseph Salvador thanked the Committee in the name of the Elders and Body of the Portuguese Jews for the assistance rendered by the Officers of the London Infirmary."

The scheme appears to have fallen through, for in 1756 arrangements were made for the treatment of

Jews in the Hospital. There were no special wards for them, nor was special food provided; but there is a minute which says: "Jews are to be allowed 2½d. a day in lieu of meat and broth, but to receive bread and beer, like the other patients."

The Jews are not referred to again in the minutes for forty years, when the Medical Staff of the Hospital reported to the committee that the 2½d. per day was insufficient for Jewish patients to provide themselves with meat. The allowance was therefore increased to 4d. a day. This was not to be paid, however, unless the patient was on a meat diet; patients who were on milk or fever diet were not to receive the grant. If patients' diets were changed then as often as they are now, the steward must have found his time fully occupied in keeping accounts of these small payments. In 1816 there was a conference between "Gentlemen of the Hebrew Nation" and the committee, to consider what further accommodation could be afforded, and the result of the conference was that the committee " entirely relinquishes all idea of a separate ward or wards."

Nothing is heard of the subject until 1837, when a very influential deputation of Hebrew gentlemen attended the committee and read the following communication:

"The Committee, for the more effectual relief of the sick poor of the Jewish community requiring medical aid in and about London, are very desirous of having a ward in the London Hospital appropriated exclusively for persons of their Faith, to be divided into two compartments, being for males and females, the former to be attended by a Jew nurse, the latter by a Jewess nurse, as also a separate kitchen under the care of a Jewess cook, and the meat to be supplied by a Jewish butcher; by which means the Jewish in-patients would, on their sick- and often on their death-beds, receive that consolation and peace of mind which would prove most consonant with their religious feelings. They are also desirous of having out-patients to the Hospital for such poor whose cases do not require their becoming in-patients. The Committee have been informed that the average number of Jewish patients in the different wards of the London Hospital have been about forty for some time, to whom the Hospital kindly allows 9d. per day each in lieu of diet.* The Committee are aware that their present request would be attended with extra expense to the Hospital, and therefore purpose to make an annual payment as some compensation for the required boon, or would recommend their body to pay immediately (as much as their funds will allow) a sum of money in lieu of an annual payment. The deputation of the Committee now in attendance leave the amount of compensation in either case to the known liberality and generosity of the Governors of the London Hospital, and they only regret that their present means are such as to oblige them to use every economy in the distribution of them. But, as the Governors of the London Hospital are aware that the Jews have been liberal donors to their excellent Charity, the Committee think they are warranted in believing that, should the present request be granted, the generosity hitherto displayed by the more opulent of their brethren will be considerably augmented, not alone by them, but by every member of the Jewish community."

* There is no reference in the minutes of this change from 4d.

A special committee was appointed to consider this communication. This special committee reported in three months as follows:

" With every possible desire to meet the wishes expressed by the gentlemen of the Hebrew nation for peculiar accommodation for patients within the walls of the Hospital, the committee is of opinion that the present means of the Hospital do not afford the power of granting the request; but the committee will be ready to resume consideration of the subject whenever the funds of the Hospital will enable them to extend the building."

In 1840 a Building Committee was appointed to consider the extension of the east wing, "including a ward for Hebrew patients."

In 1842 this Building Committee reported (the east wing having been built):

" Having had under consideration the arrangement for the Hebrew patients as formerly proposed by the Surveyor, we are unanimously of opinion that it would be more for the interest of the Hospital, as well as for the comfort of the Hebrew patients themselves, and more convenient for the medical officers and servants of the Hospital, to appropriate Sophia Front Wards for the female Hebrews, and Talbot Front Wards for the male Hebrews."

Mr. Ellis, "on behalf of the Gentlemen of the Hebrew nation, approved of this arrangement." The Jews had separate wards in the Hospital from this date until 1853.

In the latter year the House Committee complained

" of the great inconvenience resulting to the Hospital from the practice of keeping an entire ward exclusively

HISTORY OF THE JEWISH WARDS

for male Hebrew patients, whether there were applicants for the beds in such ward or not, and suggested that no injury could accrue to Hebrew patients if, upon application for admission, they were placed in one allotted portion of certain wards, the other beds in such wards being given up for Christian patients, when not required by the Hebrews, and *vice versa*."

As to this, the representatives of the Jews, through a Mr. Helbert, replied, in a broad-minded spirit, " that it was by no means their wish that beds should be kept empty to the detriment of patients requiring them."

The arrangement was adopted, and the wards hitherto used for Jews exclusively were now used for Christians as well, when necessary.

The plan did not succeed, however, and within a year—*i.e.*, in 1854—the Jews again approached the committee by deputation, asking for the allotment of separate wards instead of only distinct portions of certain wards. The committee replied that it was impossible to accede to the request. The refusal was considered by the Jewish Vestry to be unfair, as the wards had once been opened, and the following letter was sent to the governors of the Hospital :

" That this Vestry, having heard with great regret that the wards at the London Hospital, agreed to be set apart for Jewish patients, have been opened for the admission of patients of other religious denominations, this Vestry request that Mr. Ellis and the other Jewish members will represent to the committee of the London Hospital that the admission of such patients is contrary to the spirit of the arrangement between the Committee of the London Hospital and the Jewish Community, and earnestly hope that they will use their best influence with a view to prevent its recurrence."

The House Committee sent the following letter in reply to this resolution of the Jewish Vestry:

" *To the Secretary of the Great Synagogue.*
" SIR,
" Mr. J. H. Helbert having handed to the House Committee the copy of a resolution passed at a meeting of the Vestry of the Great Synagogue held on the 19th instant, I am instructed to inform you that such resolution has received the fullest consideration. In pursuing your inquiries, the following facts have been made evident to the House Committee—viz.: that since 1842, the year when the Hebrew wards were established, the number of in-patients generally has very much increased; that the several changes in the appropriation of the wards have been adopted under circumstances of pressing necessity; that every precaution is taken to render those portions of wards allotted to Hebrew patients as distinct as possible from the other parts of such ward; and that very great benefit has resulted to the general body of patients from the present arrangement. With reference, however, to these several views of the question, or to their own desire to meet the wishes of the Jewish Community, the Committee have reluctantly to confess that, with the limited accommodation afforded by the present building, surrounded as it is by a rapidly increasing population, it is impossible to allot separate wards to Hebrew patients—a conclusion at which the Committee have arrived not without very sincere regret. The utmost, therefore, which the Committee can now do is to express their determination, in the event of

an enlargement of the Hospital being effected, which, for the present, has been placed in abeyance, to give the fullest consideration of the subject of providing suitable separate accommodation for the patients of the Hebrew persuasion."

The Vestry replied :

"The difficulty in which the Hospital has been placed with reference to this subject having been explained, it is suggested that a screen, reaching nearly to the ceiling, with a door, might be provided, movable, so as to make that portion occupied by Jews quite distinct and separate, which would meet the exigencies of the case."

This plan was temporarily adopted. This, too, did not prove a satisfactory arrangement, and in 1856 the question was again raised. Mr. Sebag attended

"with the Hebrew Trust Deed and other documents, which were read, and from which it appeared that in the year 1842 certain Trustees had been appointed to apply the funds of a Society, now extinct, for the relief of Sick Poor of the Hebrew Persuasion in aid of the funds of the London Hospital, so long as certain conditions involving separate accommodation, etc., for Hebrew patients should be adhered to. The minutes of the House and Building Committees were then also examined, from which it appeared that no legal engagement to adhere to the conditions of the above-named Trust Deed had ever been entered into by the Governors, the Hebrew wards, kitchen, and other accommodation having been provided solely under certain recommendations from the House and Building Committees."

This was quibbling, I think, on the part of the Committee, or else they had not all the facts before them.

The following extract from the old minutes, dated April 21, 1842, of the " Institution for the Relief of the Distressed Sick of the Jewish Persuasion," seems to show that there *was* an agreement :

" Mr. S. H. Ellis attended on behalf of the Committee of the London Hospital, and officially announced to the meeting that four wards in that Institution were now completed and ready for the admission of Jewish patients on the anniversary—the 28th instant—and that the same wards would be named on that day by His Royal Highness the Duke of Cambridge as follows : Two male wards—the one Goldsmid and the other De Rothschild ; and the female wards—one Hannah, in compliment to the Baroness de Rothschild, and the other Esther; and that, further, one Hebrew nurse was already engaged, and that other arrangements were in progress for the Jewish patients, with due regard to their religious habits ; whereupon the following resolutions were moved and unanimously adopted : Resolved, ' that in consideration of the Governors of the London Hospital having appropriated four separate wards for the sole use and admission of male and female patients of the Jewish faith, and undertaking to provide Hebrew nurses and cooks, that the provisions and comfort of the Jewish poor may be provided for according to their custom, it is resolved by this Committee that the interest arising from £700 in the Reduced $3\frac{1}{2}$ per cent. standing in the names of Trustees and £500 in the hands of the Great Synagogue Trust be transferred in the names of Trustees, and that the interest arising therefrom be paid half-yearly by the Treasurer of this Society to the Treasurer of the London Hospital for the time being, so long as the said wards are appropriated for the reception of the Jewish patients.' "

HISTORY OF THE JEWISH WARDS 135

As the Hospital had been receiving the income derived from this trust since 1842, one cannot see what right the committee had to say the governors had not entered into any agreement. The income from the Hebrew Trust, now known as the Rothschild Fund, is still paid to the Hospital.

At last wards were reopened exclusively for Jewish patients about 1860. Later they were situated in the Alexander Wing, soon after its opening in 1866 until 1904. The four splendid new wards for Jews, situated in the west wing of the Hospital, were opened in 1904. The late Mr. Edward L. Raphael contributed the magnificent sum of £20,000 towards their endowment, and his son, Mr. Louis Raphael, a present member of the House Committee, has contributed generously to their equipment.

CHAPTER VIII

RELATIONS BETWEEN HOUSE COMMITTEE AND STAFF

WILLIAM BLIZARD

THE relations between the Lay Committee and the Medical and Surgical Staff were not always so cordial as, fortunately, they now are. Many of these disagreements between committee and Staff arose out of differences between the members of the Staff themselves, who called in the assistance of the committee to decide their quarrels. Whichever side the committee took, trouble arose, and one or other section of the Staff was offended. It seems to us strange nowadays that the Lay Committee should take upon themselves the duty of acting as judges between the surgeons and physicians in purely professional matters. The quarrel between the surgeons and physicians as to what each might do has been referred to already. This particular trouble must be mentioned again, however, as it led to further disagreement.

In 1750 the physicians passed a resolution that " the surgeons be not permitted to prescribe to patients under their care any internals except purgatives." The surgeons objected. The dispute was laid before the House Committee, who " maturely considered the arguments on both sides," and gave their decision in favour of the surgeons.

The physicians then sent a private report to the President, the Duke of Richmond, complaining "of the method of practice of physick and surgery at the Hospital, and of other irregularities." It was bad enough to send in their private report of the dispute, which had been considered by the House Committee, but it was worse to drag in " the other irregularities," whatever they may have been.

The committee got to hear of this memorial, and demanded a copy of it from the physicians, who refused to give it. Application was then made to the President himself, who ignored the letter. Therefore a subcommittee was appointed to " investigate the behaviour of the Hospital Staff," which was done very thoroughly, and reported on, certainly without fear or favour.

The subcommittee reported that the physicians attended on two days a week each only,

" and they surmised that this might be prejudicial to patients' interests, particularly in fevers, when the necessity of altering a prescription frequently occurred, were it not that they found that each physician, after visiting his own beds, visited others, if his attention was required, and they altered each other's prescriptions; and this was often done by the apothecary, whose skill and acquaintance with the method of practice of the several physicians sufficiently qualified him for that post."

Those must have been fine times for a patient, when any physician who passed his bed, not to mention the apothecary, had the right to pour a little more physic into him! One can appreciate the heartiness with which he returned thanks " to Almighty God and the House Committee " when he got out of the place safe and sound.

The subcommittee referred incidentally in their report to the complaint which had been made concerning the treatment of one Michael Bourdon, " a patient of Dr. Sylvester's." He was a lad of fifteen, who " had a shortness of breath owing to a dropsy." A swelling was noticed in his cheek, and the physician stated that he had asked the surgeon to look at it, but he had neglected to do so, and the patient subsequently died. The subcommittee, having given the matter their attention, soon settled that the death of the patient was not due to any neglect upon the part of the surgeon, but that " the patient died of a fever, shortness of breath, and a broken constitution." With such an omniscient committee one wonders what need there could have been for coroner, surgeon, physician, chaplain, or apothecary.

With reference to the action of the physicians in sending a memorial to the Duke of Richmond, the committee reported as follows :

" We also took into consideration the action of your physicians in presenting a memorial to His Grace the late Duke of Richmond, President of the Hospital, and the physicians, being called in, did acknowledge that some expressions of heat had passed from them in their memorial, which they were sorry for, and they engaged to submit themselves in future to the directions of the House Committee. This acknowledgment was deemed as sufficient satisfaction in the opinion of your committee, who recommended to the physicians a particular caution against making any complaints whatsoever for the future relating to the Hospital, except first to the House Committee."

The subcommittee closed their lengthy report by a long list of rules as to the general management of the institution and as to the behaviour of the members of the Staff, medical and lay.

Every member of the lay Staff had to appear before committee every three months, to hear his standing orders read over to him, and to be questioned as to whether he had kept them the preceding quarter. Among these rules was one to the effect that the apothecary and the "dresser for the week" were to go round the hospital every morning and examine every patient. It would seem that the apothecary played into the hands of the physicians, and the dresser championed the cause of the surgeons, for it is stated

"In case of any dispute which shall at any time arise under whose care a patient ought to be, the same shall be determined at the next meeting of the House Committee."

Until the year 1768 no medical qualification or degree was demanded of gentlemen who were candidates for appointments on the Staff. In this year a Dr. Samuel Leeds was appointed, and was asked to sit for his examination before the College of Physicians before the next Quarterly Court, and it was at the same time decided—

"That no person be in future admitted a candidate for the office of physician until he has been examined by the College of Physicians in London, has their approbation, and has been admitted by them to practice."

Dr. Leeds failed to pass his examination, and resigned, although an extension of time was allowed him.

In 1784 there were two candidates for a vacancy caused by the death of Dr. Thomas Dickson; they were Dr. John Whitehead and Dr. John Cooke. Each had to *show* his certificate from the College of Physicians before he was allowed to be a candidate. This election was interesting for another reason : 586 votes were recorded, as follows :

Dr. Whitehead	293
Dr. Cooke	292

One vote was disqualified. A protest was lodged immediately that the voting was unfair, and a court of inquiry was held, which reported " that in the opinion of this court, Dr. John Cooke had a majority of *legal* votes, and is duly elected physician." The illegality of the election was in connection with some of the proxies.

The great distress throughout the country at the beginning of the nineteenth century is reflected from time to time through the minutes. In 1800 the Staff approached the committee as to the urgent need of opening more beds, if only temporarily, " during the present winter, so peculiarly distressing to the invalid poor on some obvious and afflicting reasons." But the committee were at their wits' end to keep the beds open which were already in use, on account of the great increase in the cost of all provisions and other necessaries, and they not only had to refuse the request of the Staff, but were driven to make more stringent rules than ever to lessen the expenditure. The use of foreign wines was forbidden. Spirits and porter could only be used for the most urgent cases, on the special request in writing of the surgeon in charge. On certain days every week no meat was to be served to patients on any account whatever, and these meatless days were known as "banyan days." So great was the pressure on the beds that two patients were put into each at times, and the "matron complained that the blankets were so small that they would scarce cover one patient." The committee decided to go round the wards every week "and discharge all patients who appear to be in the Hospital for reason of maintenance rather than for the cure of disease." The committee, out of their own pockets, made grants to patients when leaving the Hospital, on account of the fearful distress. The purchase of pewter plates, spoons, and porringers was forbidden; wooden vessels only were used. Soldiers were to pay 4d. a day while in Hospital, as "a contribution towards their cure." The Overseers of the poor of Whitechapel were urged to do their duty more efficiently, and the Hospital authorities refused to treat patients who should rightly be cared for by these Overseers. Help was refused, for instance, "to all such as ask alms in the streets," and if such had to be admitted for urgent medical reasons, the Overseers were to be charged 4d. a day, like the soldiers, for the cost of the patient's keep. No bread was to be given to any patient until he had eaten up what had been given him on the previous day.

The charge of 4d. a day for parish patients was soon increased to 6d., and the Overseers had to deposit one guinea on the admission of such patient. But patients of the French nation " are to be paid for at the rate of 2s. per day, as arranged with Chevalier Sequier, the French Consul." Convalescent patients were to be set to work in order to relieve the wages bill. The apothecary's laboratory was a favourite place for the employment of such convalescents, and one cannot wonder at the repeated complaints of the Staff that the medicines were unsatisfactory, and that cases of poisoning are reported from time to time throughout the minutes.

Not often does one come across any definite reference to current events in the records, but occasionally such reference is found. In 1748 there was a thanksgiving service for the deliverance of the country from great peril, and at this time there was a Guildhall subscription " for the sufferers in the late rebellion." The Hospital received £100 of this appeal, " as it had relieved so many objects who were sufferers in the late Rebellion." This, I presume, referred to the march of the Young Pretender into England as far as Derby, and his final defeat at Culloden. Then, in 1798, the Hospital received £100 " from the fund raised for the benefit of the sufferers in the action of July 1st " (the Battle of the Nile).

In 1810 the following letter was received by the committee :

" GENTLEMEN,

" It being found necessary to assemble a body of troops round the Metropolis, amongst whom a number of sick are to be expected, we request you will be pleased to inform us whether under this emergency such men can be received into the London Hospital,

and to what extent accommodation can be provided. Should you accede to this proposal, we beg you to say if it be your desire that the sick shall be under the sole care of the Medical Gentlemen of the Hospital, or if Military Medical Officers shall be ordered to attend them.
"We have the honour to be,
"JOHN WEIR,
"THEODORE GORDON,
"ARMY MEDICAL BOARD OFFICE."

The following reply was sent:

"SIR,
"This moment your letter of the 10th inst. has been delivered to me, and I have the pleasure to inform you that there is room in the London Hospital for 100 to 150 men. Unfortunately, there are no beds, but if His Majesty's Government will undertake to provide them, and to make also a provision for the men, I will undertake that they will be cheerfully received and placed under the care of the Medical Gentlemen attached to the Hospital, who, with that liberal sentiment for which they have always been distinguished, have undertaken to give them every possible attention and assistance. I have the honour to be, etc.,
"QUARLES HARRIS,
"*Chairman of House Committee,*"
"41, CRUTCHED FRIARS,
"*April* 11*th*, 1810."

The offer was accepted. The Government agreed to supply the beds and all else that was needed, with servants and attendants, and to pay 10d. a day for each man admitted. The wards were prepared. Nothing came of it, however. No sick soldiers were admitted. This massing of troops had to do with Lord Chatham's expedition to attack the French in Holland.

Neither is there often reference in the minutes to the prevailing diseases of the time. When such reference is made it is usually on account of the disease having reached the magnitude of an epidemic, and cholera is often referred to in this way. The following reference to hydrophobia, dated October, 1808, is interesting :

" The physicians and surgeons respectfully represent to the House Committee of the London Hospital that there have been received into the Hospital within the last three months several cases of hydrophobia; that many instances of the same dreadful and fatal disorder within a short period have come to their knowledge; that several persons and animals have very lately been bitten by dogs unquestionably mad; and that in their opinion it is highly necessary that these facts should be stated to persons in high authority, in order that proper measures may be taken for the public safety."

A copy of the above, which was signed by William Blizard, surgeon, and others, was sent to the Lord Mayor, and was inserted in the morning and evening papers.

Many reports which had to do with the public welfare were received from time to time by the committee from this same William Blizard on cleanliness, on drainage, on fresh air. Some more detailed reference to this wonderful man and surgeon is necessary, and I am indebted to a memoir published by William Cooke for most of the following information.

William Blizard was born at Barnes Elms, in Surrey, in 1743. His father, William Blizard, was an auctioneer, and had five children, of whom the future surgeon was the youngest but one. His early education was neglected, but in later life he made up for the loss by doing all in his power to educate himself and to improve his general knowledge. He became proficient in the reading of Latin, and undoubtedly was a great botanist and a great chemist.

At an early age he was apprenticed to a surgeon and apothecary at Mortlake, a Mr. Besley. He afterwards came to London and became the assistant of a surgeon practising in Crutched Friars. While practising as a surgeon, he was studying under Mr. Henry Thompson, one of the surgeons of the London Hospital, and a man of considerable talent and eminence in his day. On the death of Thompson in 1780, Blizard was elected surgeon in his stead. He performed all the operations at the Hospital for many years, his two colleagues, Mr. Grindall and Mr. Neale, leaving this duty entirely to him. He always took the deepest interest in systematic medical education, and when quite young connected himself with a Dr. Maclaurin, a well-known teacher of anatomy, in giving lectures on surgery at a small house in Thames Street, and afterwards in Mark Lane. His greatest honour in this respect was that he founded, in 1785, the first regular medical school connected with a great Hospital—viz., that connected with the London Hospital. The House Committee gave the ground; the building was erected at an expense of some thousands of pounds, chiefly supplied by himself, at a time when he could ill afford it. The foundation of the Medical School will be referred to in another chapter.

It is of interest to note in passing that at first

Blizard's anxiety to teach in the Hospital met with no favour from the committee. He was not allowed to teach on cases *in* the Hospital, and although he was permitted to use a room for his lectures, he had, at first, to bring his cases with him. He seems to have considered the opening of the school on October 27, 1785, as the great event of his life. He wrote an ode on the occasion " expressive of humane and correct sentiment." Here is a quotation from this ode :

> " Hail the return of this auspicious day !
> Now let the grateful, gen'rous heart record,
> In heartfelt strains, how Providence befriends
> This seat of commerce and benevolence !
> In this fam'd city dwells such social love
> As smiles alone in climes of liberty.
> The genial patronage of every art
> That tends to soften the rough paths of life
> Bids the wide dome with lofty columns rise,
> Fann'd with refreshing air, and ev'ry charm
> Which the lax nerve and drooping frame can ask :
> She, kinder still, bids industry prevail,
> Without whose aid all other aids are vain :
> Sacred to her be this auspicious day !"

The ode was set to music by Dr. Samuel Arnold, and was performed at the London Tavern, a house which for 150 years has been strangely connected with the history of the Hospital. About this time Blizard received an invitation from Guy's Hospital to occupy the Chair in Chemistry, which he declined.

" As a practitioner he was discriminating and decided in forming his opinions, energetic and skilful in the application of his means, and studious of as much simplicity as possible. . . . The last year he operated in public was in the year 1827, at which time he was eighty-four years of age. It was the removal

WILLIAM BLIZARD, F.R.S.

President of the Royal College of Surgeons, and for fifty-three years Surgeon to the London Hospital

of a thigh, and the stump healed perfectly in a fortnight. As an operator he was remarkably cool and determined, never losing his presence of mind. His hand never trembled, and it is said to have been as steady the last year as at any period of his life. It was highly to the honour of Blizard that when called into scenes of suffering or to the infliction of pain in operative surgery he was never insensible to the sympathy and kindness of the man, when he had to exercise the cool intrepidity of the surgeon. He had often the satisfaction to notice how the kind and sympathizing word appeared to mitigate anguish and to inspire with fresh courage under the required incision; and the gratitude subsequently felt for the kindness of the manner was sometimes more prominent, in the acknowledgments of the patients, than for the dexterity and success of the operation."

Blizard was a bad lecturer, but an excellent teacher. Cooke says of him:

"He was most happy and appeared to greatest advantage in the wards of the Hospital; his clinical remarks and his oral instructions were much valued.... The aptness and vivacity of his remarks, and his ready tact in directing the attention of students to the leading points in the case under his care, rendered his visits at all times instructive."

The great surgeon John Abernethy says of him (in 1814):

"My warmest thanks are due to him for the interest he excited in my mind towards those studies, and for the excellent advice he gave me to direct me in the attainment of knowledge. 'Let your search after truth,' he would say, 'be eager and constant. Be wary of admitting propositions as facts before you have submitted them to the strictest examination. If, after this, you believe them to be true, never disregard or forget one of them. Should you perceive truths to be important, make them the motives of action, let them serve as springs to your conduct. Many persons acknowledge truth with apathy; they assent to it, but it produces no further effect on their minds. Truths, however, are of importance in proportion as they admit of inferences which ought to have an influence on our conduct, and if we neglect to draw those inferences or act in conformity to them, we fail in essential duties.'"

Abernethy says of him further :

" He contrived by various means to excite a degree of enthusiasm in the minds of his pupils. He displayed to us the beau-ideal of the medical character—I cannot readily tell you how splendid and brilliant he made it appear—and then he cautioned us never to tarnish its lustre by anything that wore even the semblance of dishonour. He caused the sentiment of the philanthropic Chremes of Terence to be inscribed on the walls of the Hospital surgery, that students should have constantly before them an admonition to humanity drawn from a reflection of their own wants : ' Homo sum ; humani nihil a me alienum puto '" (I am a man ; and all calamities that touch mankind come home to me.—G. COLMAN).

That line from Terence has been the motto of the Hospital ever since.

I must apologize for digressing for a moment. The mention of the Hospital motto reminds me of an amusing incident. A much harassed and very weary Receiving-room Officer was reported for being rude to a man in the Receiving-room. He acknowledged that he had been rather "short," but the patient had exasperated him beyond all endurance; among other things, had insisted on being thoroughly examined at 3 a.m. for some trivial complaint which he had had for a week, but had not found it convenient to attend to before.

The officer was reminded that to keep his temper at all times was part of his medical training—that he must be polite to all sorts and conditions of men. What was the Hospital motto? It was rightly quoted, but in asking for the English equivalent, I was told: "As I'm a man, I don't believe an alien's a human being!"

Blizard's exertions were not limited to the foundation of a great teaching school nor to his routine Hospital duties. He loved the Hospital with his whole heart, he was jealous of its honour, and his energies were unceasingly devoted to the extension of its sphere of usefulness. His own interests were repeatedly sacrificed to promote this object. He induced most of his wealthy patients to become governors. At a period when its funds were greatly depressed, he made innumerable applications for support and assistance, and spared neither means nor labour in urging its claim upon public attention. He once said his connection with the London Hospital was the pride of his life.

He received the honour of knighthood in the year 1803.

" During several years he was in the habit of contributing extensively from his own pocket, to relieve the pressing necessities of patients, who, on leaving the Hospital, still perhaps but convalescent, or in a lame or incurable condition, penniless, houseless, and not unfrequently without friends, were exposed to wretchedness exceeding that of their condition before they were admitted. These were objects of great commiseration to him, and it was to relieve such distress that he founded the Samaritan Society in the year 1791."

Now known as the "Marie Celeste" Samaritan Society, on account of the munificent gift of Mr. James Hora, in memory of his wife Marie Celeste Hora, this Society still administers such relief to the patients of the London Hospital as does not fall under the actual work of the Hospital, by sending convalescent patients to sea or country; by assisting patients to provide themselves with surgical appliances in accordance with the recommendation of the surgeon; by supplying the poorer patients with clothing, if necessary, when leaving the hospital; or by making small monetary grants to patients who may be in urgent need of assistance.

One cannot imagine how the usefulness of the Hospital could be maintained without such a charity. Last year (1909) over 2,000 cases were sent to convalescent homes on their discharge from hospital; 3,500 surgical appliances were supplied (artificial limbs, expensive splints for hip-disease, etc.); monetary grants were made to seventy-four patients, chiefly with a view to save the home while the husband or father was a patient in the Hospital, the result of an accident, etc. The Queen herself has generously contributed to its funds to help poor patients to bear the expense of travelling up to attend the Finsen Light Department.

Such work was exactly what Blizard had in view when he founded this most useful society. In doing so he made an appeal to the public, from which the following may be quoted as showing what he desired should be the aim of the society, and, incidentally, the kind of man Blizard himself was :

" To learn all the varieties of wretchedness, to remove it, or to soften its pangs, the ear must be unweariedly inclined to tales of woe, the hand must be ever ready to succour, and the heart and understanding to advise, to comfort, and to guide. In the lustre of public charities, misery, of a nature not immediately to attract the eye, often remains unnoticed. The greatest exertions of art and the most diligent care are extended to poor, sick, and hurt fellow-creatures. But skill and tenderness will hardly avail against disease whilst the mind is continually depressed by reflection upon a hopeless prospect in life, or upon the condition of a family pining with grief or want."

Soon after Blizard's appointment to the Staff of the London Hospital he was made Professor of Anatomy to the old Corporation of Surgeons, and he was chiefly instrumental in obtaining a charter for the new college. He was one of the two first appointed professors to the chartered institution, now designated the Royal College of Surgeons, and he twice served the office of President, an honour which has fallen to other " Londoners " since. Blizard was the founder of the Anatomical Society, a Fellow of the Antiquarian

Society, a Fellow of the Royal Society, a Fellow of the Royal Society of Edinburgh, the founder of the Horticultural Society, and one of its first Fellows, and was one of the founders of the London Institution.

He was tall in person, with features strongly marked, a man of strong emotions, and " prone to jocularity."

" Allusion has been made to his high sense of professional honour. Abhorrence of quackery in any form was a leading feature in his character. He could not endure to have kept secret any remedy adapted to the relief of human sufferings, nor bear with the self-commendation, or the detracting innuendo, designed to place another practitioner in a false light, or to subvert his interests. Everything which militated against pure integrity and unsophisticated courteousness incurred his marked disapprobation."

He was a man of strong religious feeling, and everything that had to do with the betterment of mankind was of interest to him. Sunday-schools, infant schools, the reclamation of the fallen, the reform of the prison system—all appealed to him as they did to his great friend John Howard, the philanthropist. He entertained great respect for the clergy, and was always ready to befriend them, knowing many to be poor and well deserving of kind consideration. He was a man of Catholic spirit, and as readily gave his counsel to a suffering minister of any other religious persuasion as to one belonging to his own Church.

Many anecdotes cling to a personality so marked.

Cooke, in the memoir from which I have quoted, tells the following:

"Many years ago, when the vicinity of London was greatly infested by footpads, Blizard was travelling alone on the Essex Road, and his carriage was stopped by three men. Having placed a pistol against the breast of one of them, it missed fire; he therefore gave up his watch and purse. Afterwards recollecting that the watch, though not of much value, had been given him by an esteemed friend, he asked for it back again. The man to whom he had given it up replied: "There, my honest fellow, take your watch," at the same time returning it. The man had been under Blizard at the London Hospital, and had recognized him."

At this time it was dangerous to travel in the vicinity of London at night unarmed. There is a reference in the minutes of a complaint from Blizard that, coming to the Hospital during the night to see a patient on whom he had been operating during the previous day, he was kept waiting at the outer gate of the Hospital for some time, to his great inconvenience and danger. The gates were always locked at night, and a "watcher" from one of the wards went to the gate every hour or two to see if anyone were there. After Blizard's complaint a bell was hung at the gate. Blizard always carried a weapon when he visited the Hospital.

"One night," says Cooke, "on leaving the Court of Examiners at the College, he missed his favourite hanger, which had more than once served him as a weapon of defence in early life. His servant was unable to give any account of it, which induced Blizard to exclaim with some energy: 'It must be found, for with it I am in fear of no one, not even of the devil himself.' A member of the Court who was by remarked : ' If that is the case, he had better have it put in his coffin with him."

Sir William Blizard died on August 28, 1835, at the age of ninety-two, and was buried in a vault under Brixton Church.

CHAPTER IX

BREAK OF DAY

MENTION has been made of William Blizard's friendship for John Howard. This great reformer paid a visit of inspection to the Hospital in 1788, which is thus referred to in the minutes :

" Your Committee beg leave to acquaint the Court that John Howard, Esq., a Governor of the Charity, who has visited all, or at least the greatest part of, the hospitals in Europe, did, in the month of September last, visit this house three separate times. He suggested to Mr. Blizard, who accompanied him in one of his visitations, many useful observations with regard to rendering such Asylum of the afflicted sweet and salutary, and upon principles, too, ye most economical. Your Committee, anxious for the welfare of the Charity, and wishing to profit by the experience of one whose life has been spent hitherto in such benevolent exertions, have adopted some of his useful regulations, which will be laid before you in a subsequent report."

John Howard's visit led to many improvements in ventilation, cleanliness, and the prevention of the accumulation of refuse and rubbish. The following letter was sent to him :

" Sir,

"The Committee of the London Hospital, duly sensible of the value of your endeavour to make hospitals answer the end of their establishment, return you their sincere thanks for your attention to the Charity under their special care, and particularly for your representations for its improvement. They are now executing everything in their power which you have suggested as necessary to be done, and they trust that this proof of their sincerity in their work of charity will secure them your future regard and communications, to which they will always pay the greatest deference. It is their earnest wish to see the Hospital and its government merit your entire approbation, and your good word with the discerning and humane part of mankind. They then shall not despair of that support of which they stand greatly in need, not only as affording them means of doing what is judged proper, but also as encouraging and giving energy to their undertakings."

Many of these recommendations of Howard show how far advanced he was of his day. He condemned the raising of dust in the wards, dust being somehow or other the conveyer of disease; he advocated cross ventilation; bedding was to be laid in the sun "on the grass newly mown" as often and as long as possible; the flock from the mattresses was to be washed in water, dried in the sun, and then baked. The last words of Howard's report are important, and as true in hospital management to-day as they were in 1788.

"All these several articles, however seemingly insignificant considered individually, are, nevertheless, the important constituent parts which compose the chief amount of the sum of welfare which arises from public charities to the numberless objects of human sympathy."

We who to-day enjoy the merciful benefits of aseptic surgery, which is nothing but cleanliness raised to a science, cannot but be interested in the work of these pioneers. They noticed and recorded the facts. Lister, who was to explain the facts, was not yet born. For instance, a year before Howard's visit, the Physical Committee reported:

"Your Committee are of opinion that as the recovery of the patients greatly depends on a free circulation of fresh air, that the present disposition of the beds is improper by causing a stagnation of noxious effluvia, and in consequence thereof, often producing putrid diseases, the frequent effects of confined air."

And two years before Howard's visit, namely in 1786, William Blizard, speaking for the surgeons, wrote to the committee as follows:

"In the discharge of our duties as surgeons we have for a long time past, and particularly of late, observed with great concern that many of our patients who had met with accidents—particularly compound fractures when the broken bone has pierced the outer skin, or those who had undergone certain operations, particularly that for rupture—have lost their lives through being placed in wards in which were persons ill of fevers, and that men have been principally the sufferers from this cause, being more frequently the subjects of the above accidents and operations, and breathing a more impure air from a less degree of cleanliness than women."

At this time medical and surgical cases were all nursed together, so he goes on to ask for a small ward of ten beds in which these cases could be nursed apart from the general cases in the main wards, and, incidentally, he asks that more efficient nursing may be provided, complaining that

"Lately an infirm old woman, nearly seventy years of age, had the care of two persons who had been cut for the stone, and who required constant attention both night and day."

In order that lay-readers may appreciate the importance of the struggle which was beginning, it may be of interest to give some particulars here of the precautions which are taken in modern surgery. There was a long period between Blizard's and Lister's day, during which there was little or no advance. It has been stated that the experienced surgeon of fifty years ago was possessed of an operative skill and a knowledge of anatomy that the modern surgeon can hardly hope to surpass. However that may be, the results obtained by the surgeon of that time, as shown by the following statement of facts, are quite appalling to us nowadays: "The idea of a wound was inseparable from that of fever"; "the healing of a wound without inflammation was not known, and wound fever seemed to be the normal reaction of the injured organism." Pirogoff, a most experienced surgeon, actually wrote a treatise on "Luck in Surgery," in which, after long years of surgical practice, he expressed his opinion that the influence of the skill of the surgeon was as nothing as compared to that of chance in determining the success of an operation, and he goes on to state that the scourges of suppuration, hospital gangrene, erysipelas, and tetanus, dogged the steps of the surgeon and frustrated his efforts. At the private hospital—nursing-home we should call it—of a well-known surgeon at Munich " 80 per cent. of all wounds were attacked by hospital gangrene, and erysipelas was so common that its occurrence was considered normal." "The mortality after compound fracture amounted to 40 per cent." Moreover, wounds which did eventually heal took so long to do so that patients were kept in hospital as many weeks as they are now kept days. Now all this is changed. We now know that the cause of wound infection is due to the entrance of minute organisms into the wound, which, growing there and multiplying, produce each its own toxin. The aim of modern surgery is to prevent these organisms from so entering.

By what means may these micro-organisms gain access to a wound, and how may they be prevented ? In the first place, can a wound be infected by contact with the air ? To answer this question innumerable experiments have been performed, and the answer is : " No, a wound cannot be infected by the air unless the air contains particles of dust." It was firmly believed that contact with the air did infect the wound long after Lister's discovery—indeed, Lister himself believed it—and his custom of performing an operation with a spray of carbolic in the vicinity was intended to destroy the myriads of organisms which he believed to be floating around. We still possess in the Hospital, curios now, several of these old Lister's sprays. This belief in contamination by the germs in the air died hard. When several patients in a ward were attacked by erysipelas or hospital gangrene, the air of the ward was blamed, and it was customary to perform all operations with as small an incision as possible, in order to admit as little air into the wound as possible. Now we are accustomed to see incisions freely made several inches in length, and wounds are exposed to the air in the theatre sometimes for as long as three hours.

The method by which the number of micro-organisms in the air may be counted is a very simple one theoretically. A bottle of known capacity is filled with sterilized water; the water is slowly drawn off from a tap at the bottom; an equal volume of air, obviously, is drawn in through the neck of the bottle; the entering air is made to pass across the surface of, or through, "culture media." These culture media are fluids or jellies (broths, meat extracts, gelatine solutions, etc.), in which germs will freely grow, if present, just as seeds will grow in potting mould in a greenhouse. The culture media are themselves rendered sterile by heat before the experiment, and proper precautions taken that they may not be infected by anything else than by the micro-organisms which may be in the air as it passes into the bottle. The tubes containing the culture media are then removed and placed in an incubator, and under such conditions each retained microbe grows into a colony, which may be seen even by the naked eye, and the colonies may be counted. Thus we are in a position to say that the air in such a place contains a hundred, or a thousand, or twenty thousand micro-organisms per cubic yard or metre, according to the size of the bottle. Moreover, the colour, shape, and method of growth of the colonies give much information even to the naked eye as to the identity of the germs present. Simple as the experiment may appear, it has to be performed with infinite care if the results are to be relied upon. Having devised a plan for counting the germs in the air, it became easy to apply the test in various ways. It was soon found that—

1. The air was richer in germs in cities than in the country.
2. In dry weather germs are more numerous in the air than in wet weather.
3. They are more numerous when wind is blowing than in a calm.
4. Far out at sea the air contains no germs at all.
5. The air at the summit of the Alps, above the snow-line, is free.
6. On the sea-shore wind blowing off the land is germ-laden; that blowing in from the sea is germ-free.

All these experiments seemed to point to one conclusion—namely, that air which was free from dust was free from germs, and that air which contained suspended dust contained germs. This theory was therefore put to the test by a very noted set of experiments, by which it was found—

7. That the air examined in the middle of the city of Berlin contained about 1,000 germs in each cubic yard, while the air in the drains underneath Berlin was entirely free.

It is now understood that these micro-organisms require warmth, moisture, and also some substance on which to feed and grow. These conditions do not exist in the air. When germs *are* found in the air their presence there is temporary and accidental, and may be accounted for by the fact of their food material having dried up, and their subsequent dispersal by the process of sweeping or dusting, or by the wind; but they will settle as soon as they are allowed, and leave the air free again. Germs do *not* fly about of themselves; they will never leave a damp surface to pass into the air, for the air is not in the least congenial to them as a dwelling-place.

Long before Lord Lister explained the reason why, the old surgeons considered dust to be a carrier of disease and infection: Blizard believed this to be the case. More than one surgeon had insisted that no one should enter his theatre for some hours before an operation was to be performed, but it never struck him that his own finger-tips and his instruments were the most important carriers of infection.

Now that the reason of wound infection is known, every endeavour is made to prevent the access of micro-organisms to the wound. At the London Hospital, and at all great hospitals, this sterilization of all material used is in the hands of experts. Every corner in the theatres is rounded, to make cleaning easy. All water-pipes and shelves are carried on brackets away from the walls for the same reason. Air coming into the theatres is warmed and strained through fine gauze, and the water used is boiled and cooled again out of contact with the air (no harmful micro-organisms can resist five minutes in boiling water). Instruments are boiled and not touched again by anyone except the surgeon himself; dressings are sterilized by heat from steam under high pressure in boxes of copper, which

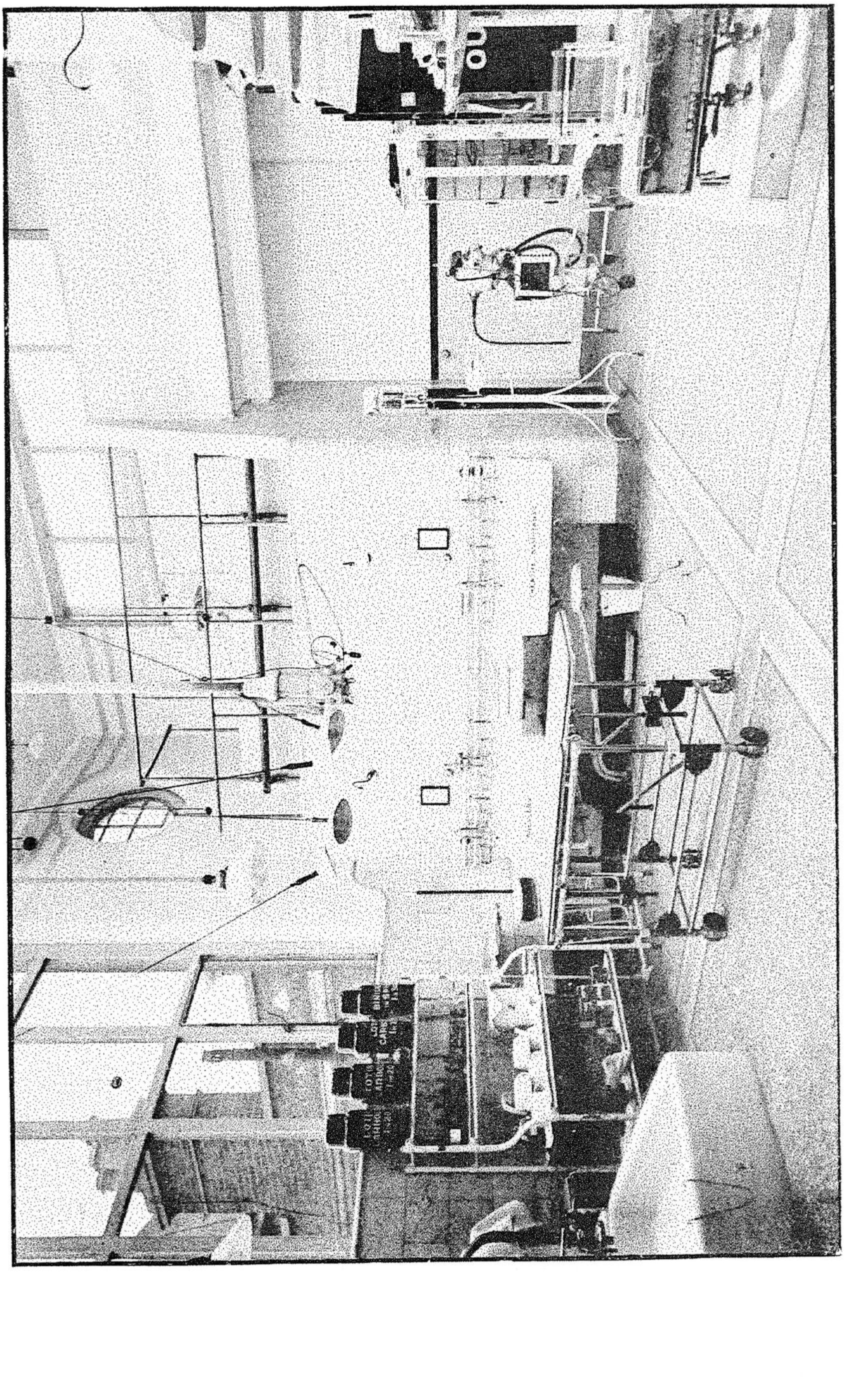

are sealed down after sterilization, and the seal not broken until the time of the operation. The patient's skin, in the vicinity of the incision, is also rendered sterile by means of ether and various antiseptics, in order that no germs may be washed into the wound. The surgeon's own hands are cleaned by long scrubbing and by antiseptics. Sometimes the cleaning of the surgeon's hands will take longer than the operation itself. There are many materials used—such as sponges and catgut—which cannot be sterilized by heat, the most efficient method. Sponges, which are used in thousands, are never allowed in the theatres at "The London" until they have been washed by hand in at least fifty changes of water, to remove all grit and sand, and have then been allowed to stand for not less than seven weeks in strong solution (5 per cent.) of carbolic acid. All these precautions being taken, wounds heal with a regularity that is almost monotonous. The average residence in hospital of a surgical in-patient has been lowered since Blizard's day from sixty days to nineteen, so that each bed is taking nineteen patients each year instead of six. As there are nearly 1,000 beds at "The London," the gift to the country from this voluntary charity in returning the wage-earner to his family is not an insignificant one.

But to return to the old records. In reading through the minutes, I find no less than six references in the Hospital's history to fearful epidemics of cholera. The close neighbourhood of the river and docks may partly account for this. In 1832 cholera was raging at Newcastle, and the committee of "The London" sent one of its physicians, Dr. Cobb, to Newcastle to thoroughly investigate the cause and treatment of the disease—

" In order that the Committee may be prepared to make the best arrangements and provide the most efficient remedies in the event of the appearance of this most fearful disease within the London Hospital, or in the densely peopled district in which it is situated."

At this time Sir William Blizard presented the committee with a paper on the subject of cholera,

" which contained suggestions so valuable in reference to the duty of the directors of a public institution at this crisis that the Committee ordered that it be printed and published."

Two hundred and fifty copies of Dr. Cobb's report were also printed and circulated. He was given fifty guineas for his expenses. Fifty of the surrounding parishes were communicated with—from London Bridge to East Ham—and warned *not* to send any cases of cholera from their district to the Hospital, as all the beds available for such patients were in use for cases occurring in the Hospital itself. Every patient arriving at the Hospital had to be examined by one of the Staff or the apothecary to make sure that he was not suffering from cholera. In spite of the warning sent to the parishes, patients came to the Hospital suffering from the fearful disease, and all the parishes were again written to, the committee asking where they were to send the patients, since the Hospital was full. Eventually each parish arranged for the treatment of cholera in its own workhouse, and the

Hospital referred a patient to the workhouse of his parish. One cannot help wondering how this was arranged. It is difficult to imagine a conversation with a man dying from cholera to ascertain what parish he came from, and it is still more difficult to understand how he was sent through the public streets without spreading the disease. Quite likely this was one source of infection.

In 1848 there was another cholera epidemic. This time the committee were bolder, and decided to meet it more efficiently. Special arrangements were made for the reception and treatment of all patients who might come to the Hospital. The secretary was instructed to use his discretion, and open one ward after another for cholera, and the committee was to be summoned at twenty-four hours' notice, should the secretary require further advice. The apothecary seems to have been the most influential and important person during this epidemic, for the Court passed a special vote of thanks to " our Apothecary, Mr. Burch, for his very zealous exertions, and for his unfailing attendance during the period." That is all I can find of Mr. Burch, but it is " honourable mention." But all the Staff, lay and medical, were heroic in their exertions. When this epidemic had lasted a year, the Medical Staff were worn out, and begged

" that when the number of cholera cases admitted to the Hospital reached one-tenth of the total beds, no more should be admitted, on account of the insufficiency of Medical Aid."

Cholera was raging again in 1853 and 1854, and here I note that a nurse—her name is not mentioned—is thanked by the Court "for her great service."

But the most awful visitation of all was in 1866. Canon the Rev. Thomas Scott was chaplain of the Hospital at the time, and he has very kindly given me the following description of this epidemic:

"*The Cholera in the London Hospital*, 1866.

"It was on Friday, July 13th, that the first case of Asiatic cholera was brought to the London Hospital. I was Chaplain at the time, and earlier on the same day had been drawing up a Form of Service for the opening of the Alexandra Wing.

"I lost no time in writing to Mrs. Gladstone (whose husband had only just ceased to be Chancellor of the Exchequer) to warn her not to continue her usual visits to the patients, as it was very unlikely that the present case of cholera would be the only one. I had an answer by return of post saying that, though she knew that her visits could be of no direct advantage, she thought that her presence might help to cheer the nurses, and, as a fact, she was in the Cholera Ward the very next day, and was a very frequent visitor during the whole outbreak.

"In ten days' time we had had sixty-seven cholera cases, and by the 30th of the month two hundred and thirty, and one hundred and ten deaths, which, by the 2nd of August, numbered one hundred and fifty.

"The Alexandra Wing was to have been opened about the same time by a member of the Royal Family, but it was opened by King Cholera.

"On the 3rd of August there appeared in the *Times* a letter from Mrs. Gladstone asking for help towards opening a Home for Children who had been left orphans by *both* their parents dying in the Hospital of this terrible disease. How liberally her appeal was answered may be realized by the fact that my wife and I sat up the next night till twelve o'clock acknowledging the donations which had already been sent in, and for days afterwards we could only keep pace with the task by the help of various friends.

"It was at Clapton that Mrs. Gladstone opened the Home, which she kept open for several years, till the inmates were old enough to leave it to earn their living. It was not then closed, however, but was continued as a Convalescent Home for general patients. It is now known as Mrs. Gladstone's Home for Convalescents. It has been removed from Clapton to Mitcham.

"But Mrs. Gladstone was not alone in this good work. Rather later in the outbreak, Miss Marsh (whose name is well known for her charities and her writings) became a welcomed visitor in the wards, and a letter from her to the Papers brought a liberal response, which was the means of establishing a second Convalescent Home at Kemp Town, Brighton, which, like the other, is still doing useful work. At the time it was arranged that men should be sent to the one and women to the other; and if I remember right, the Authorities at Brighton did not welcome our arrival! I recall this the more clearly because Mrs. Scott and I had the chief share in arranging the fitting up of the Home!

"But I have said nothing of the work which fell to the Chaplain during the terrible time of the outbreak—about three months in all.

"It was a remarkable instance of the way in which the Divine promise may be fulfilled—'As thy day so shall thy strength be'—that all nervous fear of infection, which up to that time had been one of my many weak points, was entirely removed. I was well aware of my danger, but all nervous fear was absent; and though constantly in the wards, and, so far as it was possible, ministering to the spiritual wants of the patients, I kept my health the whole time.

"Terrible was the scene, for the agonies of the sufferers were often very great. Death not unfrequently followed the attack in a very short time. As an instance of this, one of our laundry-women came to her work at seven o'clock one morning, to all appearance in good health, but was dead by the middle of the day. And I saw two little children lying dead in the same bed (where they had been placed for want of more accommodation), the second having died before there had been time to remove the first. I had to watch my opportunity for speaking with the sufferers, or for offering a prayer, because it was only now and then that they were free enough from pain, or in a state of sufficient consciousness, to listen to or understand what I might say.

"I was not left to minister to the sufferers alone, for, besides the excellent City Missionary who was attached to the Hospital, several clergymen from the neighbourhood, and even from the country, volunteered their help.

"The mortality was so great that Pickford's vans came early every morning to take away the dead. On one morning there were forty, and it became a serious difficulty to get coffins made fast enough.

"But it cannot be necessary to write more, for I have written enough to recall to my own mind, and to give some notion to anyone who may read it, of a very terrible and solemn time, but of a time full of mercy from Our Father in Heaven, and of sympathy and help from numberless friends known and unknown."

"T. S."

The mortality in this year rose from 10 per cent., at which it had been for many years, and has been nearly ever since, to 37 per cent., of all the patients admitted.

The London Hospital, from its close proximity to the docks, has always had a share in quelling epidemics of cholera in London. Before me as I write is a letter dated September, 1909, from the Metropolitan Asylums Board, asking permission to send any urgent case arriving at the docks to the Hospital by ambulance at once. Permission was at once given, of course, and necessary arrangements made for such admission.

I cannot resist setting down some further reminiscences of Canon Scott:

"When I first came to the London Hospital as Chaplain in 1860, it was not much more than half its present size. The Grocers' Wing had not yet been built, and 400 In-patients were as many as could possibly be accommodated at one time.

"Mr. Fowell Buxton was Chairman.

"It was a great change from Brighton, where I had been a curate for some years, though in a parish of at least as poor people as in Whitechapel.

"If I remember right, Mr. Adams, Mr. Curling, and Mr. Hutchinson were Senior Surgeons, and Dr. Fraser, Dr. Davies, and Dr. Andrew Clark (he was not then Sir Andrew) were Senior Physicians. It was in the early days of anæsthetics, and they were not always made use of, one of the older surgeons going so far as to say that he 'liked a good honest scream'! The prejudice against anæsthetics was general, and lasted for some time.

"There was a chapel on the first floor, with an organ-gallery and a lady organist (Miss Bell), and a choir of boys. A much larger proportion of the patients were able to attend than can now venture to St. Philip's, and my congregation must have resembled, as I used to think, the multitude of impotent folk at the Pool of Bethesda. On Wednesday and Saturday mornings, which were the usual days for convalescents to leave the Hospital, they attended a short Thanksgiving Service and shook hands with the Chaplain. For years afterwards I used to be stopped in the street by former patients, and to have a bit of chat about the Hospital.

"Almost every morning and evening were spent by me in the wards. In the morning, when dressers and nurses were about, I went from bed to bed, and had an advantage over what I have often had since, in there being no back-door at which the man I wanted to see could slip out when he saw the parson coming. It was my own fault if I did not make friends with him, and I hope I did not often fail to do so. To propose finding him an interesting book from the shelves was often a first step towards getting on friendly terms, and the beginning of more serious intercourse. In a good many instances, when a patient's answer to my offer to find him a book had been, 'Worse luck, I can't read,' I was able to persuade him that his time in the Hospital gave him such a chance of learning as he might never have again. And by other more literary patients undertaking to teach him, such a man has often left the Hospital an accomplished reader.

"In the evening the wards were much more free, and I could generally speak or read from the desk between each two divisions, and thus be heard by a good many at once. Besides this, I was always liable to be called to special cases. And thus, in one way or another, my time was pretty fully occupied, and very happily to myself.

"The Chaplain's work was made pleasanter, and the patients were cheered, by the frequent afternoon visits of a number of ladies, including Mrs. Gladstone (the wife of the Rt. Hon. W. E. Gladstone) and her friend Miss Smith, the Hon. Miss Lyttelton, Miss Pole-Carew, Lady Robartes, and perhaps others whose names I do not remember, their visits often ending with afternoon tea in the Chaplain's room. During the cholera outbreak Miss Marsh was also a frequent visitor.

"There had been for many years a Special Service in the Chapel on some week-day afternoons in the summer, at which a well-known clergyman was preacher, and which was attended by members of the Committee and friends of the Hospital. The last preacher whom I happen to remember was Dean Goulbourn.

"One meeting of the Committee at which I was present, and one only, I will mention. It was when the building of the West Wing was contemplated, and the Chairman suggested that it was now time to consider how much they themselves proposed to give. Two gentlemen were sitting next each other, and one of them asked the other how much he meant to give. To this the reply was, 'I will give the same as you.' 'Well,' said the other, 'I'll give £5,000.' 'And I'll give the same,' was the reply. As much as £23,000 was promised round the table, if I remember correctly."

CHAPTER X

SUNDRY INCIDENTS AND EVENTS

CANON SCOTT in his reminiscences referred to the administration of anæsthetics, and their unpopularity at first with some of the Surgical Staff.

The references, or rather the scarcity of them, to anæsthetics in the minutes is a good illustration of a fact which is often noticeable in reading the Hospital's records—namely, the frequent lack of appreciation of that which was important and fundamental, and, on the other hand, the great amount of attention given to what has since been proved to have been but trivial and transitory.

The introduction of anæsthetics is undoubtedly one of the two most important factors contributing to the advance of surgery, the other being the introduction of antiseptics. The great abdominal operations were impossible when patients had to be strapped to the table, or held down by volunteers, while the surgeon did his awful work. The patient's inability to bear unlimited pain, and the surgeon's inability to inflict unlimited pain—for, strange as it may appear, some of the surgeons shrank from this part of their work, and would never perform any large operation—entirely prevented advancement in surgery beyond a certain point. There are still ghastly relics in the Hospital of these terrible days: the great wooden operating-table with its straps; the bell which was sounded before an operation to call assistants to hold down the patient—a bell whose dreadful clank could be heard by every shivering patient in the building, including *the* patient, often a little child; a bell with a voice loud enough and harsh enough to make all Whitechapel shudder; and then there are the instruments used by the iron-nerved, although tender-hearted, Blizard himself.

It is undoubtedly true, also, that the honourable profession of sick-nursing by tender, good, refined women could never have developed but for the introduction of anæsthetics. Few women could have faced those shambles.

And yet there is no reference of any sort in the minutes to these merciful drugs for many years after Simpson's discovery, and then not in wonder and thankfulness because of the new era which was dawning, but because of a petty quarrel between committee and Staff as to whose duty it was to administer the anæsthetic. The Staff wrote to the committee to say that it was not the duty of members of the Staff, nor of house-surgeons, to give anæsthetics, and that the apothecary ought to be made responsible. The committee would not agree to this, and said that the apothecary's duties were sufficiently onerous already, as they certainly were. The committee insisted that it was the duty of the house-surgeons to administer chloroform, and further, that it was the duty of the Staff to teach the house-surgeons to administer it properly. The Staff were no doubt offended, and some of the surgeons continued for years after to operate without an anæsthetic.

The apothecary's was the most thankless appointment in the Hospital. There was no end to his duties, and every advance in any department added to them; and, for all, he was badly paid and badly treated.

He slept "on a settee-bed placed in the physicians' parlour." He was allowed to increase his slender stipend by taking an apprentice; but even his apprentice was bound by humiliating rules like his master, for although he were permitted "to follow the box and attend all chyrurgical operations, he was not allowed to bleed patients nor to apply dressings."

This "following of the box" referred to the custom of the surgeons having a box of instruments carried before them as they went round the wards, with which they used to perform lesser operations then and there. Instruments so used would be put back into the box, to be used again, possibly, on some other patient! Sometimes the apothecary very mildly protested, but he belonged to a dying race, and was easily cowed into submission. For instance, "The apothecary was severely reprimanded because he objected to carry water for the hot bath"; and "the apothecary's assistant was reprimanded in that he considered it as not part of his duty to carry dead bodies."

In an advertisement for one of these gentlemen in 1821 we find that he was expected "to have attended lectures in anatomy, physic, chemistry, and midwifery; he was to produce a certificate of his moral character, and was to be careful to attend chapel daily." And yet with such qualifications this officer was responsible for all sorts of petty and insignificant duties. He was to see that patients' heads were clean and their feet and legs washed before they were admitted into the wards. He was instructed to procure twelve flannel garments in which in-coming patients were to be clothed while he examined their clothes for vermin. In 1828 still further duties were placed upon him. He "was to report to the Committee weekly on the conduct of the nurses towards the patients, and was to superintend the warming and ventilation of the house." Among his many duties and accomplishments, his knowledge of drugs seems to have been considered the least important, and yet some of these old apothecaries were excellent druggists. Quackery, however, appealed most to the committee, evidently, for

"Mr. Seal of Blackwall having offered to supply this Charity with an approved remedy for the ague, it is the sense of the Committee that he should be admitted a Governor."

One of the greatest difficulties which the poor apothecary had to meet was to keep a supply of lint; he had to engage a woman to scrape lint, and she was expected to produce three-quarters of a pound of lint a week. So important a person was a lint-scraper that she was paid more than a nurse, and was engaged by the quarter, not by the week. One quarter's salary was always held back, and was confiscated if she failed to supply the allotted amount per week. In 1837 the Staff complained that the apothecary had made three serious mistakes in one day in making up his medicines, and that it was important that a "Chemist and

Druggist" be engaged, as "being more likely to be skilled in the making of medicines than an apothecary."

In 1854 the committee, on the request of the Staff, abolished the title of apothecary altogether, and he was henceforth known as resident medical officer, because, as the Staff said,

"The said officer is, in reality, *not* an apothecary, but a Medical Practitioner, whose chief and most important duty consists in prescribing for the patients, in the absence of the physicians."

The question of lighting the Hospital with gas was first raised in 1822, when a subcommittee was appointed "to look into this new invention." Hitherto candles had been used, and very precious they were, and their consumption was carefully checked. The Family (the resident staff, steward, apothecary, and matron were always spoken of as "The Family") were allowed seven candles (seven to the pound) each in winter, and five in summer; seven candles per week were allowed to each ward, and "no extra allowance of candles at any time of the year except those required for operations by the order of the surgeons." Imagine a surgical operation by candle light! Now an operating theatre at night is as light as day, and the surgeon has the further assistance of a multitude of extra lights—head-lights, hand-lights, bull's-eyes, and various electric devices for illuminating internal organs.

The subcommittee appointed to consider the question of lighting by gas invoked the assistance of the medical Staff.

INCIDENTS AND EVENTS

The Staff did not object to the lighting of the corridors by gas, but would have none of it in the wards.

After considering the subject for a year, the sub-committee recommended the adoption of twenty gas-burners for the whole Hospital. This was not extravagance—it included one burner for the entrance-hall, one for the theatre, one for the kitchen, and one for the dispensary. The cost was 40s. per 1,000 cubic feet. Gas was not introduced into the wards for many years after.

Soon after the introduction of gas the committee received a deputation from the inhabitants of Whitechapel, asking that the great clock over the main entrance of the Hospital might be lighted at night. The request was at first refused, but was afterwards granted on the inhabitants contributing £30, which they had collected, towards the expense.

It may be of interest to mention that this clock was the gift of the workmen of John Ellicot, F.R.S., the great clock-maker, in 1757. John Ellicot was a great friend and supporter of the Hospital from very early days; he was Chairman of the House Committee in 1757. He presented a clock of his own make for the Committee-room, and the House Committee time their sittings by the same clock to-day.

John Ellicot was a great personal friend of Benjamin Franklin, and Benjamin Franklin, who was Postmaster of New York, when he came to this country, was introduced to the Hospital by John Ellicot, and ever after took the deepest interest in it. We have a letter framed in the Committee-room from Franklin to Ellicot.

In 1823 a very serious disagreement between committee and Staff occurred, and echoes of this storm were heard for twenty years.

It has already been explained that patients were admitted to the Hospital on the recommendation of one of the governors, and patients were admitted once a week only—viz., on Tuesday—and discharged once a week only also. Both on admission and discharge patients had to appear before the committee. The only cases on whose behalf exception was made were those of sudden accident. At the end of the year 1822 the committee discovered that nearly 300 cases had been admitted *without* recommendations from governors, and that the Staff were making use of the Hospital as a sort of private nursing-home for cases in which they were interested. A special meeting of the governors was called to consider the matter. As a result the following resolution was passed at a large Court:

" That no person shall be admitted a patient into the Hospital without a recommendation from a Governor, nor on any day except the weekly day of meeting of the House Committee, cases arising from accident only excepted, and such excepted cases only on the authority of a surgeon of the Hospital, notice being given by him to the Secretary in the usual manner of every such occurrence, and a ticket in such case to be filled up by the clerk superscribed with red ink ' extra case from accident,' and affixed to the bed of the patient."

The rule was extended, and cases of sudden illness might be admitted in this irregular way. For many years after this, every patient who was not admitted by the committee in the usual way was distinguished by a card printed in red, " Extra case, essential for the preservation of life," and the officer in charge had to fill up the following form and present it at the next meeting of committee :

" By virtue of the discretionary power in me reposed by the Governors of the London Hospital, I hereby certify that A. B. is afflicted with . . . and that . . . admission is essential to the preservation of life.
" (Signed) . . . .

The House Committee in 1839 refused to take such a certificate from assistant surgeons and assistant physicians, insisting that such discretionary power was vested in the full Staff alone.

The following resolution was passed by the Court every two or three years from 1803 onwards :

" Resolved, that the right of admitting patients into this Hospital is vested solely in the Governors thereof, through the medium of the House Committee."

Not until recent times, in 1896, did the governors choose a more honourable way. Then they gave up their letters of recommendation, threw open the doors of the Hospital, and made " the right of admission " depend upon poverty and sickness alone.

There were those who foretold disaster to the Hospital when the change was made. " Who," they asked, " would pay to be a Governor of a Hospital where Governors had no rights ?"

The disaster has not come, for there still are found men and women who are charitable for Charity's sake, and love to support a great almshouse whose gates stand open always. To the few who objected answer was made that they ought not to complain because, whereas formerly they could only recommend that number of patients corresponding with the number of the letters, now they would be able to recommend as many as they liked. But what about abuse ? The Hospital has very complete organization to check abuse, but had it not, the abuse would be far less than in the old "letter" days. Now every case is treated on its merits. The Hospital had ceased to be a huge sick-club which received pay for services rendered. It has become a charity, and its work is a gift to the people, and every patient within its walls is a guest. How long this may last it is impossible to say. The outlook is not cheering. What will England be when there are no *gifts* between friend and friend, but only rights demanded and paid ?

The Charter of the Hospital was obtained on December 9, 1759. The question of obtaining a charter was first raised by the energetic Harrison in 1742, but it fell through. In 1756 the matter was again brought forward in a report of the House Committee to the Quarterly Court. The committee drew attention to the great inconvenience of not being an incorporate body. The Hospital could not sue or defend an action, could not recover a disputed legacy, could not purchase lands. A committee was appointed to consider the matter, and meetings were held at the Pontack Tavern, Abchurch Lane. A draft was drawn up and submitted to the Court and approved. The Duke of Devonshire, then President of the Hospital, appealed to His Majesty, George II., who consented to grant a charter. The draft

"was delivered to the Right Honble. William Pitt, Esq., one of His Majesty's principal Secretaries of State, who promised to lay the same before His Majesty."

This was done. The King, on the advice of the Attorney-General, approved, and the Charter was granted. The Charter cost the Hospital £398. The most important provisions of the Charter are :

A benefaction of 30 guineas entitled to the privileges of governor for life, and an annual subscription of 5 guineas for the period during which such subscription was continued.

The Corporation was empowered to purchase lands to the yearly value of £4,000, to sue in courts of law, to use a Common Seal.

Quarterly Courts were to be holden, at which alone the Common Seal might be used, and at which bye-laws were to be framed.

Special General Courts might be called for election of officers.

General Courts were to elect committees.

Elections were to be by ballot.

Noblemen, members of Parliament, and ladies, being governors, might vote by proxy.

Fifteen governors were to constitute a General Court, whether Quarterly or Special.

Accounts were to be audited quarterly.

The meaning of any expression in the Charter being disputed, the construction most beneficial to the Hospital was to be adopted.

It has been pointed out that when the Hospital was first erected on its present site, it stood alone, and was surrounded by fields which extended at the back almost to the river.

The committee, as they were able to afford it, bought up this land bit by bit. The first to be so bought was a farm, which stood immediately behind the Hospital, for £1,442. This was in 1754. In 1772 a second farm was bought for £2,800. The size of these farms is not given in the minutes, but they were certainly very extensive, for they were relet, in portions, to various tenants, and the sum of these portions makes a very large area. There is nothing interesting to the general reader in these agreements and leases except that in a good many cases light is thrown on the kind of district Whitechapel was at the time: "Mrs. Mary Webb offers £13 a year for 2 acres of the field known as 'Ten Acres'"; the same lady also offered £8 a year for a piece of land near the new road leading from Whitechapel Road to the Turnpike, for the purpose of a Tenter Ground. "Mr. Perry takes the several parcelles of land situated on the East Side of the New Road, with the dwelling-house, barnes, cow-houses, and all other buildings"; "a bill is to be put up at Mile End Turnpike making known the desire of the Governors to let the Red Lion Farm, with several pieces of meadow land."

In 1787 the committee decided that all this pastureland around the Hospital should be let on building lease. Before this was done the directors of the London Dock Company wished to purchase the whole of the estate of the Hospital. The governors refused, as they did not consider "that the Act for making the Docks at Wapping warranted the Dock Company in making

THE LONDON HOSPITAL FROM THE BACK

a compulsory purchase," and application was made to various members of Parliament, asking them to watch the interests of the Hospital.

In 1802 there was an Act "for making and maintaining a road from the West India Docks in the Isle of Dogs to Whitechapel," and the trustees of the Commercial Road purchased from the Hospital a piece of land for this road.

In 1807 the leases on the estate for ninety-nine years were sold by auction, and the whole estate mapped out. The Commercial Road Trust complained that the arrangement of the roads on the Hospital's estate enabled persons to evade the turnpike on their road, but the committee replied that the Trust must make their own arrangements about that, as the Hospital could not be expected to lay out its estate to suit the Trust's turnpike.

In 1822 Blizard persuaded the Court to pass a resolution that the open space immediately at the back of the Hospital, the part now known as "The Field" and "The Garden of Eden," should not be built on, this "being of the utmost importance to the health of thousands of patients in succession."

This piece of ground between the College and the Nurses' Home has been turned to many uses. It was once larger than it is now, and included "The Garden of Eden" and the site of the Isolation Block, there being no Oxford Street between. It was let out until comparatively recent years for grazing sheep. It was once the kitchen garden of the Hospital, and it was for many years the burial-ground for patients who died in the Hospital. There are several references in the records of cases of body-snatching from this burial-ground, in two instances the culprits being found to be porters of the Hospital itself, who had exhumed bodies at night in order to sell them to the students for dissecting.

For many years the offices of chaplain and secretary were filled by one and the same person, as has been said, and this secretary-chaplain conducted hundreds of burial services on this ground, at which all patients who were able were bound to be present.

The London Hospital, like many other of the hospitals in London, is heavily rated. In the year 1908 more than £1,400 was paid in rates. That a voluntary hospital should be rated at all is an extremely unfair thing, considering that all its work, freely given, tends to enable the poor to keep off the rates, and to remain working members of society.

So long ago as in 1763 the churchwardens of the parish of Whitechapel threatened to distrain for rates if the Hospital would not pay. The committee of that day treated the threat with scorn, and replied that "this Charity will stand a lawsuit with them." But the churchwardens did not bring an action, and for nearly a hundred years we hear no more of these churchwardens.

In 1853 the Whitechapel Improvements Bill was before Parliament, and the solicitor of the Hospital reported that in all probability the Hospital would become rateable under the provisions of that Bill. Therefore the governors who had previously supported the measure immediately withdrew their support. The evil day was postponed until 1866, when the

Hospital first had to pay rates, in spite of a petition to Parliament, "for special exemption from Parochial Rating or for a continuance of that exemption which the Hospital has hitherto enjoyed." From that day onwards the rates have steadily increased year by year. Some parts of the Hospital are exempt.

That a charitable institution should have to pay legacy duty also seems hard lines. Legacies form a very important part of a hospital's income. In going through the records some very strange legacies have fallen to the Hospital. One of the strangest was "the plantation called 'Spring,' in the Parish of Hanover, in the Island of Jamaica, which contains by estimation 110 acres, *and all the slaves thereon.*" This property paid a profit to the Hospital for thirty years, and then ceased to yield any profit, "because of the unjust attempt in operation upon the slave population." How strange that the Hospital should have been partly supported for many years by the labour of slaves! Stranger still that John Howard, "the philanthropist," should have been one of the trustees of this estate, and saw nothing incongruous in holding such a position.

CHAPTER XI

THE MEDICAL SCHOOL

The Medical School attached to the London Hospital was founded in 1783, chiefly by the exertions of Sir William Blizard.

Before that time the members of the Staff attended the meetings of the House Committee week by week, and asked permission that one or other of their own private pupils or apprentices might be allowed to " walk " the Hospital for the sake of experience. The length of time during which a pupil " walked " was at first one year, but later, as the number of pupils who were allowed about the Hospital was limited by the committee, and on account of the popularity of the Hospital, the requests of the Staff to be allowed to take pupils became more and more frequent, and the length of time was cut down. Within ten years of the foundation, Harrison was taking pupils for eight months, and a little later Blizard himself, who was said to have made more by his pupils than by his practice, took pupils for six months.

Every pupil was introduced to the House Committee with great solemnity and form, and received the " charge " from the chairman which has been set down in a previous chapter.

This loose system very soon led the authorities into all sorts of trouble, as may very easily be imagined. A pupil would take no orders from any member of the Staff except the particular one to whom he was apprenticed. The Hospital was broken up into factions and parties, not working for the good of the Charity as a whole, but only for the benefit of his party, against every other party. There were Harrison's men, and Andrée's men, and Grindall's men, and Neale's men. The strong feeling running between these groups of pupils aggravated quarrels and jealousies between the members of the Staff.

The medical pupil of a hundred years ago was not the gentleman he is now. That Bob Sawyer was a picture from real life is abundantly proved by the minutes of this Hospital. Many of his misdeeds cannot be written here. He frequently appeared before the committee to be expelled, and to be forbidden entrance to the Hospital for ever. He was frequently " disguised in liquor," was insolent to everyone but his own chief, held all lay authority in great contempt, was often cruel to the patients (but there were many honourable exceptions to this last), and was generally as insufferable a cad as can be imagined.

And there existed no sort of educational facilities : no lectures, no demonstrations, no teaching, clinical or otherwise, no system of any kind. The pupil just lounged about the Hospital, doing nothing in particular, and was a nuisance rather than a help. His delight was to invite friends of his own, who had nothing to do with medicine, and to take them round the Hospital to " see the show." The " show " consisted of all the horrors he could find, and the fearful butchery of the operating theatre was his *pièce de resistance*. The entertainment ended with a drinking carousal in the Pupils'-room, and he did not hesitate to put his friends up for the night in the ward beds if they were too intoxicated to go home.

Sometimes these friends whom the pupils invited into the Hospital did more than see the sights ; they actually interfered in the treatment of patients. The committee objected, and passed a resolution " that no young gentleman who is not an apprentice to one of the Surgeons be suffered to dress any patient, or dispense any medicine in the surgery."

Although the School was not founded until 1783, the very lax state of affairs just referred to was put an end to twenty years earlier. The committee insisted that the pupils of any member of the Staff were under the authority of the whole Staff when such pupil was at the Hospital, and, further, that all fees from pupils which were paid for Hospital practice were to be equally divided between all members of the Staff. The pupils were to be pupils of the Hospital, not of individuals, although the Staff took all fees.

A little incident in 1769 shows the sort of respect these gentlemen had for all authority. It was found that the pupils were borrowing Hospital instruments to use on cases outside. A notice was put up accordingly by the committee in the Pupils'-room forbidding the practice. The notice was promptly torn down. A second notice was put up. This also was torn down. The pupils were at last summoned before the committee, and the chairman censured them severely.

THE PRESENT MEDICAL SCHOOL

One of the pupils then began to discuss the question with the chairman, and was grossly impertinent. The chairman, Mr. Robert Salmon, however, was a strong man, and the pupil "caught a Tartar." The hall-porter was called in, and told "that Joseph Gibbs was to be removed from the Hospital within half an hour, and never admitted again under any pretence whatever." There was no more trouble during the tenure of office of that chairman, but, strange to say, the incident was repeated with other pupils and another committee exactly seventy years after. On this occasion two pupils were expelled, and all the rest informed that "the Committee had a determination to make a severe example of anyone who might be convicted of such conduct in future." The committee also decided that no pupil was to be found in the House after 5 p.m.

In 1783 the following petition was received from the physicians and surgeons of the Hospital:

"We beg leave to state to the Chairman and Committee of the London Hospital that we are of opinion that teaching the several branches of physic and surgery by lectures at this Hospital would prove to the interest and credit of the Institution. That at present there are many obstacles in the way of such an undertaking for want of room and conveniences. That by estimation, the expense of a proper building would not exceed the sum of £600, and therefore we request of the Committee—That the said sum may be raised by subscriptions for the above application, and that such persons as shall subscribe 30 guineas or upwards may be deemed Governors for Life."

The Court of Governors gave permission to the physicians and surgeons to build a lecture theatre at the east end of the Hospital, near where the Pathological Institute now is, and a subcommittee was formed to collect subscriptions for this new theatre. A separate account was to be opened at the bankers', however, and the Court would *not* agree that subscriptions to this fund entitled the donor to be a governor of the Hospital.

Blizard issued an appeal in pamphlet form—" An Address to the Friends of the London Hospital and of Medical Learning "—on this occasion, from which the following may be quoted as being true to-day, when we find it so difficult to get money for the endowment of our Medical School :

" As all those advantages and that superiority which distinguish one nation from another have arisen either directly or ultimately from their knowledge of the sciences or their skill in the arts, so the comparative reputation of nations, and the consequent advantages of such reputation, will be in proportion to the degree of perfection in which they possess the arts and sciences. . . . But, amongst the various arts, those which contribute most to the good of mankind should claim our first attention. The importance of the arts of Physic and Surgery, from that degree in which they may be made to contribute to the good and happiness of mankind, is universally acknowledged. The cultivation and advancement of these, therefore, are objects highly deserving of the consideration of good and wise men in every country. . . . But however great may be the importance of these arts, and however strong the desire of the humane to promote their cultivation and improvement, yet if proper and effectual methods be not adopted for the education of young persons who are to practise them, they may, with the generality of practitioners, be in a very imperfect state, and even prove pernicious and destructive, instead of useful and salutary. It unfortunately happens with respect to the Art of Medicine that it is not with it as with many other arts ; as, for example, those of the painter and of the pleader at the Bar, where the spectator or hearer can judge of the abilities of the performer. On the contrary, in Medicine, no bystander who is not skilled in the art is capable of drawing any tolerable certain conclusion as to the comparative merit of the most skilful and knowing and the most unskilful and ignorant practitioner. But whilst we wish to promote the cultivation of Physic and Surgery, and make provision that practitioners in them may not be ignorant and unskilful, we should certainly endeavour to promote and facilitate the means of attaining the qualifications which are necessary to such as intend to practise these arts. A skill in the practice of Physic or Surgery cannot be acquired without an attendance at an hospital. But that degree of skill which can be acquired from an attendance on hospital practice, without a proper knowledge of principles, as it is the result of mere imitation, must be comparatively very small. It is necessary, therefore, that principles be studied. But the principles of Medicine and Surgery cannot be taught but by means of lectures publicly read. The experience of learned men from the beginning of science to the present time has proved this to be the only true and effectual method of instruction. By means of these the several discoveries that have been made respecting any art or science are properly brought together and preserved, and new ones continually added, which otherwise might in time be lost and forgotten. But lectures on the principles and practice of Physic and Surgery cannot, consistently with the advantage of the student respecting his improvement, be properly given in any other place than the hospital which he attends. . . . These are some of the reasons from whence it has been judged proper that Lectures should be read at the London Hospital, the situation of which, as being remote from places of dissipation, is uncommonly well calculated for a medical school. But there are additional reasons which relate more immediately to the Hospital itself. The Governors of an Hospital depending upon public favour should be able to make every possible plea of public utility, and should employ every rational means of promoting its interest among all ranks of people. If Public Lectures on the various branches of Medicine are delivered at the Hospital, its reputation will be raised, its fame extended, and it will become an object more generally noticed. But, farther, the giving of public lectures at the Hospital will conduce to the good of the patients and the interest of the Charity, for the great number of gentlemen who will receive their education at the Hospital, and who from that circumstance will have formed an attachment to it, may be a means of greatly promoting its interest. This effect has already been experienced from gentlemen formerly educated at the Hospital. But hitherto the conveniences for the teaching of the several branches of Medicine were wanted. The Physicians and Surgeons therefore made application for and have obtained leave of the Governors to erect by subscription a Theatre for that purpose. By this means a valuable building will be added to the property of the Hospital without the smallest expense or detriment of any kind being incurred by the Charity. . . . It is already in great forwardness, and it is intended that the Theatre shall be opened some time in September, with orations from some of the Physicians and Surgeons."

THE MEDICAL SCHOOL 193

Exactly two years before this, however, Mr. Blizard had obtained permission from the committee to deliver two courses of lectures on Anatomy and Surgery. He had to undertake not to use any patient of this Hospital in these demonstrations.

Blizard's appeal was successful, and, with the help of liberal gifts from himself, the theatre was built, and regular courses of lectures commenced.

The School was started, and grew, but we have very little reference to it in the minutes for fifty years. There appear to have been great dissensions amongst members of the Staff as to who had the right to lecture in the theatre, and the House Committee appointed a special committee to investigate the whole matter. This special committee reported (in 1834) as follows :

" In furtherance of the objects delegated to them, your Committee have instituted a diligent inquiry into the nature of the tenure under which the buildings at the East End of the Hospital, at present occupied as a museum, theatre, dissecting-room, and chemical laboratory, are held, and from careful investigation, and by examination of witnesses, the following facts appear to be satisfactorily established.

That at a General Court held February 5, 1783, permission was granted, on application by memorial from the Physicians and Surgeons, for the erection by subscription of an Anatomical Theatre; that under the authority of the said Court, and under the superintendence of a Committee appointed at a subsequent Court of March 5, 1783, the buildings were accordingly erected on ground belonging to the Hospital ; that the precise amount of subscriptions cannot now be correctly ascertained, but it appears from the evidence of

Sir William Blizard, then one of the surgeons, that, the amount proving inadequate, the deficiency was supplied by himself and his friends ; that for a long period after its erection the School remained in the possession of Sir William Blizard, and it has since passed through various hands, without any express permission from the Governors, into those of the present managers, consisting of a portion of the Medical Officers of the Hospital, who officiate as lecturers, possession having always been retained by sufferance only. The scanty information afforded by the Hospital records in relation to the School has caused considerable difficulty, but your Committee feel perfectly warranted, from what they do afford, in now repeating their conviction that the whole of the buildings are the undoubted property of the Corporation, the fixtures and fittings, with the contents of the museum, belonging to the Lecturers.

" Under the next head of inquiry—namely, the dissensions reported to have existed among the Medical Officers—your Committee have found that from time to time, for a considerable number of years past, dissensions and jealousies have unfortunately prevailed, which to a great extent appear to have originated in the possession of the Theatre by a portion of the Medical Officers only. Your Committee are therefore of opinion that such cause of disunion should be henceforward removed by placing the management of the School equally in the hands of all the Medical Officers of the Hospital. In order to accomplish this object, two plans are proposed by your Committee :

" Either, 1st, that the present possessors of the Theatre should continue to hold it, admitting henceforward the other Medical Officers, on the latter paying a certain proportion of the capital or expense, to be

THE MEDICAL SCHOOL

determined accordingly as they may be more or less interested in the profits of lectures ; or—

" 2nd, that the Governors should acquire by purchase such interests in the theatre and museum as have been declared in this report to be private property.

" Your Committee found much difficulty in decidedly recommending either of these plans, and therefore they submit them to the consideration of the Court of Governors. In any case, your Committee recommend that the management of the Medical School should be entirely in the hands of all the Medical Officers, who should constitute a Medical Board for that purpose. All regulations which originate with such Medical Board should be submitted to the House Committee for their approval, to enable them to see that such regulations do not interfere with the due discharge of Hospital duties.

" Your Committee further report their opinion that some improvements may be made in the Medical Department of the Hospital by the observance of certain orders ; that the certificates of the attendance and competency of Pupils shall be issued under the authority of the Medical Board ; and that the delivery of lectures be prohibited during the time in which the attendance of pupils is required on their Hospital duties.

" Your Committee, in conclusion, beg leave further to state in unqualified terms that, deeply regretting that any expressions should have been used during the heat of discussion tending to reflect upon the professional character of the Medical Staff of this Hospital, nothing whatever has transpired in the course of this lengthy inquiry to impeach their high character for latent humanity and attention to the duties they have undertaken to perform."

Nothing was settled, however. After all the trouble taken by the subcommittee, the Court simply resolved " that this report do lie on the table," and there is no further reference to it.

The beginning of the custom of having a resident staff of house-physicians and house-surgeons seems to have been in the decision that two of the pupils should be resident, and so always ready " to attend accidents and extraordinary cases." These men were not " qualified," and had little in common with modern resident officers. They were in office for one week only, and received the following charge from the Chairman of the House Committee :

" You are, agreeably to the Standing Orders, recommended by Mr. ——, one of the Surgeons of this Hospital, as Gentlemen competent to discharge the respective duties of Senior and Junior House Pupils for the ensuing week. The Committee consider this recommendation as an assurance that you are qualified for the fulfilment of the several important duties thus confided to your care ; they accordingly admit you to the exercise of these duties, trusting that, by devoting your best attention to the comfort and relief of the patients, and showing due respect to every authority and regulation constituted for the preservation of good order within the Establishment, you will evince a becoming regard to the interests and reputation of the Hospital, and to your own character as destined to an honourable profession. On your thus realizing these expectations of the Committee, you will secure to yourselves their approbation, with that of the Covernors of the Hospital ; but if otherwise, the Committee have determined that the privilege of residence shall in future be withheld."

By 1837 the Medical School seems to have been fairly started.

It is interesting to note that in 1845 there were two kinds of pupils—dressing pupils and visiting pupils. The dressing pupils, who corresponded to the modern students, were limited in number; no surgeon could introduce more than six. Visiting pupils could enter the wards, operating theatre, and Out-patient Department, but "were not permitted to dress nor direct for any patient in the Hospital."

The House Committee claimed the right to recommend three students annually to be appointed, without fee or reward, to attend daily in the Out-patient Department. If they served with satisfaction, they were to receive, also gratuitously, the appointment of dressing pupil for one year. In 1849 this arrangement caused great annoyance to the Staff, who wrote by one of their number to the committee as follows :

"GENTLEMEN,

"The regulation respecting which I have already addressed the Committee, and which my colleagues and myself desire to have altered, is that contained in the Standing Orders for Pupils, by which the Surgeons are required to forego their fees for three students when entering upon their studies in the Wards of the Hospital, in consideration of their diligent attendance as Dressers to the Out-patients for one year. The Surgeons beg to state that they consider the fees received from Students as afforded for the instructions which they impart, and they regard these fees as an indirect though inadequate means of remuneration for the services which they render to the Hospital. They are of opinion that no part of these means should be withheld from them for the payment of duties in the Out-patient Department, which they cannot be expected themselves to discharge. The Surgeons beg, therefore, to suggest that, if the appointment of Dressers to the Out-patients be continued, with the present condition of the Dressers receiving gratuitous dresserships to the In-patients, the expense of the arrangement be no more expected to fall on the Surgeons, but be defrayed by the Governors. The collateral advantages to the Hospital School of gratuitous dresserships which induced your former surgeons to consent to these appointments are now materially diminished by the regulations of the Royal College of Surgeons, and they are consequently, as respects the attractions of the School, of little value, and improperly curtail the remuneration of the Surgeons. Had the collateral advantages continued, the Surgeons would have been unwilling to interfere with the existing regulations, but under altered circumstances they consider themselves fully justified in requesting a different arrangement.

"(Signed) T. B. CURLING."

The committee, having maturely considered the statements made before them in the above letter, unanimously resolved that it was inexpedient to make any alteration in the regulations.

In 1851 the Hospital Staff approached the committee, asking the committee to sanction the payment of a grant to the Medical College out of the Hospital funds. The letter making this request is of sufficient importance to be quoted:

"*To the Secretary of the London Hospital.*

"SIR,

"I have been requested to submit to the House Committee a table showing the amount and nature of the support and assistance afforded to the Medical Schools in London by the Authorities and Governors of the Hospitals to which they are attached. The information was obtained and the Table constructed by one of the Lecturers of the Westminster Hospital School. It shows the great disadvantages under which the Lecturers of the London Hospital Medical School labour in competing with the other hospital Medical Schools in the Metropolis, from having to bear entirely the heavy expenses connected with the business of Medical Instruction. The grounds upon which the Governors of the other Hospitals have either borne the whole expenses of the Medical Schools, or afforded them large assistance, are understood to be the advantages derived by the Hospitals, not only from the educating and training of Gentlemen in order to qualify them for undertaking the higher and more responsible duties of the Medical Staff, but from the great and important services rendered gratuitously by well-instructed Pupils in the capacities of House Surgeons and Dressers, which services, without the adjuncts of Medical Schools, could be obtained only by a heavy outlay of the Hospital Funds. The Medical Officers entertain a confident hope that a fair and liberal consideration of the circumstances here represented will induce the House Committee to recommend that assistance be granted for the maintenance of the Medical School, in some degree commensurate with the advantages derived by the Hospital from the Association and the value of the services rendered by the Pupils. The Committee need scarcely be reminded that, in consequence of the great amount of patients admitted into the London Hospital—an amount exceeding that of the In-patients of any other hospital in London, with the exception of St. Bartholomew's—of the large proportion of Surgical cases and Accidents, and of the immense number of Out-patients, the duties required of the Dressers are very onerous, and equal to, if not greater than, those performed at any similar Institution. The Medical Officers, in making this application, have no intention at the present time of calling the attention of the House Committee to the subject comprised in the last column of the Table—namely, " Honoraria received by Medical Officers of Hospitals "; but as the services of the Medical Officers of the London Hospital are not acknowledged in this way, they trust that will be regarded as an additional reason for the Medical School receiving the support and countenance of the Governors.

" T. B. CURLING,
" *Hon. Sec. to Medical School.*"

The committee did not send a favourable reply. After giving the matter due consideration, they did not consider they were justified in passing any pecuniary vote.

That decision has long since been reversed. It is now understood that the interests of the Hospital and the Medical School are one. A good medical school stimulates the hospital to good work. A hospital doing good work attracts students to its school. Without students it would be impossible to secure men of the same standing for the Staff, and the patients would thereby be great losers. The Hospital from 1880 until the recent Commission upon " Hospitals and

Medical Schools" in 1905 made an *annual* grant (it had made an occasional grant before) to the School for services directly rendered by the School to the Hospital. For instance, the Medical School has to supply the London Hospital annually, and without salary, with 14 Receiving-room Officers, 8 Resident Accoucheurs, 10 House-Physicians, 14 House-Surgeons, 8 Emergency Officers, 40 In-patient Clinical Clerks every three months, and 30 In-patient Dressers every three months, besides Out-patient Clerks and Dressers, Maternity Assistants, Post-mortem Clerks, and many others. But for the School the Hospital would have to pay for the services of these gentlemen. Their medical education at the College is closely associated with their work at the Hospital. It is of considerable interest that, when the Commission decided that no grants were in future to be made from the general funds of a hospital to a medical school, many subscribers, and those who best understood the value of this School to this Hospital, wished that in future their subscriptions should be given to the School, and not to the general funds of the Hospital at all, if the House Committee so wished. They well understood that they were supporting the Hospital most usefully in insuring continued success of the School.

In 1853 the Medical College was erected on its present site. The old building, with which Blizard had so much to do, had long since been inadequate.

Since the erection of the new building in 1853 it has been enlarged on four occasions, and is to-day one of the finest schools in the kingdom for affording medical education.

There are the following departments under the control of specialists :

1. *Biology.*—Laboratory, museum, and class-rooms for general and University students.

2. *Chemistry and Physics.*—A lecture-theatre and laboratories for general students, University students, and students of public health.

3. *Materia Medica and Pharmacy.*—A pharmaceutical laboratory, and a museum containing all the substances described in the Pharmacopœia, and plates of officinal plants.

4. *Anatomy.*—Dissecting-room, class-rooms, and lecture-theatre, fully equipped for teaching anatomy to University or general students, and for research.

5. *Physiology.*—Class-rooms and laboratories for general, chemical, and experimental physiology; rooms for special research; and a lecture-theatre, supplied with electric light and power, and with an epidiascope for lantern demonstrations.

6. *Bacteriology.*—Laboratories and class-rooms for routine instruction and for research. Annexed to the department is a laboratory for the investigation of the treatment of certain diseases by inoculation.

7. *Operative Surgery.*—A special department in which students are taught operative surgery. Special classes are also held for those preparing for the higher examination, officers in His Majesty's service, and others.

8. *Public Health.*—Laboratories, lecture- and demonstration-rooms, and museum, fully equipped for students proceeding for the Diploma in Public Health.

By the generosity of the late Rev. S. A. Thompson Yates, the laboratories have been furnished with all

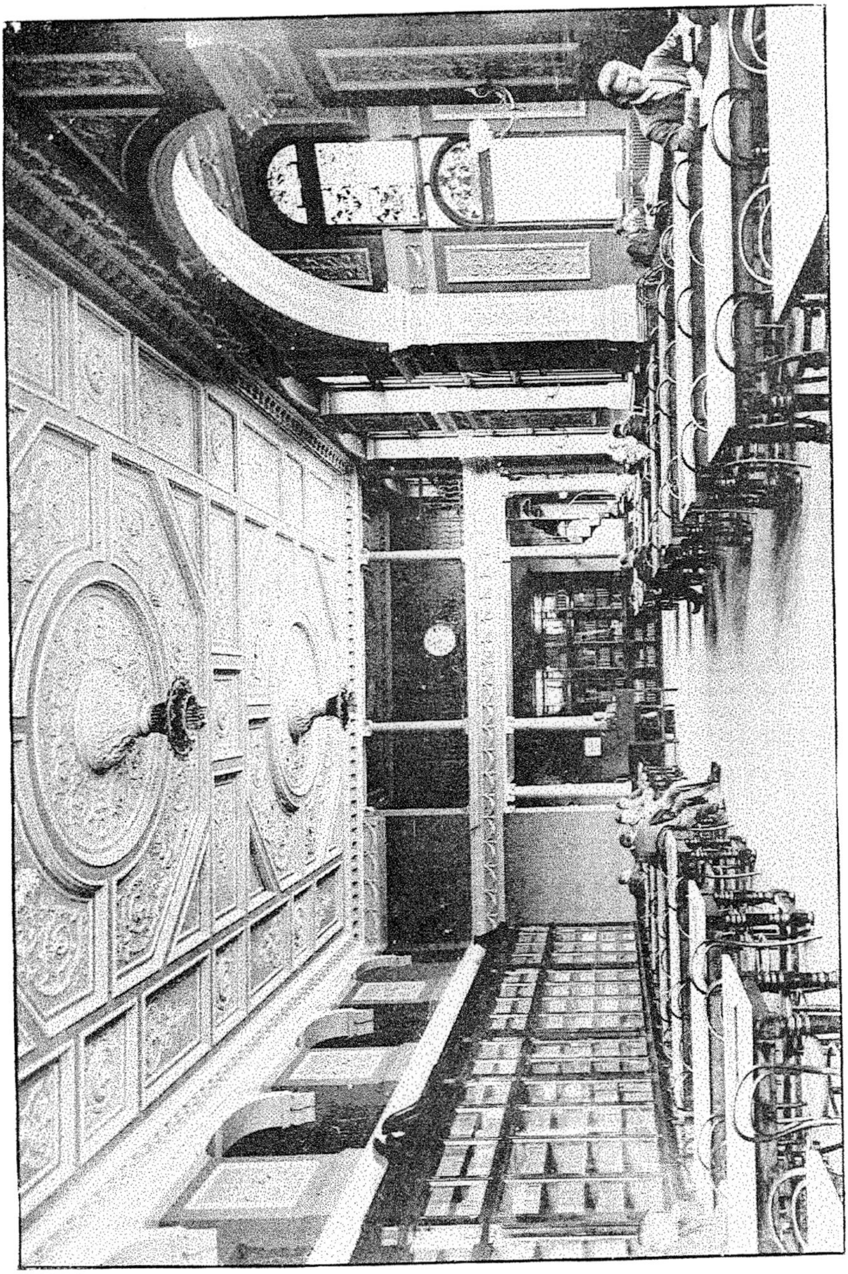

the latest and most approved apparatus, and with electric light and power.

The library, which serves also for an examination-hall, is well provided with the most modern medical and surgical works, and with a large collection of ancient authors. New works of interest to students are being constantly added to the collection.

The Medical College is managed by the College Board, which has been presided over for many years by Mr. Douro Hoare, and Mr. Munro Scott has filled the important position of warden of the Medical College for thirty years with conspicuous success.

An endowment fund has been established, and last year a sum of £20,000 was received (from a donor who wishes to remain anonymous) for the advancement of medical research.

CHAPTER XII

THE NURSING OF THE SICK POOR

As far as the records of this Hospital are concerned, we have seen that the type of woman employed as a nurse or watch at the beginning of the Hospital's career was of the lowest. She was usually an old woman who, on account of her age, and very often on account of her habits, was worse than useless to the community.

Her wages were of the smallest, and her livelihood was eked out by gratuities from the committee, tips from the Staff, and fines from the patients. If her wages were small, her number of hours on duty was certainly not.

In 1756, when she was honoured by having Standing Orders, she was expected to come on duty at 6 a.m., and was to continue on duty until her supper-time at 10 p.m. She might then consider herself free, but had to be in bed by 11.

When referred to in the minutes, she is classed with "beadles, porters, and other inferior servants." Her duties, according to the Standing Orders referred to, were, amongst other things, "to make the beds of the officers and servants, to clean the rooms, passages, and stairs, and the Court- and Committee-rooms."

THE NURSING OF THE SICK POOR   205

It was not until 1820 that the committee thought it advisable that nurses should be able to read and write (two were discharged in 1822 because they could not read and write, "which was contrary to the bye-laws"). This law had to be relaxed, however, in 1829, on account of the difficulty of obtaining nurses. Only head-nurses were expected to have this qualification. Nurses who were not able to read and write were not to administer medicines except on emergency.

Sir Henry Burdett, writing on "Nursing Systems," and speaking of these days, says:

"The only points to be settled on engaging a nurse were that she was not Irish and not a confirmed drunkard. 'We always engage them without a character,' wrote a doctor, 'as no respectable person would undertake so disagreeable an office.' Every vice was rampant among these women, and their aid to the dying was to remove pillows and bedclothes, and so hasten the end."

The training of women for the honourable profession of sick-nursing was unknown before 1840.

It would be doing a wrong to the memory of many faithful women if it were thought that every woman who nursed in the London Hospital before 1840 was of the type described above. There were brilliant exceptions. There were "born nurses" then, as now, whose names occur in the minutes from time to time with honourable mention. "Annie Broadbent was well qualified for her situation, which no one could fill with more credit to herself or advantage to the Hospital"; "Susan Jewell was very attentive, particularly with respect to administering medicine;" "Ann Maddy was very attentive, highly respectable in her character and conduct, and is very humanely disposed;" "Sarah Lowe was a very good servant, kept her ward particularly neat, and her patients in good order;" "Catherine Willis was exceedingly kind and attentive to her patients, of a good character and of an obliging disposition." All honour to these unknown women who used their only talent well. They showed a true womanliness and tenderness in times when their duties were considered degrading, and when their surroundings were abhorrent—born nurses, but untrained.

Now the pendulum has swung in the other direction. The *danger* is in thinking that training alone will make a nurse. It will not. It can only perfect the inborn nursing instinct. It can only make the woman more useful, but it cannot make the woman. A nurse must be a true, pure, self-sacrificing, cheerful woman. That comes first, middle, and last. That is her power. Her training directs her power into ways of increased usefulness, but it does not create her power. Her certificate will tell you about the one; a sick child could tell you most about the other.

On September 2, 1840, appears the following minute:

"The Committee met on special summons to consider a communication from a deputation of the Provisional Board of Management of a projected society for the establishment of Protestant Sisters of Charity, especially with the view to improve the class of women employed in nursing the sick, requesting the Committee to admit two or three respectable women to be trained under the superintendence of the Matron. Resolved that the application be complied with, under a definite understanding that it shall in no manner be permitted to interfere with the discipline or arrangements of the Hospital."

Mrs. Elizabeth Fry was the moving spirit and founder of the society, a deputation from which attended the Hospital. The minutes do not say who was on the deputation, although it is more than probable Mrs. Fry was present.

The excellent services rendered to the Hospital by these Nursing Sisters is referred to years after—namely, during the cholera epidemic of 1866 :

" Resolved, that a letter be addressed to the Lady Superior of All Saints' Home, Margaret Street, Cavendish Square, conveying the best thanks of the Committee for the very efficient services of the Sisters who attended nightly in the cholera wards of this Hospital during the period of greatest pressure, and assuring her that their kind attention to the wants of the patients and their responsible supervision of the Night Nurses were of great value to the Charity, and have been highly appreciated by the House Committee."

The Hospital, however, as yet showed no disposition to train its own nurses for their work.

In 1847 serious illness in the nursing staff is recorded. A committee was appointed to investigate the cause of this general breaking-down in health. They reported that

" The general disorder of the health of the nurses is brought on from excessive fatigue, induced by having to perform both Day and Night Duty, with but a short and hurried interval of rest between those periods of attendance in the wards."

They recommended that a sufficient number of nurses be engaged, especially for night duty. Consequently, fourteen women were engaged to act as night nurses. They were not resident, but came in every evening. They were paid weekly, at the rate of 1s. 6d. per night. And this was but sixty years ago! About this time there is a note which says that only the older nurses were allowed to go into the men's wards, and that nurses were paid £2 a year more for nursing men than women. But within the next ten years the great change was to burst on the world, owing to the work and example of Miss Florence Nightingale.

In 1863 the governors agreed to the principle of pensioning nurses who had long been in the service of the Hospital. No pension could be given until after twenty years' service, and the maximum for nurses was 12s. a week, and for assistant nurses 7s.

In 1865 the committee received a memorial from the nursing staff, craving to be allowed one week's holiday in the year. This very unusual request was postponed for a year, but was eventually granted.

In 1866 is found the first sign that the authorities thought it would be a good thing to train our own nurses:

"Resolved, that a system of training Assistant Nurses be adopted in the Hospital, in accordance with the terms of a report from the Matron" (Mrs. Nelson).

The following is part of this report:

"The difficulty of procuring qualified Assistant Nurses has been long brought to your notice, but it is only now that I am in a position to submit for your approval a plan which has been for some time under the consideration of the House Governor and myself, and which plan, when fully carried out, will, I firmly believe, obviate this pressing inconvenience. I would suggest that we should have a small training establishment for our own purposes in the Hospital, to consist of from four to six probationary assistant nurses. These women, after two months' training, would, if required, be sufficiently qualified to be placed in wards under the Head Nurses, but, of course, they would become more valuable as they became more experienced. It is proposed to put these extra assistant nurses on the same footing as regards pay and allowances as the other assistant nurses, with this difference : that they shall not have dresses supplied to them until they are appointed to wards, and that they shall not be entitled to gratuities until they have been six months in a ward, or twelve months in the service of the Hospital."

It is strange that the committee should have been so slow in deciding that it was advisable to train nurses for the Hospital's own work, when it was constantly receiving requests, and granting them, from all sorts of outside charitable organizations for permission to send women to the Hospital to be trained.

In 1874 a new wing was added to the Hospital (the Grocers' Wing), and when the plans for this wing were being considered, the Court decided

" that in carrying out the proposed extension of the Hospital the House Committee be empowered to include, either in the same or in a separate building, arrangements for a training-home for nurses, for the special benefit and service of the London Hospital."

Very few nurses could be accommodated in this wing, however, and in a small part of what subsequently became the first Nurses' Home. The greater number were accommodated in houses in the district. In 1875 there was a serious outbreak of typhoid in some of these outlying homes, and several nurses were attacked, two with fatal results.

Although the committee referred to a "training-home" for nurses in 1874, there was no proper and systematic training until 1880, when courses of lectures on nursing subjects were commenced by the present Matron, Miss Lückes, and, at her instigation, by members of the Medical and Surgical Staff.

In 1895 a preliminary training-school was opened at Tredegar House. The advantages of such a preliminary training-home cannot easily be overestimated. Here probationers attend for seven weeks before entering the Hospital wards, and are taught all that is possible of routine work apart from the embarrassing surroundings of a great hospital. Here are given lectures on anatomy, physiology, bandaging, and sick-room cookery. One of the advantages of such an institution is that probationers are taught the necessity of discipline, punctuality, system, and accurate observation.

For the benefit of those who may contemplate entering the nursing profession, some particulars of the conditions of a nurse's life in the London Hospital to-day may be of interest.

Having been accepted as a candidate suitable for training (all particulars as to age limits, etc., can be obtained by applying to the Matron, and there is

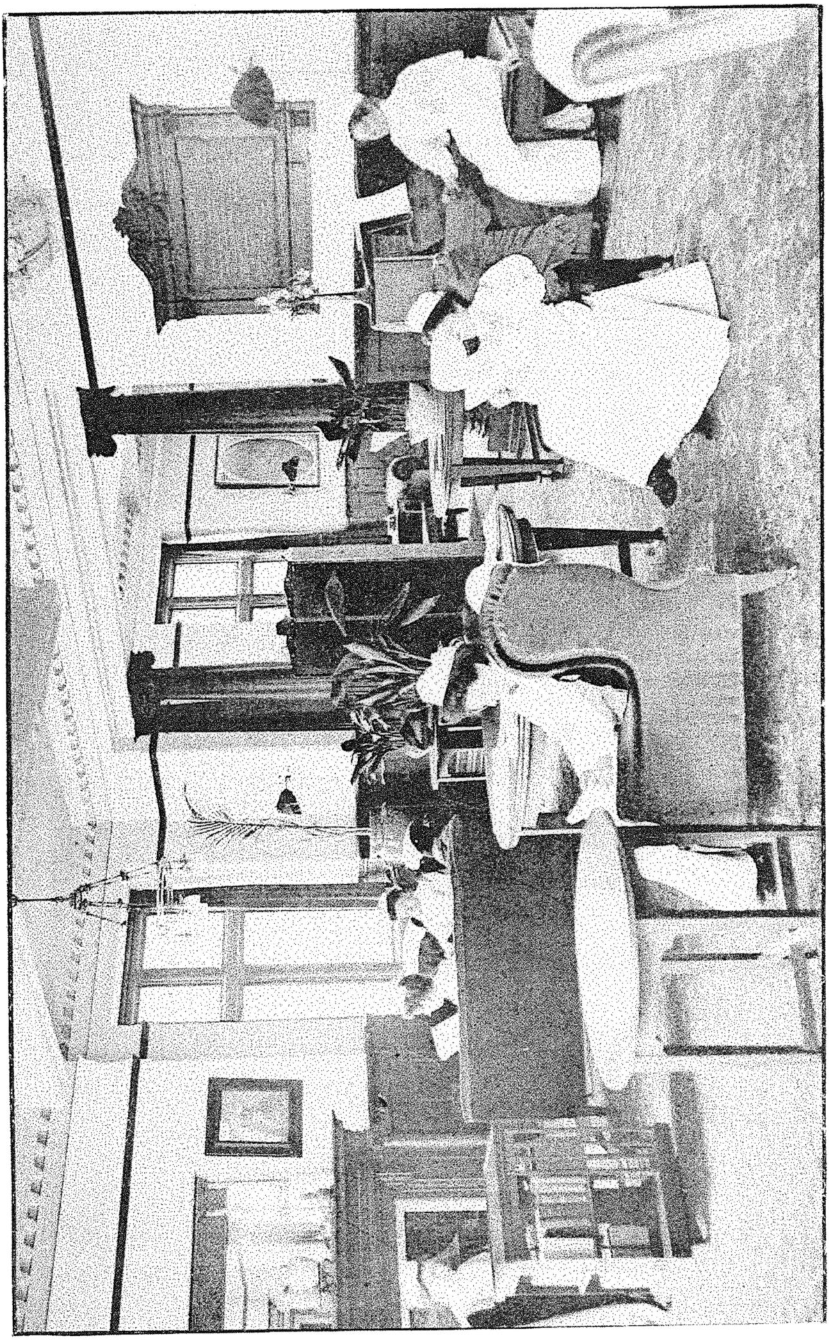

always room for suitable candidates), the pupil probationer would be sent to Tredegar House for her seven weeks' preliminary training. Parties of twenty-eight such candidates are received at a time. She would then come to the Hospital itself, and after a month's trial, if satisfactory, would sign an agreement to remain in the service of the Hospital for four years —that is, for two years of training, and for a further two years after obtaining her certificate. This last two years compensates the Hospital for expenses incurred in giving the training, free of all cost, to the probationer, and for paying her while she is being trained.

From the day she enters the Hospital the probationer is provided with a separate bedroom, and excellent sitting and reading rooms. The domestic arrangements generally are exceedingly comfortable.

The hours of duty are so arranged as to give all nurses and probationers three hours off duty daily, always by daylight. Nurses (a probationer becomes a "nurse" on the completion of her two years' training), as well as three hours daily, have a half-day off duty every week, and every fourth Sunday. They are allowed to have the half-day of that week on the Saturday preceding the Sunday off duty, so that they may spend the night away from the Hospital, should they desire to do so. Probationers have their daily three hours, and also a whole day off duty every fortnight.

In addition to the lectures given to pupil probationers at Tredegar House, three courses of lectures are given at the Hospital annually—on the General Details of Nursing, by the Matron; on Elementary Anatomy and Surgical Nursing, by one of the surgeons; and on Elementary Physiology and Medical Nursing, by one of the physicians. After each course of lectures an examination is held, and at the end of the first year's training the probationer sits for the annual examination.

As I have said, no fees are charged for training. On the contrary, a salary is paid from the first. A probationer is paid £12 the first year, and £20 the second. A nurse is paid £24, increasing by £1 per annum to £27. Sisters are paid £30 the first year, £35 the second year, £40 the third year, as a maximum. Nurses who are sent out to nurse private cases—that is, those who are appointed to the private staff—are paid £30 the first year, £35 the second, £40 the third, and £45 the fourth, as a maximum.

A certain amount of uniform is provided to all members of the Staff, and, of course, full board, with an allowance of 2s. 6d. per week for washing.

In order to encourage the best nurses to remain on the Staff, an addition of £5 to her salary is made to every nurse after six years from the date of her entrance as a probationer; a second increase of £5 per annum is given after the completion of her twelfth year; and after the expiration of eighteen years' service, at a minimum age of forty-five, all members of the Nursing Staff are eligible for pensions, the pension being full pay for life.

The training of the nurses at the London Hospital to-day is on lines laid down by one of the

THE NURSING OF THE SICK POOR 213

Hospital's best-known governors, Miss Florence Nightingale, who has always taken the keenest interest in the work of the Hospital, and in the nursing especially.

Miss Nightingale was made a life governor in 1856, when she was still carrying out her nursing work at Scutari. On acquainting her with the wish of the House Committee to make her an honorary life governor, the secretary received the following letter from her:

"SCUTARI, BARRACK HOSPITAL,
"*March* 20*th*, 1856.

" SIR,

"I beg to acknowledge the receipt of your letter of March 5th, and to request that you will be kind enough to convey my best thanks to the Governors of the London Hospital for the honour they have done me in entering my name on the list of Governors of that Institution.

"It is an honour especially gratifying to me, since the objects of the Hospital are those which have been the strongest interests of my life. And to receive such a tribute of sympathy in these interests of cordial feeling from an Institution which commands the respect and admiration of all who have witnessed the manner in which it is conducted is a peculiar satisfaction, which I appreciate most highly and heartily. If I live to return to England, when this work in which I am engaged shall be at an end, I shall have great pleasure in receiving from the Governors of the London Hospital the documents mentioned in your letter, and in hearing whatever they may have the kindness to say to me concerning that Hospital.

" FLORENCE NIGHTINGALE."

No living woman has done more for the betterment of the conditions under which nurses work, the shortening of their hours, the lengthening of their holidays, the improvement in the domestic arrangements, than Miss Lückes, the present Matron, and she has been encouraged in this work by our present chairman, who has made the improvement of the conditions of nursing one of his main objects in devoting his life to hospital work.

CHAPTER XIII

THE LAST TWENTY YEARS

THAT more has been done in the great task of fighting disease in the last twenty years of the Hospital's life than in all the years since its foundation will be conceded by those acquainted with the work. And yet such a statement is not true altogether. It is more accurate to say that the result of the work of the last hundred years is shown in the last twenty. The blossom and fruit which we see and admire are only proofs that the root was quietly doing its work underground in the dreary winter days.

Twenty years ago every hospital in London was beginning to see that it needed weapons in its combat with sickness the lack of which it had never felt before. Up to that time a hospital was essentially a collection of large rooms in which patients could be put to bed, kept warm, and well fed. Surgery rarely interfered, except in cases of accident. The cure of the patient was left to "Nature." How Nature assisted was not clearly understood. The treatment was negative, not active.

From twenty years ago onwards great discoveries have been made almost every year, and there is occasion in a great hospital for the discoveries in all branches of science to find application—physiology and anatomy, chemistry and biology, bacteriology, pathology and histology. Discoveries have been made in all of these which are of use in the healing of sick folk, and in destroying the causes of disease. Consequently, every hospital, efficient as may have been its work hitherto, according to the light it had, suddenly found itself out of date, inefficient, and incomplete.

Until twenty years ago the deliberations of the committee were chiefly concerned with routine questions of discipline and standing orders; of purchase and storage of coals, and meat, and bread, and bedding; of appointments and resignations; of income and expenditure. These questions still occupy, and must always occupy, much of the committee's attention. But now to these were added long and anxious considerations as to the possibility of introducing some new and hitherto unknown system of attacking some loathsome and hitherto unconquered disease. And it was not simply a question of deciding on the purchase of this or that apparatus, or the enlargement of this or that room. One single step forward on the part of one investigator would lead to a greatly increased *permanent* expenditure. For instance, Lister makes the discovery that wounds are infected by micro-organisms which enter at the time of operation; that these micro-organisms produce suppuration, which may end in death; therefore, their entry is to be prevented. What has followed? The whole system of surgical operation was immediately changed. Before his day a simple well-lighted room, a wooden table, and a dirty old coat for the surgeon to wear for his dirty work, sufficed. Now the operating theatres must have mosaic floors, tiled walls, and rounded corners; all theatre furniture must be enamelled and rounded. Hot and cold water must be supplied in unlimited quantities, and there must be conveniences for washing in running water, and all the water must be sterilized first. This is done by boiling, and then cooling out of contact with the air, and the coal bill is thus affected. The life of the instruments is shortened from years to months, because each instrument has to be boiled before use. The instrument sterilizers are always boiling in both theatres and wards, and so the gas bill is increased. No one may enter a theatre unless wearing a sterile calico smock. Some hundreds of these smocks are used in the theatres every week, and so the washing bill goes up. Dressings have all to be subjected to the action of steam under pressure, and for this expensive steam sterilizers must be provided. Highly trained assistants must be engaged, who are alive to the danger which may lurk in a piece of inefficiently sterilized catgut or sponge. Large numbers of unskilled assistants must also be employed for keeping the theatres clean.

Now, the above illustrates what has happened in nearly every department. The first simple discovery has led to enormous expenditure, which becomes a fixed and permanent expenditure. Is it worth it? Yes, it is. The Hospital has doubled the number of patients it passes through each of its beds each year, because of the shortening of the time of "average residence" by half. In other words, recoveries are more rapid. But that is not all. Patients recover who previously would not have recovered at all. The enormous advances in abdominal surgery have made recovery possible in cases which were once considered hopeless.

Now, all these things began to force themselves upon a committee, already perplexed, about twenty years ago. The committee was already perplexed because it had been gradually driven to the conclusion that the work of the Hospital had outgrown the resources of the Hospital. Every ward was overcrowded; the little underground Out-patient Department was full all day and every day. Mr. John Hampton Hale, one of the most devoted chairmen the Hospital ever had, was elected to the chair in 1893, and it is said of him, and I believe truly, that he never missed, except during his holiday, being at the Hospital for some hours of every day. Never did a distressed ship depend more on the judgment and skill of the captain than did the Hospital at that time depend upon its chairman. When Mr. Hale took office the time had come when something had to be done if the work was to go on at all, even in the old non-scientific method. Before he retired the new era had come, and the difficulties had increased a hundredfold.

Up to now the Medical and Surgical Staff had been capable of teaching nearly all that a medical student ought to know. No better proof of the changes which were taking place can be given than the altered opinion of the Staff on this point, and the following extract from the Quarterly Report of the House Committee may be quoted :

" During the last quarter the Medical Council asked the House Committee to receive a deputation of the whole Medical Staff, to discuss the present and future of the Medical School. The House Committee readily acceded, and at the interview it was pointed out very forcibly by the Medical Staff that it was absolutely necessary to strengthen certain of the teaching departments ; that so much was now required of teachers that it was no longer possible for a man to be a Professor of Science and do his teaching fairly towards the students, and also to be in practice as a physician or surgeon ; and that it has become necessary, if the Medical School was to maintain its high position, to support and adequately pay professors of physiology, bacteriology, biology, practical anatomy, and of chemistry."

That report shows quite well what was going on. The healing forces were taking to themselves allies, and room had to be found in the old camp for the increased army.

This sudden advance in medicine and surgery was reflected everywhere throughout the Hospital. There was a general awakening and a desire to do better. Disease was to be fought, not suffered. Overcrowding had been referred to years before, but only as an inconvenience, as a man might complain that his orchard was too small. Now it was more than that ; it was preventing good work from being conscientiously performed, when there was so much to be done. Everywhere was greater keenness. So we note all sorts of minor and apparently disconnected improvements. Modern bedsteads were supplied throughout the Hospital, which gave greater facilities for good nursing ; hair and spring mattresses were substituted for the old flock ones ; feather pillows were introduced. The conditions of the nursing service were improved, and the quality of the training of probationers changed for the better. It was in the chairmanship of Mr. Hale that Tredegar House was opened (1895) as a preliminary training-school for nurses, and also it was from about this time that nurses were enabled to take a course of sick-room cookery. Much greater attention was given to cleanliness, and now commenced the practice, still in vogue, of scrubbing the Hospital corridors, staircases, waiting-rooms, and Out-patient Department during every night between the hours of 11 p.m. and 5 a.m. The Lords' Commission on the Metropolitan Hospitals awakened a keener interest in the work of these great charities, and the committees of them all strove to increase their efficiency.

In 1896 is the first reference to the treatment of disease by serum, diphtheria and tetanus being the diseases first attacked.

This treatment has so revolutionized the treatment of certain diseases, diphtheria especially, that some fuller reference to it may be of interest to lay readers. The principle on which the treatment rests is this: that when a micro-organism grows, it first produces a substance which is poisonous. The symptoms shown by man after the invasion of these micro-organisms are due to the action of these "toxins" which have been produced, and which affect nerves, kidneys, liver, stomach, or other organs. After a certain time a substance is produced by the man which is antagonistic to the further action of the toxin, and eventually neutralizes it. This substance is called antitoxin. Each kind of organism produces its own special toxin and antitoxin. In the case of a person suffering from a disease due to the presence of one kind or another of these minute bodies, the recovery or the death of the patient depends largely upon his capacity for " holding out " until sufficient antitoxin has been produced to neutralize those toxins which are causing the disease. If a horse be inoculated with the diphtheria bacillus, he shows symptoms of the disease, and recovers, and in his recovery antitoxins have been produced in his blood. The animal is again inoculated with the disease, and again and again, until it is not possible to give the animal the disease at all, because the protective antitoxins have been so developed as to be able to resist entirely any diphtheria bacillus with which he may be inoculated. When this condition has been arrived at, blood is drawn from a vein in the neck with a suitable vessel, and allowed to stand until clotting takes place; the clear, yellowish serum is drawn off, and sterilized by being passed through a special filter. This serum, when injected into a child suffering from diphtheria, gives to the child the resisting power or immunity gained by the horse. By this, the now recognized treatment, the mortality in infant diphtheria in London was reduced from 59 per cent. in 1888 to 11 per cent. in 1901. It should be stated that every horse used for the production of antitoxin serum is first of all tested by means of tuberculin and mallein, to insure his own freedom from tuberculosis and glanders.

But to return to the Hospital. In 1894 the Staff asked that the Hospital should be lighted by electricity. The old gas-burners were antiquated, and the surgeons urged that in the theatre especially (there was only one) more efficient lighting was absolutely essential. The question was carefully considered, but the committee came to the conclusion that the expense was prohibitive. Two years later, however, incandescent gas-burners were established throughout the Hospital instead.

Electricity was now becoming an important agent in the treatment of disease, and again, in 1894, the Staff attended the committee, asking for the provision and equipment of an electrical department. This was granted after careful consideration. A temporary building was built and equipped, and in the following year (1895) the first Medical Officer in charge of the Electrical Department was appointed. This, like every other new department, has grown enormously, and now engages the whole time of six assistants.

At this date, also, is the first reference in the minutes to the Röntgen rays, and still another department had to be founded for the application of these rays. Once their uses were known, no hospital could afford to neglect so useful and important an aid in diagnosis and treatment. Now the Röntgen rays are in use at the Hospital from morning to night. Every fracture is examined on admission by their aid, and again examined after the bones have been put into position for uniting. X rays are in constant use, too, as has already been stated, to discover the whereabouts of the odds and ends which Whitechapel children, like little ostriches, delight to swallow—buttons, pins, coins, etc. They are largely used now, too, in the treatment of certain diseases—cancer, ringworm, and certain forms of lupus.

In December, 1896, the Honourable Sydney Holland was elected chairman, on the resignation of Mr. Hale. Mr. Hale had been chairman through the most strenuous years which the Hospital had known since its foundation. Everything was " pressing," and at every meeting of the committee some new development had to be considered. When he retired from the chair, the Court passed the following resolution :

" On the occasion of the retirement of Mr. John Hampton Hale from the position of Chairman of the House Committee, which he has occupied since December, 1892, it was unanimously resolved to place on record the very high appreciation of the splendid services rendered by Mr. Hale to this great Charity. The Committee acknowledged with deep gratitude the untiring zeal with which Mr. Hale has given himself up to the many interests of the Hospital, the absolute self-sacrifice with which he has devoted his valuable time to the Institution, and the able manner in which he has mastered all the many difficult details connected therewith."

On looking through the records of the work, week by week, during Mr. Hale's term of office, one cannot but feel that the praise given in the passage quoted was thoroughly deserved.

To the outside public Mr. Sydney Holland is best known as the " Prince of Beggars." That such a man should take up the responsibility of the chairmanship at such a time was a piece of great good fortune to the Hospital. Money was sadly wanted, and here was the man with a great power of interesting sympathetic people in what he himself was so keenly interested in.

To those who work within the walls of the Hospital Mr. Holland is known as a man of untiring energy, of broad views and high ideals, and of great kindness of heart. His appeals hit hard, and cannot be resisted. That is because he has himself been hit hard. The suffering poor appeal to him, and he appeals to the charitable. When he asks for help, it may be safely assumed that he has done his own share in helping first, and a great deal more than his share. His pocket and his time have been at the service of the Hospital since he was elected chairman in 1896. He is chairman now in 1910, and works as hard to-day as he did thirteen years ago. On the desk before me as I write is a note of things Mr. Holland wants to know, and to know soon : Was that operation on So-and-so successful ? Is anyone doing anything for that man's wife while he is in Hospital ? Cannot we help that poor woman more ? Why has Mr. A. cancelled his subscription ? The Budget ! " Absurd ; give me his address." Are we not using too many chickens, and would not rabbits, which are cheaper, do as well in some case ? Are the dinners served hot in Rowsell Ward, which is a long way from the kitchens ? Are the residents' meals properly cooked and served ? and so on. All at " The London " work hard, but no one so hard as the chairman.

From the first he devoted a great deal of his energy to improve the conditions under which the nurses worked. The hours on duty were shortened, the time off duty by daylight increased ; the holidays were extended, the salaries raised, and the accommodation enormously improved. A sick-room was provided

THE HON. SYDNEY HOLLAND, CHAIRMAN

THE BOARD-ROOM

for the nurses, with the advantages of a hospital ward, and the privacy and cosiness of home. For thirteen years he has championed the cause of nurses, not only here, but everywhere.

Again and again the Staff attended the committee, urging the necessity of one improvement after another. They again appealed for the electric lighting of the Hospital. A fund was started. The work was commenced, and was, after some five years—for the committee had to feel their way—completed. It cost £15,000.

Then the necessity of a photographic department was urged. It was started, and its work, too, has increased beyond all expectation. Very full and careful notes are kept here, as at all good hospitals, of every case treated—of the family history, of the onset of the illness, of its progress every day, and of its termination. These notes are classified and bound, and form one of the most useful medical and surgical reference libraries in the world. Should the patient die and a post-mortem examination be held, the notes of this examination are included with the notes formerly taken. With the notes are also bound photographs taken at different stages of the illness, if such a record may be useful, so that the appearance of the patient, or some part of the patient, may be compared before and after treatment.

In 1897 affairs had reached a stage which made the most sanguine despair. Never was money so wanted since the Hospital began. There was none. Even ordinary upkeep could not be met. It was the darkness before the dawn, however, but at the time it was not known that dawn was breaking. Since then (it is only twelve years ago) the Hospital has been entirely rebuilt. Every department is up to date, and new departments, then unheard of, have been founded and have grown. The scheme cost nearly half a million to carry out, and Mr. Holland may well be a proud man as he stands in the quadrangle to-day, with this great temple of healing towering around him, as nearly perfect as such a place can be, from the huge boilers throbbing in the basement to the kitchens on the roof.

In looking through back records it seems that this huge scheme originated in a correspondence between the Prince of Wales' Hospital Fund—now King Edward's Hospital Fund—and the House Committee. The Prince of Wales' Fund wrote asking what improvements it was considered necessary to carry out in order to render the London Hospital up to date and efficient. A reply was sent giving a list of such requirements, pointing out that the *necessity* had long been recognized, but lack of funds made it impossible to carry out improvements so obviously necessary. In a reply from the Prince of Wales' Fund, dated December 29, 1897—a document of historic interest to us—it was stated that if the Hospital would spend £100,000 of its capital, the Fund promised to pay an annual subscription of £5,000. This has been paid ever since. The Staff were immediately acquainted with this good news, and were asked to appoint members to sit on a joint committee with members of the House Committee to form a Building Committee. The

THE LAST TWENTY YEARS

Building Committee was asked to consider the following :

1. Additional accommodation for about 100 nurses.
2. Another Operating Theatre.
3. Better accommodation for the Resident Staff.
4. An Isolation Block for infectious cases.
5. New Ophthalmic Wards.
6. Seclusion, Padded, and Twenty-four-Hour Rooms.
7. New Children's Wards.
8. A new Out-patient Building.

The above were the " terms of reference " to the Building Committee. That was what it was proposed should be done. It has all been done—much more than that. In the deliberations of the Building Committee it was soon decided that during the alterations not a bed must be closed. That also was accomplished. It must be noted, however, that this decision greatly increased the cost of the work. No part of the Hospital could be handed over to the builders until accommodation had been found for the patients elsewhere. Every single ward in the Hospital without exception, and every passage and every room, have been altered. The difficulty of carrying on the routine Hospital work with gangs of workmen all over the place cannot be imagined, and can never be forgotten by those who had to put up with it. Corridors were constantly being blocked, necessitating a journey to another floor to get to different parts of the Hospital. Night shifts had frequently to be undertaken in order to get some important part clear as soon as possible. In one case screws, instead of nails, had to be used to put down the floor of a new ward, at an increased cost of £40, simply for the comfort of the patients who occupied the ward below. Hammering had to be stopped every day in some part or another while a physician or surgeon went his rounds. The whole of the work was stopped on the East Wing one day for the sake of one patient, to whom sleep was a matter of life and death. Large temporary wards were built in the garden to accommodate the patients as they were turned out of each ward in turn. If there is one thing connected with this old place of which I am proud more than another, it is the fact that this vast rebuilding was done without closing a single bed.

When the improvements had once fairly started, one munificent donor after another came forward with some splendid gift. We shall never forget those days. Surely some good angel watched over the Hospital at that time, and moved the hearts of men to great effort.

To begin with, one donor offered £25,000 towards the cost of the new Out-patient Building. The gift was offered on two conditions: first, that the letter system should be abolished, and, secondly, that every out-patient who could afford it should be asked to pay some small trifle towards the cost of his medicine (3d.). And here I may add that this same generous man has since given £20,000 for the endowment of Research at the Medical College. After due consideration the committee decided to accept the gift with the conditions. This splendid department was opened by the King, accompanied by the Queen, our President, on June 11, 1903. It has been described in an earlier chapter. His Majesty's words at the opening ceremony have filled the heart of every Londoner with pride :

"It gives myself and Queen Alexandra great pleasure to be here to-day, and to open this building.

"It is a satisfaction to me to see such a great advance in hospital construction and policy; and I am glad to think that the out-patients in this Hospital will be treated with greater care and attention than has been possible in your old building.

"I am unable to thank by name the generous donor who has given £25,000 to this building, but it must be a pleasure to him to see his gift so well bestowed ; and I am specially glad to learn that the benefits of the London Hospital are open to everyone who is poor and ill, without having previously to obtain a letter from some subscriber.

"I note also with satisfaction the help the Hospital has received from the great employers in the neighbourhood, and, looking at the report, I notice as a matter of interest that your Treasurer, Mr. John Henry Buxton, succeeds his father as Treasurer, and has also a son on the Committee. I note also the very generous help the Hospital has received, especially from the Lord Mayor and several great societies.

"You have rightly alluded to the interesting fact that the Duke of Cambridge has presided over this Hospital for fifty years. We are all delighted to see him here to-day, and trust he may long be spared to continue his duties as President.

"I well remember the visit of Queen Victoria, my beloved mother, and I know of the great interest she took in this Hospital.

"Speaking for Queen Alexandra, I can say that she is very much pleased with the way this Hospital has carried out the trust she imposed on it, and it is the greatest satisfaction to me that she has been able to introduce into this country from her own country the invention of her distinguished countryman, Dr. Finsen, for the treatment of lupus, which has already produced such satisfactory results.

"We shall have great satisfaction in inspecting the building, and before declaring it open I wish to record my deep feeling of gratitude to this Hospital, which at the time of my severe illness provided me with so distinguished a surgeon as Sir Frederick Treves, with an anæsthetist in Dr. Hewitt, and with two such nurses, Nurse Haines and Nurse Tarr, whose unceasing attention I cannot sufficiently praise.

"I declare this building open; and may God's blessing rest on all who come to it for aid, and on all who work in it."

Before the Out-patient Building was finished, another great gift was received. The late Mr. B. W. Levy, in going round the wards once, was much affected by the mental distress which patients suffered who had to undergo operation. There was only one theatre; there were 400 surgical beds. Patients, therefore, had to wait some days before it came to be their turn to be taken to the theatre, and often after being "prepared for operation" the case got crowded out—previous cases had taken longer than was expected, or an emergency case had to be taken at once—so the unfortunate patient was taken back to the ward unoperated on, and had to go through the dreadful time of preparation again. It was this that so moved Mr. Levy, and he gave at once five great theatres at a cost of £13,000, on condition that these theatres should be open for all time to all nationalities and all creeds, and that his

BALCONY OF MARIE CELESTE MATERNITY DEPARTMENT

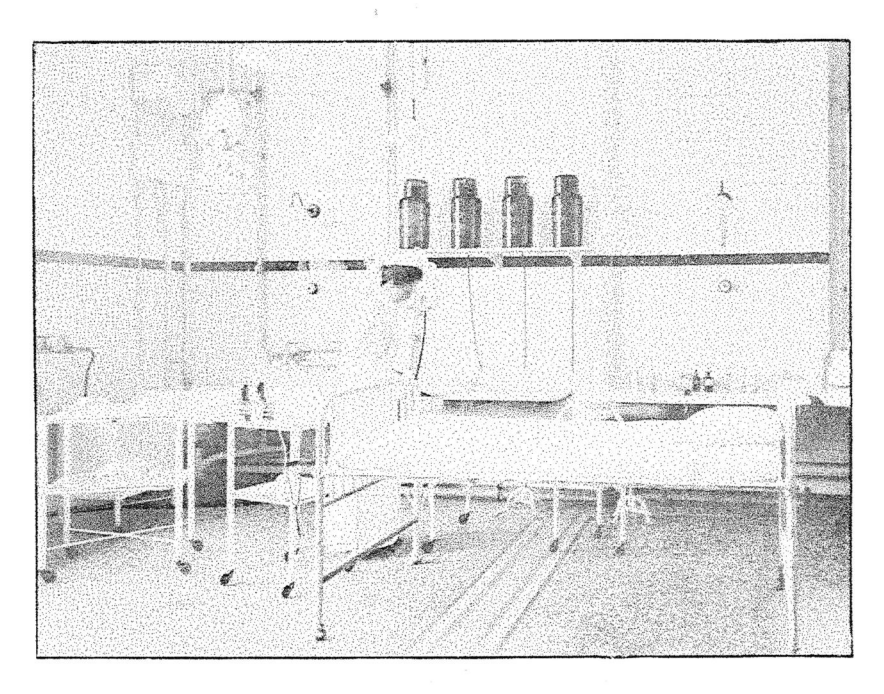

LABOUR-ROOM OF MARIE CELESTE MATERNITY DEPARTMENT

name should not in his lifetime be mentioned in connection with them.

Once again the Staff came to the committee, this time to urge the necessity for the provision of a separate building for the nursing and care of cases which were infectious, or which, although not infectious to healthy individuals, might be infectious to open wounds. The committee appreciated the necessity, but were again met with the difficulty of expense. Again help arrived from an unexpected quarter. Mr. J. A. Fielden, at that time a stranger to the Hospital, came forward, bought the site, paid for the building, and furnished it throughout. It contains about sixty beds. We also owe to him many of the balconies outside the wards—an incalculable boon to patients.

It had long been the intention of the committee to improve, to rebuild if possible, the wards reserved for Jewish patients, when sufficient funds were forthcoming. In 1899 came a gift of £10,000, afterwards increased to £20,000, from the late Mr. Edward Louis Raphael (for the endowment of these wards when built), whose son, Mr. Louis Raphael, then joined the committee.

One of the most touching gifts was one of £10,000, which was received about this time from Mr. James Hora, for the endowment of the Marie Celeste Wards, in memory of his wife, Marie Celeste Hora.

As has been stated, these wards are lying-in wards, and admit women from a radius of one mile of the Hospital. Hardly could a more beautiful method have been found for perpetuating the name and memory of anyone. The wards are to be called Marie Celeste

Wards "as long as the Hospital shall exist," and as long as the Hospital shall exist that name will be associated in the minds of hundreds of poor women with memories of tender care and loving help.

And there is yet another of these great and special gifts to record. The executors of the late Baroness Julia de Stern gave £60,000 for the erection and endowment of a Convalescent Home for patients from the London Hospital at Felixstowe. This Home is of incalculable value to the Hospital. We are enabled to send patients who are not sufficiently convalescent to go to ordinary convalescent homes — patients with wounds not yet completely healed, and who require very special nursing. It is really a country branch of the Hospital, and is managed on the same principles as the mother Hospital itself.

I need not enter in further detail into these magnificent gifts which the Hospital received about this period, each given for some definite object.

In 1894 Sir Andrew Clark, one of the Hospital's most noted physicians, died, and a large sum of money was collected in order to erect some suitable monument to his memory. It was considered fitting that such a monument should be set up in the Hospital in which he had worked so long. After considerable discussion it was eventually decided to build a Pathological Department. This has been done. The building contains a post-mortem room, in which, if necessary, six post-mortem examinations can be carried out at the same time; it also contains laboratories for the carrying out of research, and is equipped with everything necessary for investigations in this direction. It cost

£10,000. The work here has been largely assisted by the generosity of Lord Northcliffe and the Right Hon. Sir Hudson Kearley, Bart.

In 1899 our Queen, then Princess of Wales, during one of the many visits she has paid to the Hospital, urged the adoption of the new treatment for lupus which had been discovered by her countryman, Dr. Finsen of Copenhagen. Two of the physicians—one was the late Sir Stephen Mackenzie—at once went to Copenhagen to study the system under Finsen. The authorities sent two Sisters for the same purpose. As a result the committee decided to instal the light cure. The Queen herself gave the first lamps, and has ever taken the kindest interest in the department and in the sufferers from this awful disease. The Queen's lamps are in use to this day. It is a very costly department to run. Since its foundation an endowment fund has been formed, to which Lord Northcliffe gave the sum of £10,000, and for which Mr. Percy Tarbutt collected nearly £8,000.

A Bacteriological Laboratory has been established, and an Opsonic Department opened, and later, an Inoculation Department.

A Statistical Department has been added to the already existing Registrars' Quarters.

In 1903 Mr. John Henry Buxton resigned the post of Treasurer, and Lord Stanley (now Lord Derby) was unanimously elected Treasurer. He is the Treasurer to-day, and has taken, ever since his election, the keenest interest in the Hospital's welfare, and has used his great influence to further its interests.

In 1904 our Queen graciously accepted the position

of President, vacant by the death of H.R.H. the Duke of Cambridge, who had been President for fifty-four years.

At the conclusion of the rebuilding, the committee, the Staff, and other friends of the Hospital, set up in the quadrangle a statue of the beloved President and friend of the Hospital, Her Majesty the Queen.

The Hospital has been honoured many times by her visits, and those of other members of the Royal Family.

That Great Lady has been the good angel which has watched over " The London," and it is " The London's " honour to do her pleasure, and watch over her poor in the East End.

THE LONDON HOSPITAL FROM WHITECHAPEL ROAD

CHAPTER XIV

THE ADMINISTRATION OF A MODERN HOSPITAL

EVERY secretary of a large hospital is constantly receiving letters asking for information on certain points of administration and management. Such letters arrive daily, and they come from every part of the globe, and especially from India and the Colonies. In one week letters asking such questions have come from Bagdad, from Calcutta, from Hongkong, from Auckland, and from Sydney. The questions asked refer to the nursing arrangements, the power and duties of the Staff, to the advisability or otherwise of paying wards, to the system of buying, storing, and distribution, to the dietary, and so on.

It may be of some advantage, therefore, to some who may be interested enough to read this little book, if I set down the chief points in the administration of the London Hospital to-day. They are more or less the same at all large hospitals. Much that I shall state in this chapter has been touched upon in preceding chapters, but it may be a convenience if the various points are again mentioned in their order.

Within the last few years much deeper interest than heretofore has been taken in the treatment of the sick poor, and the voluntary hospitals have recently occupied public attention as to their management and administration. The public are, as a rule, well disposed towards hospitals, and support them magnificently. Nevertheless, the feeling exists that the hospitals are somewhat extravagantly managed. Officials have been charged with showing a lack of ordinary business methods, and it has been said that money, so generously subscribed, has not always been spent to the best advantage.

Perhaps, on the whole, these criticisms have done good, in spite of the obvious danger of the hospital boards being influenced thereby into thinking that cheapness in itself was meritorious.

How do those who charge the hospitals with extravagance come to the conclusion that a hospital is expensively managed? In only one way—namely, by comparing the cost of one hospital with that of another. The total ordinary expenditure per annum of a hospital is taken, and this sum is divided by the number of beds occupied. A quotient is arrived at, and this is called " the cost per bed " of that particular hospital. Then the cost per bed of various hospitals is compared. That which has the lowest is taken to be right, and those who have higher are condemned more or less vigorously for " expensive management."

Now, this " cost per bed " comparison is misleading to those who do not thoroughly understand hospital work, as I have previously tried to show. True, the low figure may be due to good management, but it does not in the least follow that it is so, and it certainly does not necessarily follow that the high cost per bed points to extravagance.

The comparison is wrong for this reason, that the word "hospital," being a word of wide application, is used for institutions which are not doing the same kind of work, and are not intended to do the same kind of work, and so are not fit subjects for comparison.

Moreover, to the question "What is efficient management?" many answers may be given. There is no standard of efficiency, and those who know most about hospital work will be the last to attempt to fix a standard. These know, better than the public, that medical science is progressing so rapidly that what is "efficient" to-day may be culpably "inefficient" to-morrow.

To illustrate. Until within the last few years all hospitals treated the terrible disease of lupus by the rough method of surgical scraping. As this was then the only means available for treating this disease, all hospitals were, to the best of their knowledge, efficient. Then Finsen came and worked, and published to the world the discovery of the light cure. Those hospitals which were governed by keen and progressive boards at once fitted up a Finsen Light Department. Such a department would immediately and materially raise the "cost per bed." Were they guilty of extravagance, or had they merely done their duty in a broadminded spirit? This is only one instance, many of which might be given. By this instance may be seen the danger referred to above—namely, that the public may press so urgently for a low "cost per bed" that progress in medical science may be hindered, unless a board is strong enough to be willing to sacrifice a certain amount of popularity for what they feel to be right.

It is necessary to draw attention to the very varied work which hospitals are doing. It is all good work, but it is not all equally costly work.

For instance, one hospital is satisfied to receive certain patients who are sick, to heal them if possible, and finally to return them to the community well or relieved. This is a most commendable aim, and it is a splendid work. But it is not very costly work, and it must be noted that such a hospital is enabled to do it as cheaply as it does because other hospitals have expended much in investigation and research. All big hospitals have now their Finsen lamps, but it was a few pioneer hospitals which bore the chief expense in finding out what were the best lamps to use.

But some other hospitals have a somewhat loftier aim, and take a broader view of their duties than those just referred to. They are not content with simply returning their patients cured or relieved. They not only attempt to cure the disease from which the patient is suffering, but their wish is to investigate that disease, to trace it to its cause, to discover what favours it, what destroys it. The aim of these hospitals is higher; so, of necessity, is their "cost per bed." One hospital is attempting to destroy the disease in the patient; the other is doing this, and is also trying to eradicate the disease from the community altogether, to stamp it out of existence, just as tubercular disease of all kinds is being stamped out by those hospitals which are energetic enough and independent enough to establish an Opsonic Department. These hospitals must have their Bacteriological Laboratories, Clinical Laboratories, Pathological Laboratories, Physiological Laboratories, Sterilizing Rooms, etc. All these adjuncts to Research require a large staff and expensive material. It will be one of these hospitals which will give to the world one of these days the discovery of the cause of cancer.

And here I may draw attention to a statement which is often made—namely, that the work of the cheap hospital must be as good as that of an expensive hospital, because the " death-rate " of both is the same. Now, it is a curious fact that the death-rate at most hospitals is about one in ten of the patients admitted, but perhaps, from what has been said above, it will be seen that the death-rate is not the only test or measure of a hospital's work. The condition of the 90 per cent. who do not die would perhaps be a better test, if taken, say, five years after they left the hospital. I will go further and say that the hundreds of happy people who never have to go to a hospital at all may actually owe their good fortune in this respect to the good work which these hospitals are doing in discovering and spreading the principles of hygiene.

Further, the comparison between the various hospitals by the " cost per bed " method is misleading, in that some of them are much more than houses for the cure of sick people, more than establishments for the investigation of disease. They are also schools whereat the future physicians and surgeons of this country are being trained for their life-work. It may be said that to train medical men is no part of a hospital's work. But where else can they be trained if not at the hospitals ?

It is true that those hospitals which have schools attached are more costly than those without, although the increase in expenditure is not wholly due to the presence of the students, but largely to the energetic policy of the board which has attracted the students.

There is yet one other reason which has made it misleading to compare the cost of the hospitals in the way mentioned. This is, that there is no standard as to the degree of " brotherliness " with which the sick and injured poor should be treated. Hospital boards have different views on this matter. Some, perhaps—one hopes they are few—would regard the sick poor man as little more than a damaged machine, to be mended as cheaply and as quickly as possible. Such a board, if it carried out its views logically, would dispense with the services of a chaplain. Change of diet would be considered unnecessary, flowers in the wards an extravagance. Expenses of cleaning, of lighting, of nursing, would be reduced to a minimum. There may be other hospital boards who go to the opposite extreme, and may treat patients in a way which, coming from the homes some of them do, may not be entirely appreciated. Somewhere between these extremes is the right line to take, and the King's Fund, in comparing the expenditure of the most important London hospitals in all their departments, has been of service to the various boards in their attempt to decide where this line should be drawn.

But while it may not be advantageous for the public to compare one hospital with another, the comparison by a hospital's officials of that hospital's expenditure at different times is one of the most important duties of those officials who are anxious to prevent waste.

There are two things to be borne in mind in controlling expenditure : Firstly, the method of buying must be sound—to insure this is not very difficult ; secondly, the methods adopted to prevent waste must be sound—the devising and carrying out of these methods is extremely difficult.

The whole secret of hospital economy lies in a keen appreciation of the importance of these two points.

I will deal with the question of general administration first, and of buying and the prevention of waste when each department is considered.

As to general administration : The Hospital is the property of the governors. A governor is a subscriber who gives 5 guineas a year, and he is a governor as long as he continues to pay his £5 5s. a year. A life governor is a donor of 30 guineas. Courts of governors are held quarterly, and at these Courts the whole of the administration of the Hospital is decided. At the Courts all appointments to the Medical and Surgical Staff are made, and also the more important lay appointments. At the Courts, too, resignations are received.

The Courts are responsible for all standing orders, and none of the Hospital's capital may be touched but by their permission and authority. Should the Charity be incorporated, the Court sanctions the use of the Corporation Seal to all documents.

At the last Court of the year—the December Court—is chosen the House Committee for the following year. The House Committee consists of thirty governors.

They sit weekly, and at their first sitting after their election in December choose their own chairman for the year. The whole Medical and Surgical Staff, too, are re-elected every year at the December Court.

It is the duty of the secretary to bring before the House Committee at their weekly meeting all that has transpired during the week which it is of importance the committee should know. The ideal secretary—I have never met my ideal—must use considerable judgment in what he brings before committee. He must be able to recognize what *are* the most important things. He must draw attention to the principles involved in a certain course of action, and where such and such a course may lead to. He must be absolutely fair in reporting facts. A shrug of the shoulders may damn a man. He must have no personal likes and dislikes. That is the ideal secretary. The ideal chairman is a man who is so enthusiastic in hospital work that he inspires all those with whom he comes into contact with the same zeal. A man for whom it is a delight to work, a man who leads, not drives.

The Weekly Committee reports to the Quarterly Court all that has transpired during the last three months. The Court approves or refers back for further consideration.

If the hospital is a small one—say of 250 beds—the House Committee can keep all departments under its direct management. If a large hospital—say of 700 to 900 beds—it is wiser for the House Committee to appoint from among its members certain subcommittees which will give more detailed attention to the different departments and report to the House Committee. Thus at the London Hospital we have:

> The Nursing Committee.
> The Steward's Committee.
> The Estate Committee.
> The Surveyor's Committee.
> The Dispensary Committee.
> The Theatres Committee.
> The Out-patient Committee.
> The Accounts Committee.
> The Finance Committee.

The Hospital is divided into certain departments, each having its head. Each head of a department reports to the secretary anything in his department which is not routine. He would also report to his own subcommittee, who would deliberate. The minute-books of the subcommittee are delivered to the secretary, who brings them before the House Committee. The danger of this system is that the subcommittees work as units, and their work may clash with or overlap the work of another subcommittee. It is the duty of the secretary, who has a bird's-eye view of all, to guard against this, before the matters come before the House Committee, if possible.

Some reference should now be made to the departments and their heads.

MATRON'S DEPARTMENT.

The Matron is head of the Nursing Department, and is over all female servants—scrubbers, ward-maids, housemaids, and laundry-maids. At the London

Hospital the number of nurses, including those engaged on the Private Staff, is, at the time of writing, 780. The responsibility of engaging such a staff and of maintaining its efficiency is enormous. The London Hospital is fortunate in having the services for nearly thirty years of a lady known throughout the Hospital world for her marvellous powers of organization, and her lofty ideas as to the attributes of a true nurse. Miss Lückes, an old friend of Miss Florence Nightingale, has for all these years worked quietly and patiently, and unselfishly, for the betterment of nursing and the betterment of nurses. I see in the minutes, from week to week since her appointment, suggestion after suggestion for improvement. Every suggestion that was ever carried out by the committee has been a conspicuous success, and not one single one has ever been rescinded, hardly even modified.

The Matron sees personally every candidate who wishes to enter the Hospital as a probationer. If, after medical examination, such a candidate is approved, a date is fixed for her to commence her course of seven weeks' preliminary training at Tredegar House. Here she is taught Sick-room Cookery, Bandaging, Ambulance Work, and Elementary Hygiene. Then she comes into the Hospital itself for a trial month. If approved, she signs a four years' agreement to serve the Hospital. For the first two years she is a probationer under training. If suitable, she receives, at the end of two years, her certificate, and, after a month's holiday, commences her last two years as a fully trained nurse. This is to repay the Hospital for the expense of training her. She receives salary from the day she takes up her Hospital duties—namely, £12 for the first year, £20 for the second, £25 for the third, and £26 for the fourth. If she becomes a Sister in charge of a ward, she receives from £30 to £40; if she serves on the Private Staff, she receives from £30 to £45, and more under certain conditions. In order to encourage long service, she is given an increase of £5 after six years, and another increase of £5 after twelve years. She is well treated as to holidays.

If she stays eighteen years, she is eligible for a full-pay pension for life.

The training does not merely consist of her spending two years lolling about the Hospital, learning whatever chance may bring in her way. Every day of the two years is most carefully planned out, so that she may get a share of male nursing and female nursing, of surgical nursing and medical nursing, of adult nursing and of children's nursing, of day nursing and of night nursing. Definite courses of lectures are given and times for study classes allowed. Examinations follow the courses of lectures on medical nursing, surgical nursing, general nursing, physiology, and anatomy. The examinations are carried out by an examiner from outside, who has no connection with the Hospital.

A separate bedroom is provided for each nurse, and there are spacious sitting- and writing-rooms, and an excellent library.

In the summer, thanks to the kindness of the Tilbury Steam Lighterage Company, nurses who are off duty are taken several times a week on one of the company's tugs for trips to the mouth of the river.

These water-picnics are always looked forward to and enjoyed.

With regard to the expenditure in cleaning, and the number of scrubbers engaged, it must depend upon the Hospital's "standard of cleanliness," and upon the traffic in the corridors and wards. If the Staff visit in the morning, which is not the rule in London, the cleaning can be done in the afternoon. If the Staff visit in the afternoon, the cleaning in some hospitals has to be done at night; it cannot be done in the morning, because the wards and corridors are then crowded by students, and by porters with their trollies, distributing stores. Night cleaning is more expensive, both because a charwoman working at night must be paid a higher wage than a day woman, and also because it is necessary to employ artificial light. The scrubbers should be under supervision of a Sister or Housekeeper, who would give out to each her supply of soap, soda, etc. This Sister would obtain her supply from the stores, as the ward Sisters do. The cost of cleaning, when once the standard has been fixed, can be checked and kept stationary. As a hospital is the meeting-place of all the sick and dirty people of the neighbourhood, I would advise that the standard of cleanliness should be a very high one, certainly much higher than is usually adopted for an ordinary dwelling-house.

Under the charge of the Matron, too, is the laundry. Here is treated by efficient machinery all the Hospital washing, amounting to 60,000 "pieces" per week. The laundry is one of the best equipped in London, and we have been often complimented by managers of commercial laundries who have visited it. The comfort of the seventy-five employés is carefully considered. They are paid good wages, and are given good food, and their surroundings as to light and ventilation delight the heart of the Government inspector. It pays a large hospital of, say, 500 beds to have its own laundry. Where careful accounts have been kept, it was found that 60,000 pieces a week could be washed at a cost of about £100, which includes the cost of depreciation of machinery and interest on the building. The account for a week may be of interest:

	£	s.	d.
Salaries and wages per week	40	9	11
Food (dinners, luncheons, milk)	13	13	6
Materials: Yellow soap, 240 lb.; washing-powder, 640 lb.; soda, 7 cwt.; starch, 110 lb.; borax, 10½ lb.; blue, 3 lb.; turpentine, 1 gallon; disinfectants	12	12	10½
Electric light and power	4	5	2
Coal for boilers	21	7	6
Water	1	15	6
Interest on outlay and depreciation, say—	5	0	0
	99	4	7½

The Matron is responsible for the buying of bedding and sheeting, uniforms, towels, linen, etc. The expenses under the heading of bedding are largely affected, not only by the number of beds occupied, but also by the number of patients the Hospital puts through each of its beds per annum. This number varies at different hospitals from twelve to twenty, and is certainly a point to be borne in mind when the " cost per bed " is discussed. The expenditure in linen and bedding is also affected by what one may call the " standard of cleanliness" which the hospital adopts. This is by no means the same at all hospitals. I have seen sheets in use at one hospital which would not be tolerated at another. The following is a fair allowance of bedding for each bed at a general hospital: Eight sheets, four draw-sheets, 4 blankets, 6 pillow-cases, two feather pillows, two counterpanes. It is, of course, important that an exact inventory of the bedding of each ward and room should be taken periodically—say once in six months.

STEWARD'S DEPARTMENT.

The steward is responsible for the engagement and good behaviour of the porters. He, too, has to do with the buying of meat, milk, bread, flour, and house coal (but not steam coal), fish, poultry, grocery, and provisions; stationery, hardware, and crockery. The following notes on the system of buying may be of interest:

MEAT.—This, like all other provisions, is bought by tender. Tenders are issued every six months. Firms wishing to compete should be approved by the Steward's Committee before being allowed to do so. It is quite sufficient to allow four or five firms of good standing to compete. Open contracts cause waste of time in correspondence and in examination of samples. The meat most suitable for a hospital is—

(*a*) *For Patients.*—Best American refrigerated beef: thick flank, rounds, middle ribs, shins and lean beef for beef-tea, kidney suet. Best New Zealand mutton: legs and mutton-chops.

(*b*) *For Officers, Nurses, and Servants.*—As for patients, but with the addition of fresh pork, fresh veal, New Zealand lamb.

The tender forms must state that the meat is to be delivered as required every morning early, and should include the usual terms to be signed by the contractor —namely, that the buyer may cancel the agreement if the goods are unsatisfactory, and may purchase elsewhere, charging the contractor with the cost. The delivery each day must, of course, be checked by the steward or storekeeper as to weight and quality. It may be pointed out in passing that a stone of butcher's meat weighs 8 pounds, not 14.

FISH.—This, too, is bought by tender. The fish most suitable for hospital use are plaice, fresh haddock, turbot, brill, and lemon sole. The tender form should state that the fish is to be delivered daily as required; that heads, tails, roe, and offal are to be removed, and the fish is to be cleaned ready for cooking. The same penalty for unsatisfactory delivery must be imposed as for meat, and this applies to all contracts for provisions.

POULTRY.—Chickens are the only poultry used in the hospital. The tender should specify that the fowls should weigh about 2 pounds each when trussed and ready for cooking. Hospitals which cater for Jewish patients will have to make a second contract for meat and poultry—*i.e.*, for Kosher meat and Kosher fowls. These are more expensive than the ordinary.

BREAD AND FLOUR.—The tender form should state that the bread should be of the best wheaten flour, well baked, and made into loaves weighing about

1¼ pounds each. Long loaves, square in section, are the most economical. It must be perfectly cold before delivery. The flour should be the best wheaten and the best Vienna self-raising. Bread will, of course, be delivered daily.

GROCERY.—This form includes tenders for rice, tapioca, sago, arrowroot, sugar, pearl barley, coffee, cornflour, and all other grocery requirements of the doctors, nurses, and patients.

VEGETABLES.—Those used in Hospital are potatoes, carrots, onions, turnips, and greens. Tender forms should state that the vegetables must be clean and free from dirt, that the greens should have the stalks and outside leaves removed, and should be free from undue moisture.

MILK.—The percentage of fat and the total solids must be specified in the tender. Milk should be examined daily on delivery as to proper quantity, and daily as to percentage of fat. Microscopic and chemical analysis should be conducted periodically. It should be delivered in sealed churns. The contractor should supply a list of the farms from which his milk is obtained. The medical officers of the districts where these farms are situated should be communicated with, telling them that the hospital is obtaining milk from that district, and asking that he would give special attention to the condition of the surroundings.

COAL.—The colliery should be specified in the tender, and a certificate should be demanded from the colliery from time to time, stating that the coal is being duly supplied. The coal should be selected on the advice of a chemist, as the result of proper analysis conducted with a view to obtain its calorific power, percentage of ash, etc.

The prices for coal are affected by the hospital's storage capacity. Most hospitals unfortunately must have the coal delivered daily.

FURNITURE, HARDWARE, SOAP, ETC.—These should be bought by half-yearly contracts. Soap should be bought to sample. All samples of soap should be carefully examined for the percentage of water they contain. It will often be found that the cheapest is by no means the least costly.

STATIONERY.—This should be bought by annual contract. Each department should provide the secretary, steward, or other official with a sample of each book and printed form used, and the numbers likely to be required. Stationery is stored by the steward, and given out to the departments once a week, on written orders being given.

Now as to the methods adopted to prevent waste.

That the prevention of waste is the more important part of the work of the officials will appear when it is noted that to buy well is useless if stores are frittered away by lax systems in the hospital itself. One must be continually checking a tendency towards extravagance, which *will* creep into the hospital, as it will into any institution in which some hundreds of people are at work, and when individual carelessness can be so easily overlooked. Luxuries become conveniences, and conveniences necessities.

As to checking waste in provisions. A system which very much affects the expenditure in provisions should be mentioned first—namely, that most hospitals have what is known as a diet table. This is a table of the various diets which are intended to meet the requirements of patients in different illnesses, and in different stages of their illness. These diets are revised by the Medical Staff periodically, about every five years, and it is most important that the steward should sit on these revising committees. Few medical men, few men of any profession, are familiar with the *cost* of food, and consequently the diets may be drawn up without regard to cost. On the advice of an expert, such as the steward ought to be, in the price of foods, the cost of a diet may often be lessened by some slight modification *without in any way depreciating its value as a food.* The difference of a penny in the cost of a diet per day will amount to some hundreds of pounds a year in our large hospitals, with their five or six hundred occupied beds.

The following is a sample of a diet sheet:

DIET TABLE.

LONDON HOSPITAL.

Milk Diet.—(*a*) Milk, 1 pint, (*b*) or 2 pints, (*c*) or 3 pints, (*d*) or 4 pints.*

Diet No. 1.—(*a*) Bread, 8 ozs.; fried or boiled fish, 10 ozs.; milk, 1 pint; pudding; green vegetables at discretion. For supper soup, or ½ pint of milk, or cocoa, or porridge, or gruel. (*b*) is as (*a*), but with an extra pint of milk or one egg.†

Diet No. 2.—(*a*) Bread, 10 ozs.; potatoes, 8 ozs.; cooked meat, 4 ozs.; milk, 1 pint; pudding; green

---

* Milk costs about 9d. per gallon.
† This diet costs about 4½d.

vegetables. For supper, as in Diet No. 1. (b) is as (a), but with an extra pint of milk or one egg.*

Diet No. 3.—Bread, 12 ozs.; potatoes, 8 ozs.; meat, 6 ozs.; milk, 1 pint; pudding; green vegetables. For supper, as in Diet No. 1.†

Diet No. 4.—Bread, 10 ozs.; potatoes, 8 ozs.; meat, 6 ozs.; or fish, 10 ozs.; cooked bacon, 4 ozs.; milk, 2 pints; pudding; green vegetables. (Jews are allowed two eggs instead of bacon.) For supper, as in Diet No. 1.‡

Extras Allowed. — The following extras may be added to the diets if it is felt that the patient's condition requires them: Beef-tea or mutton-broth; extra eggs or milk, chicken, rabbit, bacon, fruit, ale or stout, cream, beefsteak, mince, wines or spirits. All orders for extras lapse on Wednesdays—diet day—and will not be served unless re-ordered by the doctor. Orders for wines and spirits must be renewed every three days.

By Order.

It will be noticed that at the end of the diet table is a list of extras which the Staff are allowed to order for cases which require some further feeding than is provided by the regular diets. This is the usual arrangement at most hospitals. It is these extras which are the source of much leakage unless carefully watched. It is so very natural for a kind-hearted resident doctor to put a poor patient on bacon or chicken, "because No. So-and-so has bacon or chicken." Moreover, in the rush of hospital work, it is likely to happen that a patient who is on an "extra" will continue to have it long after he really needs it—the

---

* This diet costs about 4¾d. † This diet costs about 5¾d.
‡ This diet costs about 8½d.

result of oversight on the part of the doctor, who is not, as a rule, present in the wards during meal-times. Therefore the necessity for the rule that these extras should lapse automatically. The secretary or steward should visit the wards on diet day with a view to noting whether the rule has been complied with. My experience is that doctors err, not from intention, but from pure oversight. It is only fair to explain to the Staff what is the value of each of the diets, and of the extras, and I have invariably found them most ready to co-operate in reducing unnecessary expenditure in this direction.

Each ward should keep a diet-book, which should be written up every evening by the Sister in charge. This is a summary of the particulars as to diets on each of the patient's prescription papers hanging at the bedhead. These ward diet-books should be delivered to the steward every morning, and the requirements analyzed by him, and entered into a book known as the "steward's diet-book." This book serves two purposes : it is the guide to the chef as to the amount of beef, mutton, chicken, vegetables, etc., which he is to cook and deliver to the wards (he is allowed 31 to 37 per cent. loss on meat in cooking), also to the storekeeper as to the amount of bread, milk, beer, etc., which he is to serve out. From this book, too, the steward compiles his weekly diet returns. This should show at a glance the cost of each ward in diets and in diet extras.

It is more economical for the dinners to be carved by expert carvers in the kitchen, and delivered to the wards in hot-water tins, than to send down joints to be carved in the wards. They are then served on to the patients' plates from the hot-water tins in the ward itself. It is more economical for two reasons: First, the carving itself is performed with less waste than if performed by ward Sisters, who cannot be expected to be expert carvers; and secondly, the bones, if they have never entered the ward, can be used for making stock. Bones *returned* from a ward can only be thrown away. It is a mistake for nurses in the wards to give large slices of bread to patients; it is generally left, and is then wasted.

There are many provisions which must be supplied to the ward which are not included in the diets, such, for instance, as tea, coffee, butter, sugar, arrowroot, etc. These should be ordered by the ward Sisters from the storekeeper on slip-forms. These orders are filed, and once a week are entered by the steward into the "steward's provision book"; and from this the weekly cost of each ward, of the residents' quarters, and of the nurses' home, and of the servants, can be obtained, for such provisions as are not included in the official "diets."

THE ESTATE DEPARTMENT.

The Estate Committee superintends the management of the hospital's estate, if it is lucky enough to have one. It superintends repairs, collection of rents, and recommends the granting of leases.

THE SURVEYOR'S DEPARTMENT.

The Surveyor is responsible for the structural repairs and additions to the hospital buildings. Under him are the engineers, electricians, blacksmiths, stokers, and labourers. He buys the steam coal, and should do so under arrangements similar to those by which the house coal is bought. He should arrange for a weekly examination of meters, both gas and electric.

The amount of coal consumed will largely depend upon the system of heating in vogue. If by hot-water pipes, it will be less than if by open fireplaces. Most hospitals are warmed by both systems—the wards by one, and the corridors by the other. The amount of coal consumed in the furnaces for the boilers must be carefully recorded day by day. No automatic stoker can be compared with a good man who knows his work. The difference in the amount of coal used by a good and bad stoker is astonishing, and, as a rule, the very fact that the consumption is being carefully watched makes the bad stoker try to improve. As to that part of the hospital which is heated by fires, the amount of coal and coke conveyed to each ward must be noted and careful firing encouraged.

THE DISPENSARY DEPARTMENT.

It is the duty of the chief dispenser to purchase drugs, chemicals, and dressings. He also is responsible for the engagement of dispensers, and for the proper supply of medicines to in- and out-patients. As to purchasing :

DRUGS, DRESSINGS, CHEMICALS, WINES, AND SPIRITS. —These should be bought by half-yearly contracts from approved firms by the Dispensary Committee, a committee composed of members of the weekly Board and of the Medical and Surgical Staff of the hospital.

Samples should be delivered a fortnight before the committee sits, to enable the chief dispenser to analyze or carefully examine them, that he may be in a position to advise the committee. Drugs and chemicals are much more subject to market variations than provisions, and the advice of the chief dispenser should be followed if he suggests the postponement of certain purchases.

The chief dispenser's most important and difficult work is the checking of waste in the dispensary.

DRUGS AND CHEMICALS.—Every hospital has its own pharmacopœia—a book containing formulæ of repeatedly ordered mixtures, pills, liniments, etc. It is intended to save the physician's time in prescribing. Instead of having to write out a long prescription for each patient, he simply orders the mixtures by the names they are known by in the Hospital Pharmacopœia. The dispenser will understand and dispense accordingly. This book is analogous to the diet table in the Steward's Department, except that in this case the formulæ run to some hundreds.

These formulæ, like the diet tables, are revised periodically, and it is the duty of the chief dispenser to be of service to the revising committee as to the *cost* of the formulæ suggested, and also (and this is very important) as to the *keeping* properties of the mixtures—important, because most out-patients take away medicine for a week at each visit. Care in respect to both of these points will save the hospital some hundreds of pounds a year.

I should like to say very emphatically that the more of its medicines a hospital makes, and the fewer it buys, the more it will save. It is cheaper for the hospital to buy crude roots, barks, leaves, and seeds, and with them make its own tinctures and infusions, ointments, lozenges, and tablets, than to buy outside.

Every dispenser knows the tendency of young doctors to try all sorts of advertised remedies. This tendency should be judiciously checked. If the doctor does *not* know the formula of some patent medicine he is ordering, he has no right to prescribe it. If he *does* know the formula, he should write it so that it may be dispensed in the ordinary way in the dispensary. As a matter of fact, he should be allowed to prescribe only—

(a) Medicines described in the British Pharmacopœia.

(a) Medicines described in the special Pharmacopœia of the Hospital.

(c) Medicines described in a list, revised quarterly by the staff, of newly-discovered remedies.

It may happen that certain commonly-used medicines rise at times to a fabulous price. The chief dispenser must report this, and it may be necessary for the Dispensary Committee, on his advice, to withdraw a drug or medicine from use on the plea of *non possumus*, until the price has fallen. Notice of such withdrawal should be sent to each member of the Staff at once.

A cause of waste in the Out-patient Department is that patients sometimes have to attend for weeks, if not months, and gradually their prescription books accumulate quite a long list of various medicines.

Pills are ordered one week, liniment is added another, lotion another, then a gargle. The temptation of the young doctor, to avoid wading through pages of back prescriptions, is to put *Rep. omnia* (Repeat everything), and to let the dispenser do the searching, under the impression that the patient will say what he wants. The patient always wants *omnia*. Once having had a gargle, he will always want it. This custom must not be allowed. The rule should be insisted upon that the doctor must write down exactly what he wishes the patient to have at each visit, and dispensers must be authorized to refuse any other kind of order.

Another possible leakage in the dispensary which must be guarded against is the tendency of dispensers to give too large a quantity to out-patients. The temptation is to give patients a few *extra* cough lozenges, a little *extra* liniment, because "the doctor said I might rub my arm as well as my leg, and take a lozenge whenever I liked." The dispenser knows quite well that he did not say so, but, to save long discussion, gives the extra. Dispensers must dispense exactly what is *written*, and no more. If the prescription says the lozenges *ter die sumendi*, he must count twenty-one, and no more. The trouble is that these tendencies *grow*, unless they are constantly checked; and if, at a hospital where the out-patient attendances run into hundreds of thousands, every patient is given a little extra for the sake of peace, a £2,000 drug account will jump to £3,000 for no apparent reason.

With regard to the medicines sent to the wards for

in-patients, the very natural tendency of the dispensers is to send too large a quantity of each prescription ordered, specially if the prescription is somewhat difficult to dispense. In the wards patients are seen daily, and medicines are repeatedly changed. Small supplies, therefore, should be sent, or the waste in a large hospital through medicines being thrown down the sink will be enormous.

There will be things required from the dispensary by the wards other than the patients' prescriptions—such, for instance, as stock bottles of various lotions, turpentine, stock ointments, glycerine, etc. These should be ordered by the Sister of each ward in an order-book day by day, and from these order-books the dispenser writes up his returns for the " dispensary sundries," supplied to each ward week by week.

DRESSINGS AND BANDAGES.—It is not necessary to dwell with any detail upon the special pitfalls into which, with a mistaken notion of economy, a chief dispenser is likely to fall in buying dressings. Suffice it to say that in dressings, almost more than in anythings else, the lowest price is *not* the most economical. Bandages may be bought so cheaply, and be so common, that a dresser *uses two or three instead of one,* and they can be so flimsy as not to stand washing, and can therefore be used once only, whereas a good bandage can be washed and used two or three times. A cheap lint will run six or seven yards to the pound. One costing 50 per cent. more will run to double the length. Gauzes, bought in 100-yard lengths, are quoted at most alluring prices, but may be so light in weight that the dresser uses ten thicknesses instead of five.

Against all this sort of thing the wise dispenser will be very much on his guard at contract time.

As to the Out-patient Department, not much in the form of dressings is used : lint, boric lint, and bandages are the most important items. It used to be the custom to keep a pile of lint on the dispensary counter already cut, and, whenever lint was ordered on a prescription a piece of this lint was given. The dispenser, with a long line of patients waiting at his window, had no time to make inquiries as to how much was likely to be required. To-day lint is kept ready cut as before, but in three sizes : (*a*) is a piece only a few inches square, (*b*) is larger, and (*c*) is the largest, and is about 18 inches square. The surgeon, on ordering lint for a patient he has examined, must state whether (*a*), (*b*), or (*c*) is to be given. This, of course, refers to dressings which the patient has to apply at home.

As to bandages, it has already been shown that cheap, thin bandages are wasteful. But a cheaper bandage than is used in the wards can be used in the Out-patient Department, because out-patients can never be depended upon to wash their bandages, so they need not be of that fine quality which is necessary to withstand repeated washing.

Coming to the in-patients, all dressings are ordered daily for each ward from the dispensary (in the same way as are all other ward requirements), and from these the dispenser prepares his weekly dressing summary.

One word as to the Dispenser's Store-rooms. Everything delivered from the manufacturers must be entered in, although it must not be put away into stock until examined and passed by the chief dispenser himself; also nothing must be allowed to leave the stores unless a voucher is received.

The dispenser should attempt to keep the cost of in-patients and of out-patients distinct.

THE THEATRE DEPARTMENT.

The Theatres Committee and the theatre supervisor are responsible for the management of the operating theatres, the purchase of instruments and appliances, the sterilization of material used in operations, and the engagement of the Theatre Staff.

INSTRUMENTS.—Orders for instruments are sent at irregular intervals. As new instruments are constantly being invented, requests from surgeons for these are made from time to time. If the instrument is below a certain value, the order is written in the surgeon's order-book, and this book and all other order-books are sent from the various departments every week to the secretary to be examined by him, and laid before the board. If the required instrument is of greater value than £5, the order must be initialled by *four* surgeons. This rule is intended to check the too ready ordering of every instrument that is put upon the market. The "life" of surgical instruments is much longer if they are carefully looked after, and it is wisest to make one man responsible for certain cabinets of instruments, of which an inventory must be taken periodically. It is surprising how few instruments are lost, even in a very large hospital, by making the individual responsible. It is important to have the name of the hospital clearly stamped upon each instrument, the chance of loss by theft being by this rule reduced to a minimum. Someone must be responsible for the instruments in the wards and in the Out-patient Department. It pays a large hospital to have a skilled instrument mechanic in its employ, responsible for all sharpening and minor repairs, and for the examination of all instruments after use in the theatres. He should overhaul all instruments allowed in the wards as stock, at least once a week, and see that they are kept thoroughly in order. By this means it is insured that no mishaps occur during an operation through a faulty instrument.

Instruments are not purchased, as a rule, by tender. They are usually required suddenly and singly, and have often to be specially made.

The responsibility of the theatre supervisor in superintending the all-important work of the sterilization of material has been mentioned, and need not be again referred to. We have two assistants for each theatre, one senior and the other junior. The junior is responsible for the rougher work—the cleaning. The senior is responsible for the instruments, " cleans up " before an operation, and acts as an assistant in passing proper instruments, threading needles, etc.

THE OUT-PATIENT DEPARTMENT.

The Out-patients Committee manages the very important part of a hospital's work—the Out-patient Department. The system of treating out-patients varies at different hospitals. At the London Hospital it is as follows, to summarize what has previously been said :

There is first of all a sieve, called the "Receiving-

Room," through which every patient who enters the Hospital must pass. It is open night and day, and is under the charge of seven senior qualified men, called "receiving-room officers." These men decide what is to be done with a patient. They have nothing to do with his social position. They may act in one of three ways, according to the urgency of the patient's condition.

1. A very minor ailment is given one treatment and sent away. They may not treat a case twice in the receiving-room for the same ailment.

2. A more serious case is referred to the Out-patient Department for more thorough examination. Such a case would be referred to a physician or surgeon, or to one of the specialists who attend for diseases of the throat, ear, nose, eyes, skin, teeth.

3. More serious cases are recommended for immediate admission.

When patients in Group 2 arrive at the Out-patient Department, they have to pass the inquiry officer, and satisfy him that their relief by a charity is justifiable. If passed, they see the medical officer to whom they have been recommended. They then pass the almoners, whose duties have already been described, and at last, on their way out, receive their medicine. A patient on his first visit is known as a "new case." Afterwards, as he comes up week by week, he is an "old case." Only new cases have to pass the inquiry officer and almoner.

Men are always seen first, in order that they may get back to work. Women afterwards.

Every patient who can afford it pays 3d. for a week's

supply of medicine. There are exceptions to this rule. Children do not have to pay. If advice only is given, there is also no charge. No patient who is out of work pays. No patient sent up by an outside practitioner pays. After all these deductions, it is found that about half the patients who attend pay 3d. a week. The total value of these payments is about £2,000 a year, and enables the Hospital to treat more cases who cannot pay at all than it otherwise would.

THE ACCOUNTS DEPARTMENT.

The Accounts Committee sits quarterly, and examines all accounts before payment. Each invoice must be initialled by the head of the department, to signify that the goods have been received, and that the price is correct.

It must, of course, happen that many articles have to be purchased during a quarter which are not included in any contract, articles the demand for which is small, or the use for which was unforeseen. All such articles are entered week by week in the order-books, which are kept by the heads of departments. These books are delivered to the secretary weekly, and are submitted to the House Committee.

THE FINANCE DEPARTMENT.

The Finance Committee advise on questions of investment, sale, and purchase of stock, loans on mortgage, etc., and generally report to the House Committee on the financial position of the Hospital.

THE MEDICAL AND SURGICAL STAFF.

Something should be said as to the rules observed by the Medical and Surgical Staff.

Each surgeon has a colleague—an assistant-surgeon.

Each physician has an assistant-physician.

Each physician or surgeon, after twenty years' service as such, retires, and his place is usually filled by the senior of the assistant-physicians or assistant-surgeons. Thereby a vacancy is created in the assistant staff, and all newly appointed officers come on to the assistant-staff first.

The physicians and surgeons—the full staff—attend on three days a week. They do not see out-patients. They have the care of about sixty beds each.

The assistant-physicians and assistant-surgeons—the assistant-staff—also attend on three days a week. They see out-patients on two of these days, and they have also twenty beds each for in-patients. If a member of the assistant-staff, while seeing out-patients, desires to admit a case, he admits into his own or his senior's beds. He may not pick out his cases. He is bound to admit in strict rotation, three cases to his senior and the next to himself.

A physician and his assistant-physician are spoken of in hospital language as "a firm"; and so is a surgeon and his assistant-surgeon. Each "firm" has a house-physician or a house-surgeon, as the case may be, who is resident in the Hospital, and who takes charge of his chief's cases in the intervals between the visits. Every house-physician and house-surgeon must see his cases twice daily. The visiting-staff are pledged to see every case once a week, and as many times oftener as may be necessary.

The "firms" are on "full duty" in rotation for half a week each. When members of a "firm" are on full duty (and the time comes round in about seventeen days), they must be in constant telephonic communication with the Hospital, and be ready to come at a moment's notice, night or day. The member of the staff on full duty would be always called in the case of a patient admitted directly to the beds from the receiving-room. They spend most of their time at the Hospital in their half-week on full duty. It is common for the surgeon or assistant-surgeon on full duty to be called to the Hospital two or three times during a night to operate on a case of emergency.

The students act as clerks to the physicians, and have to make full notes of every case and of its family history. The students also act as dressers to the surgeons. They go round with the staff at each visit and receive instruction—how the physician or surgeon is led to his diagnosis, what is the treatment, and what is the prognosis. This bedside teaching comes after the student has spent two years at the Medical College attached to the Hospital, where he has received systematic instruction in chemistry, biology, anatomy, and physiology. As some 15,000 in-patients are treated annually and about 250,000 out-patients, the value of the London Hospital as a school of medicine can hardly be exaggerated. Every student will probably see there hundreds of cases such as he will only see in isolated instances when he goes into private practice during the rest of his life. He will certainly not in private practice see a disease for the first time after spending five years at " The London."

SECRETARY'S DEPARTMENT.

In the secretary's office all accounts are kept, and these must be kept according to the system laid down by the King's Fund. The bills paid are analyzed, and the items classified under certain fixed headings. Thus the expense of each hospital, under the headings of provisions, dispensary, domestic, salaries, etc., can be compared.

As a rule the secretary is responsible for the collection of new subscriptions, but this is not so at " The London."

In this chapter I have quoted largely from a paper written by me, at the invitation of the King's Fund to all hospital secretaries, on " The Management of a Voluntary Hospital."

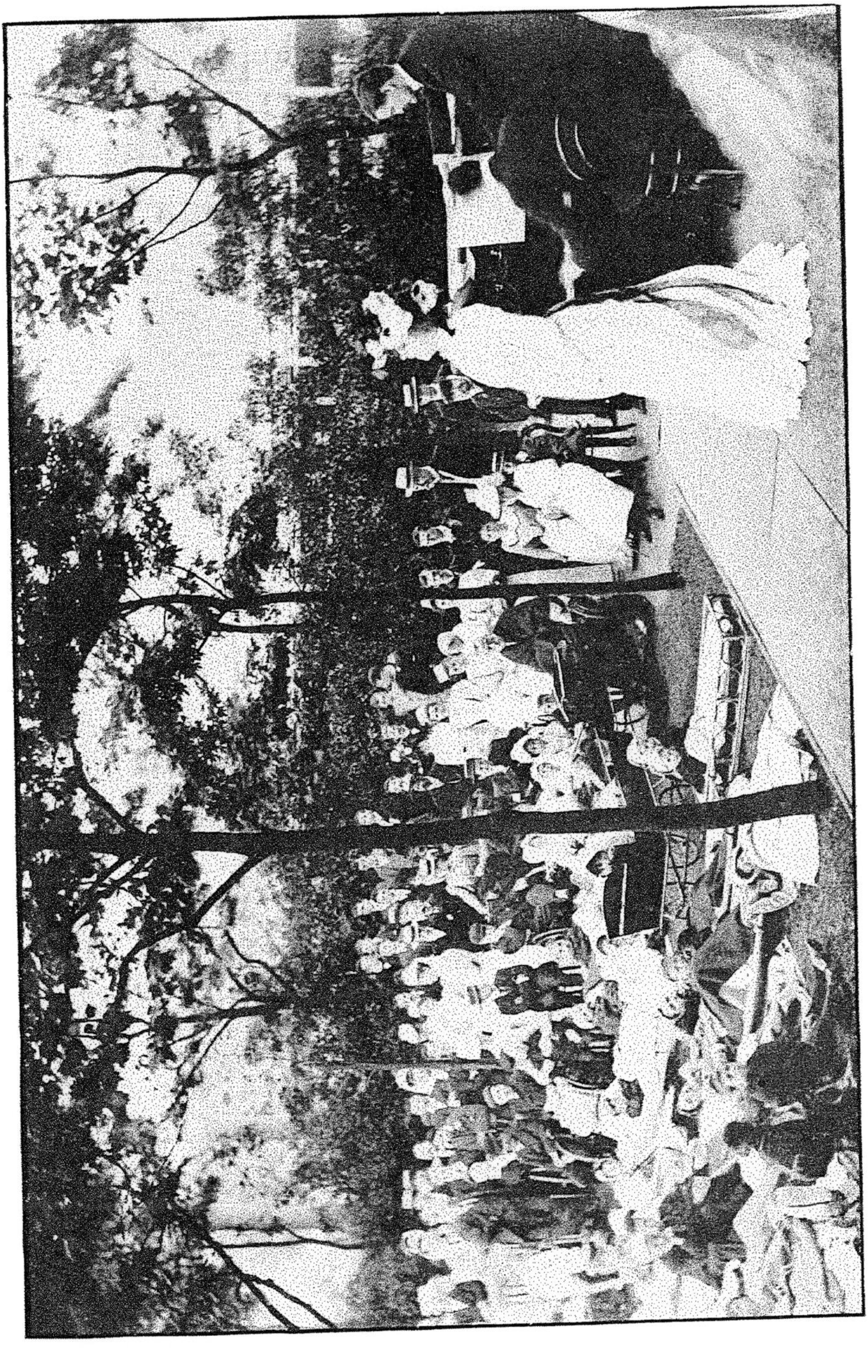

CHAPTER XV

THE FUTURE OF VOLUNTARY HOSPITALS*

WHEN we were young we were probably troubled by a mathematical master, full of curiosity, whose great quest in life was to know what would happen to a billiard-ball if it were acted upon by different forces at various angles at the same time. His question used to take this form : "If an object be acted upon by three forces of X, Y, and Z pounds respectively at angles of 25 degrees to each other, what will be the direction in which the object will move, and what will be its velocity ?" He usually added a few extras in the way of friction and so on, for those who were more advanced in solving these riddles.

He illustrated his meaning by always talking of billiard-balls. A great deal of paper was used in working out these problems, and the answer seemed insignificant when compared with the amount of brain-power and ink used in arriving at it. Personally, when giving in the answer that the object would move with a velocity of so many feet per second along the diagonal of such and such a parallelogram, I was never quite sure in which direction along that diagonal it would

* I have quoted freely from a paper read before Hospital Officer's Asssociation.

travel—to me or from me. The answer, therefore, could have been of no real use.

In trying to discover what is to be the future of voluntary hospitals, we must work out some such problem. The modern voluntary hospital is the object—the billiard-ball. The object appears to be acted upon by four forces. They are:

1. The sick poor, who cannot afford the treatment they require to restore them to health necessary to make them useful members of the community.
2. Generous people, who are willing to pay for such treatment for others.
3. The medical men, who provide the skilled treatment.
4. Medical students, who must use the hospitals as educational centres.

These are, I think, the only forces of any importance which are acting upon the modern voluntary hospital. They are not all acting in parallel directions. That is to say, they are not all pushing in exactly the same direction, nor yet in exactly the opposite direction to one another; they are acting at an angle to each other. Each influences the others. The direction in which the object will go depends upon the force of each, and upon the angles between them. It will not move in the same direction if any one of these forces be removed. That is the sum. And here is the first difficulty—that these four forces are changing so rapidly that they alter in direction and force almost while we are doing the sum.

Our guide as to how they are changing is to look back and note how they *have* changed.

First as to the sick poor.

We have seen, while considering the foundation and early history of St. Bartholomew's Hospital, that those who received the charitable help of the Hospital were poor men and women who were of the very lowest type; they were the outcasts, waifs and strays, tramps and vagabonds. When Henry VIII. seized St. Bartholomew's, the City merchants appealed to him to return it to the City, because they objected to this riffraff dying on their doorsteps. In the old inmates of our own Hospital there is the constant reference, half pitiful, half contemptuous, to the "miserable objects." This was characteristic of those old days—the wide gulf which existed between the nobles and the serfs, the rich merchants and the gutter-drabs. There were only two classes. The rich, who could pay; and the destitute, who could not—the "miserable objects" of absolute charity. Now this gulf has been gradually bridged over. Fine social distinctions have sprung up, and the growth of these social distinctions has reacted upon the system for the treatment of the sick. The class which the hospitals used to treat are now treated in our Poor Law Infirmaries. The hospitals now treat a class higher than was intended when they were founded.

What do we often see in the sick poor to-day? A person who by no means looks upon himself as a "miserable object." He is probably a member of some Trade Union. He joins associations to resist the power of Capital. He is perhaps a Socialist. He has his own Member of Parliament. He does not accept favours; he claims rights. His tendency is to claim free healing, as he claims free education for his children, and free Old Age Pensions. I am not speaking of individuals, but of some of the characteristics of the modern poor as a class.

Further, the "sick poor" of our modern hospital is often a person who is not poor *except to meet sickness*. He cannot possibly afford the heavy expenses of modern methods of treatment, whether medical or surgical, so he has gradually drifted to the hospitals, where such skilled attention could be had for the asking.

He came at first with some diffidence, but this is passing. He accepts the state of things as he finds it. The necessity of laying by for sickness, or of insuring against sickness, becomes less and less. He takes *free* relief in sickness into consideration when making up his budget. In many cases he expects free attention for his wife during her confinement, although the event was long foreseen, and should have been provided for by thrifty saving.

This class of sick poor is quite different from the class of individuals who take their blessings *as a right*. He has simply grown used to the existing state of things, and accepts them without any thought at all. He, too, is no "miserable object."

For *his* existence the hospitals are themselves largely to blame. They have assisted to make him what he is. They have said, "This struggling shopkeeper, this poor City clerk, cannot possibly afford the skilled attention, surgical and nursing, for the operation, say, for removal of appendix or for gastric ulcer; we must help him." And they did right in helping him. But were they right in doing much more than help him? Was it wise to provide also free food, free medicine, free warmth, free light, free service, and afterwards probably a free holiday at the seaside in a convalescent home? I do not wish to be misunderstood. I am not saying that all hospital patients are of these types. But hospitals should have modified their rules in assisting such people. They should have instituted some form of payment or part-payment. From the very position of the London Hospital there are probably fewer of this kind than at many hospitals, for "The London" stands in a district of poverty and squalor, and the distress which haunts the "casual." Of course, at every hospital there are hundreds of patients who have made a fine but losing fight before they asked for the hospital's help. Every hospital secretary will remember a case when he would have bitten his tongue out rather than have said what he did, not knowing all. As he gets older he takes longer before he decides to condemn. I should here like to quote a paragraph from a paper by Miss Marion Elliston on the poor of the East End. She is speaking of the casual labourer.

"Follow the programme of the day as it is being spent now by hundreds. The man gets up about four, or possibly five, according to the distance of his first work-seeking destination. There may be some strainings of long-stewed tea left from last night, and possibly a crust of dry bread. Equally possibly there may be neither. He sets out with it, or without it, as may be. If you do not know, it is well to imagine as realistically as you can the taste of November air at five or six in the morning to an unfed man. Also the feeling inside which it quickly creates. He joins the waiting crowd outside the docks or labour-yard of his special calling. The 'call' passes him and most of the others. They melt away to another yard, or some point where the road is 'up.' And on and on, from one labour-selling point to another. At last the man ceases to be conscious of his hunger. His gait grows slower. But he slouches doggedly, gazedly on, half-stupefied with his emptiness of food and his fulness of fog. Possibly he may happen on a cigarette-end in the gutter. A mate will supply the light. It eases the internal discomfort somehow. Still he goes on with that dull, dead, unhoping tramp after a vague, indefinite 'job.' That may continue all day, and many days in succession. Its only likely variation is that a mate in like plight, but not yet quite without a coin, may offer him 'a drink!' Blessed drink! The penny paid for it buys so much—the ungrudged right to a corner of a bench; the ungrudged right to the warmth of the bar-room fire; a sense of satisfiedness; and a dispelled taste of swallowed fog. You buy a great deal for a penny spent on beer if your feet have been carrying all your weight for hours and hours! Some days those of us who love temperance, and long for it, will set to work seriously at making available at the same cost as much of comfort without intoxicants. But we have been too occupied with talking about 'doing away with drink' to achieve it yet.

"At last the day ends, and the man reaches home again. Then comes a crucial moment. Such a man reached home after such a day last week. A wife and several little ones were waiting for him to come. There was no food. There was no fire. He dropped from sheer exhaustion, and from sheer exhaustion cried as his little children were doing. It happened so often that there seemed to the mother nothing left to pawn but—the shoes the little girl was wearing. The boys' had gone before. And the ha'pence lent on the little girl's shoes secured a few lumps of coal and some bread to be divided between them. All the bedclothes, too, had gone. Nothing remained but two stuffed sacks. Then to-morrow began again to carry forward the work of deteriorating the man—of killing all the good within him.

"In another home the wife was watching for her husband to come home. She explained that he had been out all day yesterday—first up to Whitechapel, and thence to Dartford and Ilford, home again to Plaistow, without a mouthful to eat. Weeping as she went on : ' And I hadn't a mouthful to give him then, so we went to bed, and this morning he went out again with nothing. I thought I must make sure of something for him this evening, so Tommy (the little boy) went up to Stratford Market and gathered up some of the cabbage-leaves dropped in the loading of the carts. The fire has burnt out, but I just managed to boil them ready while it lasted.' She showed me the plate of cold, wet-looking cabbage waiting to be a man's first meal in two days ! For herself—a neighbour had given her a cup of tea ; no, she hadn't had anything to eat ! And there was nothing left to pawn; but it used to be the nice little four-roomed home of a boiler-engineer !"

A large number—perhaps nearly all—of the patients who find their way to " The London " are just of this class. To help such is a delight. It is the duty of the authorities to see that their charitable assistance goes to such, and not to the unworthy.

But I do not think these legitimate cases should blind our eyes to the changes which have taken place in the character and the status of the sick poor as a class since our hospitals were founded.

Now we come to the changes in the second force—

the generous-minded donors, the financial supporters of the hospitals.

This force is changing because of the changes which have taken place in the first—the sick poor.

Most hospital secretaries will own that to keep up their subscription lists becomes a harder and ever harder struggle.

The fact is that the old appeal to the *pity* of the public is of less avail than it used to be. I do not think people are less tender or sympathetic than they used to be, but their pity does not, as it used to do, run in the direction of hospitals. There is a suspicion that they treat cases with which the rich givers have no sympathy. Most secretaries have received letters from former subscribers withdrawing their support because of the unpleasant attitude taken up by " the working man." One of the most forcible letters I ever had of this kind was from the late Mr. Bischoffsheim, within a few weeks of his death, pointing out that the average working man was taking such keen interest in himself, with his Workmen's Compensation Acts, and so on, that it was hardly to be expected that his hated rival, the financier and capitalist, should longer subscribe to his well-being. He *took* so much that little was left to be given. Though Mr. Bischoffsheim wrote this, he never acted on it, because his generosity and kindness were unbounded, as is that of Mrs. Bischoffsheim; and only a short time before he wrote this letter he and she had distributed £100,000 amongst charities to celebrate their golden wedding. I only quote this as typical of a new line of thought amongst thinking men.

Yes, the appeal to pity is losing power; other appeals

have to be made. We point out that the old institutions of the monastery order existed chiefly for the poor to *die* in, but now these modern hospitals *exist to restore men to their work;* we point out what an asset to the nation a modern hospital is, when by modern methods the " average residence " comes down, and the wage-earner returns to his family, not in sixty days, but twenty.

Our appeal falls flat when we are told that what probably happens is that the patient leaves the hospital a potential, if not actual, striker, and that many incomes of employers have fallen 25 per cent. on account of the uncertainty of labour.

I cannot but foresee a gradual lessening in effectiveness of Force 2, because of the changes which are taking place in Force 1.

Now we come to the third force—the Medical Staff.

I note that for long after the foundation of the Hospital the staff sat on the committee. They were themselves most liberal subscribers to the charity, as liberal as any of the laymen, and they gave their services as medical men as well. I cannot see what they *gained* in the early days by being attached to the Hospital. There were no students. They were not allowed to teach such private students who might come with them in their visits on hospital cases. If they wished to lecture, they had to bring their patients as well as their students. They were forbidden entirely to admit cases in which they were personally interested into the beds. They had letters of recommendation exactly as had other Governors.

Now all this is changed. A man, if he aims at consultant practice, *must* be on the staff of some well-known hospital, and the vacancies on the staff of any hospital could be filled ten times over if necessary. The public have just discovered—and they think themselves rather clever—that it pays a man well to be on the staff of a hospital. From a former state of adoration for the man who gave his services to the sick and suffering, they have gone to the other extreme, and fancy that every hospital doctor is very much "on the make." This view is as unworthy and untrue as extreme views always are. A man may not—he certainly does not—join the medical or surgical staff of a hospital for charitable reasons, but that is no reason that he should not be a most charitable man when he is on the staff. His work will push him in the direction of charity. We all know what a valuable asset to our voluntary hospitals is that noble *esprit* which is so difficult to define, but which marks off the voluntary hospital so distinctly from the average Poor Law Infirmary. We all know the doctor or surgeon who works for the poor, and often the grumbling poor, with no regard for hours, and who makes many a voluntary journey to his hospital, far beyond his legal obligations, for reasons of pure sympathy and large-hearted humanity. How often I have seen a member of our staff called down at midnight to see some case just brought in, and have noted that he came again voluntarily at 3 a.m. or 5 a.m., just to make sure that no more could be done. *He* did not mention it next day. It only appeared in the night gate-porter's report: "Mr. A. arrived at 12, left at 1." "Mr. A. arrived at 3 a.m., left at 3.30."

This valuable spirit in the voluntary hospitals is of such ethereal nature and delicate growth that one dreads to tamper with the present conditions of hospital life for fear of killing it.

Undoubtedly the "kudos" of being on the staff of a well-known hospital is immense. The opportunity of meeting students, the future general practitioners who will need to call in consultants, is of the greatest importance. The great benefit to the man himself, so far as his own experience is concerned, is obvious. The possibilities of his work, too, have changed for the better. He is now assisted in his researches by expert bacteriologists working in finely-equipped laboratories, and ready to prepare antitoxins for every infection. Another expert scientist works in the Clinical Laboratory, and to him is handed over the duty, performed in a more or less rule-of-thumb method by the old physicians, of examining urine, stomach contents, specimens of sputum, or of counting blood corpuscles. Many other specialists assist him.

Obviously the conditions of the Medical Staff have changed.

We have considered three forces. Already we can see the direction that the billiard-ball is *likely* to move. *All* are benefiting by the hospital, the rich and the poor. The hospitals do infinitely more good than they did a hundred years ago, and infinitely more than their founders ever dreamt of. Dives and Lazarus are both benefited, although Dives may never enter its walls.

There is one force more—the medical students. This is a comparatively new force. It has become one of great power and importance. It affects, as we have seen, the third force—the Medical Staff—strongly. The presence of that most pertinacious critic, the medical student, is the cause of much of the high quality of the work in the hospitals. You must *know* when you talk to a student; you must not *think*. He wants to know all about causes, not simply about effects; about the disease, not simply about its symptoms. His presence acts as the "fierce light" that beats on all the surgeon does. If we can rightly measure all these forces, we shall know whither the voluntary hospitals are moving.

What is the ideal? Let me try to describe an ideal hospital—a hospital where only those are treated who really and truly cannot afford to pay for such treatment themselves; where all patients who can afford to pay something will do so, disdaining to accept the whole if they can pay in part—disdaining, at any rate, to accept the hospital's charity habitually, and to lean entirely on charity. Such men will, as a matter of course, join sick clubs and provident dispensaries, and the hospital will co-operate with these as consultants. Subscribers, knowing that their gifts are wisely and honourably dispensed, will be more willing to help. The nation, recognizing that the work is national, good for the country as well as for the individual, will be willing to help, but in such a way as not to emasculate the generous giver, be he millionaire or working-man, and doing nothing to interfere with the hereditary characteristic and individuality of each hospital, nor to hamper in its help by red tape. And the Poor Law should co-operate.

The present lack of sympathy between the Poor Law and the hospitals is as serious as it is foolish.

Every hospital official knows how irritating are the difficulties when a patient has necessarily to be transferred from the wards to a Poor Law infirmary. If an out-patient is sent to the infirmary, via the Relieving Officer, that patient is almost certain to turn up at the hospital again in the course of two or three days.

The hospital's work in saving men and women from being a burden on the rates by giving them timely assistance is enormous. I asked one of our physicians to give me a list of cases which came under his care as the result of unhealthy surroundings or ignorance. Here it is :

Rickets, infantile diarrhœa, scurvy, phthisis, anæmia, tubercular diseases of hip and other joints, chronic throat diseases, scabies, favus, impetigo, pediculi, many skin diseases, many eye diseases, curvature of the spine, and some heart disease.

All of these cases the hospital helps to keep at work, and it is not fair that the hospitals should be saddled with all the expense of these " long time " cases brought about by their unhealthy surroundings and conditions of work, without any help from the Guardians of the Poor, whose duty towards the poor the hospitals are helping to carry out.

If the voluntary support goes on decreasing, there is nothing for it but the hospital to close bed by bed, and ward by ward. No one can exaggerate the magnitude of such a disaster. It would be far greater than that we should merely cease to admit sick persons suffering from this or that disease, great as that would be. It would mean that we should be ceasing to fight that disease as a disease. Hospitals are misused rather than abused. There must be part-paying beds to stop this *misuse*. There must be some more efficient system to stop the *abuse*. We have been told at the London Hospital by the Charity Organization Society, which at our request investigated the matter, that we ought to spend at least £1,000 a year on almoners. How can we spend £1,000 a year on this? It would keep twelve beds the whole year through, through each of which eighteen patients pass; 216 poor people restored to health! Somebody ought to pay it, perhaps, but the Hospital cannot afford to.

I think State aid will come; I hope not State control. The State aid should be so rendered as not to free the supporters of the Hospital from their responsibility. It might be done by adding a percentage to the subscriptions, or by an annual grant dependent upon the quality of the work as reported on by a trained scientific Government Inspector.

In London and large towns I should like to see the formation of a department or office to supervise in some *new* way the public health of the poor. This department should bring into line by authoritative powers the voluntary hospitals, which should still be voluntary, and the Poor Law Infirmaries, which should still be rate-supported, and, like the voluntary hospitals, eligible to receive State aid.

By this department officers should be appointed as " public almoners," and these should act as almoners both to the hospitals *and* the Poor Law, and to such an officer all applications for charitable medical relief, other than accidents or sudden illness, should be made.

These officers should be numerous, and their offices

easily found. Their offices should carry a conspicuous and distinctive sign, such as a red cross. This officer should have the power, with certain modifications as to the sort of illness, of sending a patient direct to the infirmary, if he can pay nothing, or to the hospital if he can pay something, and yet cannot afford all that is needed to complete his cure. He could refuse to send the patient either to hospital or infirmary should he consider it a case to be treated by a private doctor. He should also be able to send a case to the parish doctor (or medical man of similar status). These parish doctors should be much increased in numbers, and be assisted by a State grant, and be independent of the Guardians. They should treat patients in the patients' own homes. Paying beds at the voluntary hospitals should be much increased, and could be under such conditions. They cannot now. The authorities could admit a better class of patients to those at a charge which would pay all expenses, and yet be far under the exorbitant charges of some of the present so-called Nursing Homes.

The Governors of voluntary hospitals should have the right to admit "request" cases should they wish to — patients recommended by supporters of the charity.

At the risk of being thought a sentimentalist, I feel strongly that the individuality of our hospitals is such an important feature in obtaining the best help and work that I think it should be maintained. Financially it is important, because, as I have already noticed, certain families attach themselves to a hospital, and support it generation after generation; for instance, in the case of the Buxtons and the London Hospital. Less important subscribers, too, take a special pride in the hospital of their choice ; they interest themselves in its history, and watch its career with affection. This advantage would be lost if all hospitals were forced into one mould by some central governing body. With the voluntary staff, this individuality of the hospitals is of still more importance, and it would be lost were they all painted the same monotonous grey.

Country hospitals should be dotted round and well outside all large towns. These should be fed by motor ambulances by all the town hospitals, and to these country hospitals all cases should be transferred as soon as possible.

I am no believer in the theory that wounds are adversely affected by town air in these days of aseptic surgery. Wounds heal in towns just as well as anywhere else in the majority of cases. Everyone knows, however, what an immense help it is to a patient if he can convalesce in a change of air. The after-effects of a serious illness are much reduced.

The Out-patients' Departments of all hospitals should decrease. They should become more and more of consultative use, for specialists' work and for slight operation cases. The parish doctors, by the almoners' advice, should do most of the casualty work.

Of course, these alterations would necessitate alteration in the present system of medical education. The student to-day gains more information of practical use, it is said, in the Out-patient Department, where small ailments are treated, than in any other part of the hospital. But such ailments must be treated somewhere, and there the student must go.

These are the things I wish, and some of which I see ahead for our hospitals. By some such system the general poor will still be assisted, while the misuse of the hospitals by the thoughtless, and the abuse by the thriftless, would be, I think, prevented.

CONCLUSION

WHATEVER may be the future of "The London" and other voluntary hospitals, nothing can rob them of their glory for the work they have done. They got on with the work while others were discussing. England is a great deal richer for them. As for our own Hospital, readers who have been patient enough to read this little gossiping history to the end will, I think, pardon us in that we are proud of the fine, ugly old place. We are proud of its fighting power against disease and death. We are prouder still of a certain spirit that exists in it, and which pervades its workers—a spirit the existence of which, as I have said, is as easy to recognize as it is difficult to define, and which has been often referred to in these notes. This spirit exists not only in "The London," it is in St. Bartholomew's, and St. Thomas's, and Guy's, and in all hospitals with a history. It has something to do with the voluntary system, for the spirit is not the spirit of "the hireling." It is somewhat akin to the affection of a schoolboy for his school, and an undergraduate for his college, though in a hospital this affection is intensified, because the workers are mature men and women, whose work brings them habitually face to face with the more earnest and solemn sides of life.

The merriest houseman at dinner to-night will, if necessary, before the morning comes, run any risk imaginable to save a Whitechapel gutter-duck. He will not think of the risk, nor would any of his colleagues. A diphtheritic child may cough in his face as he examines it, but that will not in the least hinder him from continuing his examination. A filthy wound may poison him as he dresses it, but he will dress it; and should he succumb, as has happened, through the absorption of the poison, another man would, as a matter of course, take on the duty, and another, and yet another, if necessary. These men would be amused, and probably a little disgusted, if such action were called heroic; they would be the last to admit any heroism. The spirit of "The London" expects nothing less, and the matter rests there. There are no mottoes on their bedroom walls, nor does one notice uplifting platitudes in their speech, but "The London" has always obtained the service she demanded.

Have you ever been round a great hospital in the night? There is no glitter nor pomp. The students have all gone home. Everything is in dead earnest, and everyone who is up has something to do. Let us go now, and into the Receiving-room first. The room happens to be free from patients, but that peace will soon be broken. The "night-up" Receiving-room Officer is having a quiet smoke, and is wishing for the morning. A nurse comes down from one of the wards with a message. No. 7 Royal has been taken seriously worse, and can hardly live until the morning: can the relatives at Brixton be told? Not easy to get a message through to a back-street in Brixton at two in the morning. But long experience has taught the night-porter a wrinkle. The constable on point-duty outside is unofficially told all the facts. He strolls, or gets a comrade to do so, unofficially, to the nearest police-station. The particulars are unofficially telephoned to Brixton Police-station, and shortly a constable will be, unofficially, patrolling that little back-street, and will manage to let those relatives know that it would be wise to hurry to the Hospital. I hope I have not given away any of our good friends the police in stating this. I know they have no business to do us this favour. But many a husband has been in time to say good-bye to his wife or child through their unofficial kindness.

We will leave the Receiving-room, and go over to the Isolation Block. This is the Diphtheria Ward. There are screens round a little cot. That means failure. The little one has passsed. There is the mother talking to night-nurse. She is not crying. She is talking calmly, and is holding a doll. She is leaving now; she says she will come up in the morning. Nurse will tell us all about it. Yes, it was the mother, and her little girl has just died. She came in three days ago. A sweet little mite, with fair hair, and beautifully clean. Her mother earns 4s. a week stitching shirt-buttons. This is her only child—all she has in the world, in fact. The mother had always hoped some day to be able to buy her a doll, but had never been able. When the child was admitted, we gave her an old doll to play with, and she always cuddled it up. She died cuddling it. Yes, the mother was asking whether we could possibly spare her the doll now.

Let us go on. This is a medical ward for men. That young fellow near the door—he is only twenty-two—is on the "dangerous list." His name is at the gate, and friends may see him at any time, night or day. The old lady at the bedside is his mother; she is sitting up with him. Sister is beckoning us. She explains that she is in a difficulty. That old woman sitting by her boy is separated from her husband. They have not seen each other nor spoken to each other for twenty years. They both love the boy, but they never meet. One visits the Hospital on Wednesdays, the other on Sundays. But the boy is much worse to-night, and Sister has let them both know. The mother has arrived first. See, the door is opening—a white-haired old man. It is half-past two—one wonders how he came. Sister says that is the father, so we will move on. Here is a child who is not asleep. Sister says that nothing is wrong. He is going to Pevensey to-morrow, to a little cottage provided by one of our surgeons for convalescent children. He is very excited, that's why he cannot sleep. He has never seen the sea. His ward-mate, aged nine, went a week ago; he, too, had never seen the sea. It was a rough night when he arrived, and the sea was running high. In the morning it was a great calm. Tommie had gazed in amazement, and then said: "Now then, who's been and done that?" We turn to leave the ward. Near the door we entered by we notice an old couple on opposite sides of a bed; they are both looking into the face of a young fellow of twenty-two, who seems to be dying, and it needs no lamp to see that he is smiling. They are holding his hands, and each other's.

This is the theatre floor. There are six theatres here. One is fully lighted up, you see. Something is going on. An assistant explains that the police brought the case in an hour ago; he was picked up unconscious near the docks. Found on examination by the Receiving-room officer—we thought he would not be smoking long—to have a serious abdominal wound, a stab undoubtedly. The "full duty surgeon" was sent for at once, and is now "doing his best." Seven men have been called up to assist, and each has his definite duty, and would be missed if he were not there.

This is one of the obstetric wards. In that bed that is empty a woman died yesterday. She was only twenty-four. She had been in hospital a fortnight. Her husband was a young fellow about her own age, and he worshipped her and she him. Sister managed to get them properly married a week ago. The patient had asked that it might be so. When she died, her wedding-ring was her greatest treasure. Yes, they were together when she died.

It is six o'clock now. You notice the Receiving-room has several patients waiting. Men have dropped in as they went to work. That man is one of our own gardeners; he has been here thirty-four years, and has learned a few things. What is he doing in the Receiving-room? He is speaking to the officer, and explains that he is suffering from a "tired feeling" —it has only just gone six—and suggests that the officer would be doing a kind thing to a "brother officer, as it were," if he would just write a slip to say that "the gardener required rest"; he could then take the paper to the Steward and all would be well. The

Receiving-room officer, who was not appointed yesterday, examined his " brother officer " carefully, and feels, on the whole, that light exercise is indicated rather than rest. What sort of light exercise? " Oh, just roll the tennis lawn for one hour each day before breakfast."

We will look in at the children before we end our round. This is a surgical children's ward—much more cheerful than the medical. The convalescent children, who are running about, are excellent nurses. Here is a committee of four, telling each other fairy-tales apparently. One is telling the others that when she goes to heaven she intends to have a tea-party. Florrie and little Dick and Minnie shall all be invited, and Jesus will pour. One hopes, as I heard a good man once say, that she may be spared from going to heaven for many a long day.

We return to the secretary's quarters. This photograph in the secretary's office, you will notice, is signed by the Queen. She is the president, and is often in the Hospital. She sent that picture to one of the patients. His was a horrible case, and he was fearful to look on. But the Queen pitied him, and often spoke to him. He died here . . .

I never go round the Hospital at night but I picture the shades of the great dead walking the long corridors and down the great wards. Blizard, with sympathetic and admiring eyes, may be found any night in one or other of the silent theatres, never weary of studying how to get " 98 per cent. of first intentions." Harrison, too, I have seen there often. Dr. Andrée, the benevolent physician, may be found near the Clinical Laboratory and in all the medical wards, and the temperature charts are a never-ending source of interest and delight to him. Batson, that stickler for columns and figures, and tables and averages, may be found in the Registrars' Room and in the Statistical Department, wearing an eternal smile, for his highest flights of fancy have been exceeded.

And everywhere throughout the Hospital, wherever pain is and any trouble, you may surely meet the good and gracious Rev. Matthew Audley, who walked its corridors and visited its bedsides "during forty-nine years, carrying all kinds of consolation."

CHRONOLOGY OF THE LONDON HOSPITAL

1740. At a meeting of the Feathers Tavern, Cheapside, it was decided to " begin the Charity on One Hundred Guineas." House in Featherstone Street taken. Register of Patients commenced. Set of Rules drawn up.
Mr. Fotherley Baker elected Treasurer.
Dr. Andrée elected first Physician.
Mr. John Harrison elected first Surgeon.
Mr. Josiah Cole elected first Apothecary.

1741. Charles, Duke of Richmond and Lennox, elected first President.
Mr. Thomas Boehm elected Treasurer.
Mr. Richard Neale elected first Secretary. Banking Account opened with Mr. Frank Minors, Lombard Street. Treasurer and Chairman alone were authorized to admit patients between the sittings of the Committee. Patients were, as a rule, admitted once a week by Committee only. The Infirmary moved to Prescot Street, Goodman's Field, one house being taken at £25 per annum. First student entered, Mr. Godfrey Webb, an apprentice of Mr. Harrison. A woman to act as a nurse engaged at £14 per annum. Rev. Matthew Audley acted as Honorary Chaplain, and was made an Honorary Governor. Decided that Lady Subscribers of Five Guineas be made Governors, and might vote by proxy. Decided to hold a House Committee weekly, to be elected by the Governors quarterly.

1742. Annual Festival first held. Mr. John Harrison raised question of a Charter. Second House taken in Prescot Street. Decided that all Peers might vote by proxy.
Mrs. Elizabeth Gilbert elected Matron of one of the houses at Fifteen Guineas a year, and to provide her own diet.

Mrs. Ann Looker appointed Matron of original house, and discharged same year.

Mr. Godfrey Webb elected Apothecary.

1743. Funds started for affording a capital "in readiness for any extraordinary emergency." Committee of Accounts first formed, which still sits. Decided to appoint an Assistant Surgeon.

Mrs. Elizabeth Broad elected Matron (died same year).

Mrs. Joanna Martin elected Matron.

Dr. John Coningham elected Physician Extraordinary, and desired to attend once a week.

Mr. William Petty elected Surgeon Extraordinary.

1744. Mr. Richard Chiswell elected Treasurer. Admission to be by Governor's letter only. Physicians and Surgeons only have power to admit patients who require immediate relief. A Lint Scraper engaged. The addition of three more houses in Prescot Street decided upon. Mr. Godfrey Webb resigned. Steward first appointed at £20 per annum.

Mr. Henry Dodson elected Assistant Surgeon.

Mr. Boon appointed Apothecary.

1745. Mr. Joseph Hawthorpe chosen Treasurer.

1746. Sir James Lowther, Bart., elected Vice-President. Mr. Peter DuCane elected Treasurer. Mrs. Elizabeth Gilbert (Matron) died. Mr. Boon (Apothecary) resigned.

Mr. Thomas Shield elected Apothecary.

Mr. Walter Jones elected Surgeon Extraordinary.

Dr. James Hibbins elected Assistant Physician.

Mary Gony elected Matron.

1747. George Jennings elected Treasurer. Decided to look for a site for new hospital to be built. Influential Jews asked for information as to how to found a Charity similar to the London Hospital.

1748. Various sites for new hospital examined and reported on.

Dr. James Hibbins elected Physician.

1749. Mr. Peter Muilman and Mr. Daniel Booth appointed Joint Treasurers.

Dr. John Coningham died.

Dr. John Sylvester elected Physician.

CHRONOLOGY OF LONDON HOSPITAL

1750. William, Duke of Devonshire elected President.
Mr. Daniel Booth elected Treasurer.
Mr. Richard Neale resigned Secretaryship.
Mr. William Trotter elected Secretary.
Mr. Richard Grindall elected Assistant Surgeon.

1752. Lease of the premises at Whitechapel from the City drawn up. Foundation Stone of new building laid by Sir Richard Warren, October 15. Mr. Henry Dodson died.
Mr. Grindall appointed Surgeon.
Mr. Gabriel Risoliere and Mr. Henry Thomson appointed Assistant Surgeons. (Mr. Henry Thomson was the teacher of the future great Surgeon, William Blizard.)

1753. Mr. Robert Grosvenor elected Treasurer. Sum of money left to the Hospital for the assistance of poor patients on their leaving the Hospital. Mr. John Harrison died. Mr. George Neale elected Surgeon.

1754. Bishop of Oxford urged that there ought to be Divine Worship at the Hospital on the Lord's Day. Governors commenced to purchase the Estate around the Hospital. Mr. John Ellicot (the famous clockmaker) served on the Committee.

1755. Mr. John Dupré elected Treasurer. Rule made that no patient might remain in Hospital more than two months. In building of the Hospital, bricks were made from the clay found on the Estate. This was afterwards abandoned, as the clay was found unsuitable.

1756. Chaplain appointed at £100 per annum, to live within a quarter of a mile of the Hospital. Rev. Matthew Audley, who had been hitherto Honorary Chaplain, became first Paid Chaplain. First notice of Jews being systematically treated in Hospital. They were allowed $2\frac{1}{2}$d. a day in lieu of meat.

1757. Mr. James Godin elected Treasurer. Out-Patients first seen at the new Hospital, Whitechapel Road. In-Patient first admitted September 17, 1757, before completion of building. New building opened with 161 beds. Charter of Incorporation granted. Mr. John Ellicot designed a seal.

1758. The land adjoining the Hospital known as the Mount was now used as a Burial Ground for patients who died in Hospital.

1759. The main building of the Hospital completed (Wings not added for about ten years). The New River Water Company agreed to supply the Hospital with water for seven years at £15 per annum.
   Dr. Hibbins resigned.
   Dr. Thomas Dickson elected Physician.

1761. Mr. Christopher Roberts elected Treasurer.

1763. Mr. James Haughton Langston elected Treasurer. Benjamin Franklin, then Postmaster of New York, rendered great assistance to the Hospital with regard to a legacy. He was a friend of Ellicot, the clockmaker.
   Mr. Gabriel Risoliere appointed a Surgeon, and died same year.
   Mrs. Mark Eckley appointed Matron of the Locke.

1764. H.R.H. Edward, Duke of York, elected President. The Mount Burying-Ground was full. The Ground enlarged "quite down to the ditch."
   Dr. Andrée and Dr. John Sylvester resigned.
   Dr. Edward Richardson and Dr. Thomas Dawson elected Physicians.

1765. Dr. Edward Richardson died.
   Dr. Benjamin Alexander elected Physician.

1766. Mr. Richard Warner elected Treasurer.

1767. H.R.H. William Henry, Duke of Gloucester, elected President. Accounts show "cost per bed at this time was £17 15s. per annum."
   Mr. William Trotter (Secretary) died.
   Mr. John Cole appointed Secretary.

1768. Dr. Alexander died.
   Dr. Samuel Leeds elected Physician.

1769. Mr. John Leapidge elected Treasurer. Mr. Robert Salmon elected Chairman (previous to this Chairmen were only elected for three months). Committee decided that Physicians in future must hold a diploma of the College of Physicians.
   Mrs. Joanna Martin (Matron) died.
   Mrs. Elizabeth Paterson elected Matron. (At this time there were two Matrons, one of the general wards and one of the Locke Department.)

CHRONOLOGY OF LONDON HOSPITAL 297

1770. Mr. John Cooke elected Chairman.
Dr. Samuel Leeds and Dr. Dawson resigned.
Dr. Thomas Healde and Dr. Maddocks elected Physicians.

1771. Mr. John Coe elected Chairman.
Mr. Mainwaring, who had been the Architect and Surveyor of the new buildings, retired.
Mr. Hawkins appointed Surveyor.

1772. Mr. Devereux Bowley elected Chairman. Iron bedsteads first used instead of wooden. Large portion of the present Estate at the back of Hospital bought at Public Auction.

1773. Mr. William Loney elected Treasurer.
Mr. Joseph Sheppard elected Chairman.

1774. Mr. Timothy Mangles elected Chairman.

1776. Mr. John Swayne elected Chairman.

1777. Mr. John Cooke elected Treasurer.
Mr. Flower Freeman elected Chairman.

1778. Mr. John Baker elected Chairman.
Mrs. Elizabeth Eckley (Matron of the Locke) resigned. (Committee decided there should be only one Matron in future.)

1779. Mr. Thomas Jordan elected Chairman.

1780. Mr. John Spiller elected Treasurer.
Mr. Samuel Hawkins elected Chairman.
Court decided that Surgeons in future must be " Members of the Company of Surgeons in London."
Mr. Edward Hawkins (Surveyor) died, and Mr. John Robinson appointed.
Mr. Henry Thomson (Surgeon) resigned, and Mr. William Blizard elected.

1781. Rev. Dr. Robert Markham elected Chairman. Mr. Blizard asked permission to deliver two courses of lectures on Anatomy and Surgery. He had to bring his own patients, and had to give an undertaking that none of his Pupils should come into the Wards.

1782. Mr. Thomas Wellings elected Chairman. Surgeons' request for the building of a Theatre to give Lectures. Permission given, but the Staff were to bear the expenses of building this Theatre. Mr. John Cole (Secretary) resigned.
Mr. Thomas Hodges elected Secretary.

1783. Mr. Joseph Sheppard elected Treasurer.
Mr. James Rondeau elected Chairman.
With regard to the permission given to the Staff to erect a proper building, for teaching, in the Hospital Grounds, the Staff now asked that Donors of Thirty Guineas to *this* Building might be Governors of the Hospital. The Committee would not agree.

1784. Mr. Nathaniel Allen elected Chairman.
Dr. Thomas Dickson died.
Dr. John Cooke elected Physician.

1785. Mr. Thomas Jordan elected Treasurer, and Mr. Samuel Davy Liptrap elected Chairman. Hard times. Committee decided to close six Wards. Matron was discharged. Apothecary's Assistant discharged. Chaplain's salary reduced. Many Nurses, servants, and others discharged.

1786. The Rev. Dr. Mayo elected Chairman.
Dr. James Maddocks died.
Dr. Sir Paul Jodrell elected Physician.

1787. Mr. William Manbey elected Chairman.
Dr. Sir Paul Jodrell resigned.
Dr. William Hamilton elected Physician.

1788. Mr. Samuel Hawkins elected Treasurer. Mr. Timothy Curtis elected Chairman.
John Howard visited the Hospital and suggested many improvements, which were carried out.
Mr. Thomas Hodges (Secretary) resigned.
Rev. Mr. Buckham appointed Secretary.

1789. Mr. Thomas Coxhead elected Chairman.
Dr. Thomas Healde died.
Dr. Joseph Fox elected Physician.
Mrs. Elizabeth Paterson (Matron) died.
Mrs. Anne Guian elected Matron.

1790. Mr. Joseph Hankey elected Chairman. Much of the land forming the Hospital Estate was now let on building lease. Rule made that no Governors could vote at election who had not been Governors one year.
The Rev. Matthew Audley died, after being Chaplain forty-nine years.

1791. Mr. Nathaniel Allen elected Treasurer.
Mr. John Danvers elected Chairman.

1791. A thermometer was purchased.
   The Rev. Mr. Buckham, the Secretary, now made Chaplain as well.
1792. Mr. John Bacon elected Chairman.
1793. Mr. John Liptrap elected Chairman.
1794. Mr. Timothy Curtis elected Treasurer.
   Mr. Henry Hinde Pelly elected Chairman.
1795. Mr. Thomas Allen elected Chairman. The three Surgeons asked that three Assistants might be appointed, and the Committee agreed.
   Mr. Thomas White, Mr. Thomas Blizard, and Mr. George Vaux appointed Assistant Surgeons.
1796. Mr. Christopher Barton Metcalfe elected Chairman.
1797. Mr. Joseph Hankey elected Treasurer. Mr. Rawson Aislabie elected Chairman.
   Mr. Richard Grindall and Mr. George Neale died.
   Mr. Thomas Blizard and Mr. Thomas White appointed Surgeons.
   Mr. George Vaux resigned.
   Mr. Richard Headington elected Assistant Surgeon.
   Mrs. Guian (Matron) resigned, and Mrs. Arabella Doune appointed.
1799. Mr. William Leighton elected Chairman.
   Mr. Thomas White (Surgeon) resigned.
   Mr. Richard Headington elected Surgeon.
1800. Mr. John Liptrap elected Treasurer.
   Mr. Thomas Windle elected Chairman.
   Dr. Thomas Fox resigned.
   Dr. Algernon Frampton elected Physician.
1801. Dr. David Peter Watts elected Chairman.
   The London Dock Company attempted to purchase by Parliamentary powers the whole of the Hospital Estate without success.
1802. Mr. Charles Flower elected Chairman.
   The Rev. Mr. Buckham, who had been holding office of Secretary and Chaplain together, resigned Secretaryship, but continued to be Chaplain.
   Mr. John Jones elected Secretary.

1803. Colonel Matthew Smith elected Chairman. The Committee decided to oppose a Bill in Parliament for the formation of a canal from London Docks through the Hospital Estate to Paddington.

1804. Mr. Rawson Aislabie elected Treasurer.
Mr. Ralph Keddey elected Chairman.
Mrs. Arabella Doune resigned Matronship.
Mrs. Le Blond elected Matron.

1805. H.R.H. William Frederick, Duke of Gloucester, elected President.
Mr. Thomas Brown elected Chairman.
The Kitchen Garden to be levelled and thrown into the Burial-Ground, which was again full.

1806. Mr. Henry Hinde Pelly elected Treasurer.
Mr. Harry Charrington elected Chairman.
The City of London granted the Turner Street Opening so that the Hospital Estate at the back might communicate with Whitechapel Road.
Mr. John Robinson (Surveyor) died.
Mr. John Walters elected Surveyor.
The Rev. Mr. Buckham died.
The Rev. Andrew Hatt elected Chaplain.

1807. Mr. Charles Hampden Turner elected Chairman.
Dr. William Hamilton died.
Dr. Cooke resigned.
Dr. Isaac Buxton and Dr. Yellowly elected Physicians.

1808. Jews to have 4d. a day each, with bread and beer in lieu of diet from Hospital. Chaplain's clerk paid half a guinea a year for attending funerals.

1809. Mr. Thomas Windle elected Treasurer. £2,000 sent to the Hospital from India by old London Hospital Students then in practice in India.

1810. Mr. Quarles Harris elected Chairman.

1812. Sir Charles Flower, Bart., elected Treasurer.
Mr. John Henry Pelly elected Chairman.

1813. Mr. Thomas Coxhead Marsh elected Chairman.

1815. Mr. Thomas Brown elected Treasurer.

CHRONOLOGY OF LONDON HOSPITAL 301

1816. Dr. John Cooke elected Chairman. Cost of water raised from £15 to £30 per annum. Site of present St. Philip's Church was purchased from the Hospital for Chapel-of-Ease to the Parish of Stepney. (This site was sold for £840. Less than half was bought again by the Hospital in 1899 for an Isolation Block at a cost of £4,166 10s.). Deputation from gentlemen of the Hebrew Nation asking for further accommodation for Jews.
Mr. Thomas Blizard, Surgeon, resigned.
Mr. John G. Andrews elected Surgeon.

1818. Mr. Harry Charrington elected Treasurer.
Rev. A. Hatt resigned post of Chaplain, and Rev. William Valentine appointed. (Chaplain's duties combined with those of House Governor.)
Dr. John Yellowly resigned.
Dr. Benjamin Robinson elected.
Mr. H. Lang elected Solicitor.

1819. Mr. Charles Hampden Turner elected Treasurer.
Mr. Nicholas Charrington elected Chairman.

1820. Feather beds purchased for particular cases.

1821. Mr. W. B. Harkness elected Assistant Surgeon to Sir William Blizard.

1822. Mr. John Henry Pelly elected Treasurer.
Sir John Hall elected Chairman.
Committee appointed to consider the adoption of gas. Decided not to appoint nurses who could not read nor write. Dr. Buxton had leave through ill-health, and left the Apothecary in charge of his patients. The Brewers Company purchased a piece of land at the back of the Hospital on which to erect the Brewers' Almshouses. (These were pulled down in 1901, and the Hospital Laundry was built on the site. The land was sold to the Brewers Company in 1822 for £452. It was bought from them in 1901 for £6,401 17s. 3d.).
Dr. Buxton resigned.
Dr. Archibald Billing elected.

1823. Gas adopted in corridors, but not in wards. The Committee decided that a convalescent ward (one for each sex) would be an advantage. The Staff objected, however, and it was never instituted.

1825. Mr. Nicholas Charrington elected Treasurer.
Mr. William Davis elected Chairman.

1826. Mr. Robert Batson elected Chairman.

1827. Mr. William Cotton elected Chairman.
The House Committee desired an increase in the Medical and Surgical Staff (there were at this time three Physicians and three Surgeons). The Committee appointed three Assistant Physicians and three Assistant Surgeons. Assistant Physicians and Assistant Surgeons were to have the same qualification as Physicians and Surgeons.

Decided that a senior pupil should reside in the Hospital for periods of not less than three successive months, to take superintendence in absence of the Surgeons. George Frederick Young became a Life Governor..

Dr. James Alexander Gordon, Dr. Frederick Cobb, and Dr. Thomas Davis elected Assistant Physicians.

Mr. William Blizard Harkness, Mr. John Scott, and Mr. James Luke elected Assistant Surgeons.

Mr. William B. Harkness died same year, and was succeeded by Mr. Thomas Jeremiah Armiger.

1828. Mr. Quarles Harris elected Treasurer.
Mr. Christopher Richardson elected Chairman.
Dr. Benjamin Robinson died, and Dr. J. A. Gordon elected Physician.
Dr. John Macbraire elected Assistant Physician.

1829. Committee decided that *all* nurses must be able to read and write, but it was found impossible to get such. Decided, that only nurses who could read and write should *administer medicine.*

1830. West Wing extended to double its original length (Mr. Mason, Surveyor).
Mr. John Jones (Secretary) died, and Mr. Joseph Cecil appointed Secretary.

1831. Sir John Hall elected Treasurer.
Mr. Richard C. Headington, Surgeon, died.
Mr. John Scott elected Surgeon, and Mr. Alfred Hamilton elected Assistant Surgeon.
Mr. Thomas Jeremiah Armiger resigned, and Mr. John Adams elected Assistant Surgeon.

CHRONOLOGY OF LONDON HOSPITAL

1832. Mr. Francis Kemble elected Chairman.
Dr. Cobb sent to Newcastle to investigate Cholera.
Dr. John Macbraire resigned.
Dr. Algernon Frampton, jun., elected Assistant Physician.

1833. Sir William Blizard resigned.
Mr. James Luke elected Surgeon.
Mrs. Le Blond (Matron) retired, and Mrs. Nelson elected.

1834. Mr. William Davis elected Treasurer.
Committee adopted Filtering System, and all water used in the Hospital was filtered. Committee decided that no Physician or Surgeon could hold that position longer than twenty years. Inquiry by the Committee as to the origin of the School in 1783.
Mr. Thomas Blizard Curling elected Assistant Surgeon.

1835. H.R.H. Adolphus Frederick, Duke of Cambridge, elected President.
Mr. Robert Batson elected Treasurer.
Mr. Philip William Mure elected Chairman.
Death of Sir William Blizard.

1836. Mr. William Mitcalf elected Chairman.
Mr. Joseph Cecil resigned Secretaryship, and Mr. W. B. Bathurst elected Secretary.

1837. Mr. William Cotton elected Treasurer.
What is now the " Garden of Eden " was let to the Brewers' Company for the use of the inmates of the Brewers' Almshouses. Special communication from representative Jews asking that special Wards should be provided for Jews. The House Committee decided that it was impossible to grant the request. This decision was rescinded in 1842.

1838. Mr. Robert Hanbury elected Chairman.
Receiving-Room first instituted for the examination of accidents and extra cases. Nurse engaged for this Receiving-Room at 14s. a week, without diet or lodging; hours, 7 a.m. to 11 p.m.

1839. Dr. Davis appointed Physician, and died same year.
Dr. William John Little elected Assistant Physician.

1840. Mr. Philip William Mure elected Treasurer.
Mr. Leonard Currie elected Chairman.
East Wing extended.

1841. Dr. Algernon Frampton, sen., resigned.
Dr. Frederick Cobb elected Physician.
Dr. Jonathan Pereira elected Assistant Physician.

1842. Mr. William Mitcalf elected Treasurer.
Mr. George Frederick Young elected Chairman (still living).
Special Wards were appointed for Jews.
Rev. T. Valentine resigned Chaplaincy, and Rev. James W. Saunders elected Chaplain.

1844. Mr. Robert Hanbury elected Treasurer.
Three House Surgeons appointed. Qualification by examination was not essential; they were simply senior students.
Dr. Gordon resigned.
Dr. Algernon Frampton, jun., elected Physician.

1845. Mr. John Davis elected Chairman.
Mr. John Scott (Surgeon) resigned.
Mr. Alfred Hamilton elected Surgeon.
Dr. Patrick Fraser elected Assistant Physician.
Dr. Archibald Billing resigned.
Dr. William John Little elected Physician.
Dr. Herbert Davis elected Assistant Physician.

1846. Dr. A. Billing was requested to become a member of the House Committee. Decided that all Surgeons appointed to the Staff must be Fellows of the Royal College of Surgeons of England.
Mr. W. B. Bathurst (Secretary) resigned.
Mr. William John Nixon appointed Secretary, and is still living in 1910.
Mr. George Critchett elected Assistant Surgeon.
Mr. Henry Martin Harvey elected Solicitor on retirement of Mr. Henry Lang.
Mr. A. R. Mason elected Surveyor.
Rev. Saunders resigned Chaplaincy, and Rev. T. Ward elected.

1847. Sir Edward North Buxton, Bart., elected Chairman.

1848. Mr. Leonard Currie elected Treasurer.

1849. Mr. Charles Bradshaw Stutfield elected Chairman.
Physicians requested that a microscope should be purchased for the Hospital. This was done, and entrusted to the care of

the Apothecary. Decided that Assistant Surgeons should be required to have the same qualification as Surgeons—that is, they must be Fellows of the Royal College of Surgeons of England.
Mr. Alfred Hamilton (Surgeon) resigned.
Mr. John Adams elected Surgeon.
Mr. Nathaniel Ward appointed Assistant Surgeon.
Mr. J. G. Andrews (Surgeon) died.
Mr. Thomas B. Curling appointed Surgeon.
Mr. John Cawood Wordsworth appointed Assistant Surgeon.

1850. H.R.H. George William, Duke of Cambridge, K.G., elected President.

1851. Gas in future to be charged by meter instead of by fixed charge per annum.
Dr. Algernon Frampton, jun., resigned.
Dr. Jonathan Pereira elected Physician.
Dr. Nicholas Parker elected Assistant Physician.

1852. Mr. John Davis elected Treasurer.
Captain Richard Pelly, R.N., elected Chairman.
Medical Staff considered that the Apothecary was a proper person to administer chloroform; the Committee did not agree.
Rev. T. Ward resigned Chaplaincy.
Rev. Edward John Nixon appointed Chaplain.

1853. The House Committee, wishing to put an end to the previous decision of appointing special wards for Jews, decided that only parts of Wards should be set apart for Jews. The Jews objected to this as not fulfilling the agreement previously made with them.
Dr. Ramsbotham appointed first Obstetric Physician.
Dr. Jonathan Pereira died.
Dr. Patrick Fraser elected Physician. (It is interesting to note that Dr. Patrick Fraser's widow gave £5,000 to the Hospital, and on her death, in 1909, left another £5,000.)
Dr. James Miller elected Assistant Physician and died same year.
Dr. Septimus Gibbon elected Assistant Physician.

1854. Sir Edward North Buxton, Bart., elected Treasurer.

The title of "Apothecary" was changed to "Resident Medical Officer." New Medical College on its present site opened. Outside Maternity Department started, and first Resident Accoucheur appointed.

Dr. Frederick Cobb resigned.

Dr. Herbert Davis elected Physician.

Dr. Andrew Clark elected Assistant Physician (afterwards Sir Andrew Clark, Bart., Physician to Her Majesty Queen Victoria).

1855. Mr. James Scott Smith elected Chairman.

Staff applied for appointment of Surgical Registrars.

1856. Mr. Charles Bradshaw Stutfield elected Treasurer.

Miss Florence Nightingale became a Life Governor.

Rev. Nixon resigned Chaplaincy, and Rev. John Morrison Snody elected Chaplain.

1857. Captain Richard Wilson Pelly, R.N., elected Treasurer.

Mr. Thomas Fowell Buxton elected Chairman.

Decided that Assistant Surgeons must reside within a mile and a half of the Hospital.

Mr. Henry John Barrett appointed Dental Surgeon.

1858. Court of Governors decided that a Fourth Assistant Surgeon be appointed, and Mr. P. Y. Gowlland was appointed Assistant Surgeon.

Mr. Mason (Surveyor) resigned.

Mr. Charles Barry appointed Surveyor.

1859. Staff complained of the rule that Assistant Surgeons must live within a mile and a half of the Hospital. The Committee refused to alter the rule.

Mr. John C. Wordsworth resigned in consequence.

Mr. Jonathan Hutchinson (now Sir Jonathan Hutchinson) appointed Assistant Surgeon.

Dr. Robert Barnes elected Assistant Obstetric Physician.

Dr. Septimus Gibbons resigned.

Dr. Jabez Spencer Ramskill elected Assistant Physician. Court decided to appoint fourth Assistant Physician, and Dr. John Langdon Down elected Assistant Physician.

1860. Vaccination Department started.

Rev. John Morrison Snody resigned Chaplaincy, and Rev. Thomas Scott (now Canon Scott) appointed.

Mr. Nathaniel Ward, Surgeon, resigned.

Mr. Charles Frederick Maunder elected Assistant Surgeon.

CHRONOLOGY OF LONDON HOSPITAL

1861. Mr. James Luke resigned the post of Surgeon, and was appointed Consulting Surgeon (the first time such an appointment was made).
Mr. George Critchett was elected Surgeon.
Mr. John Couper elected Assistant Surgeon.

1862. Mr. Tanqueray Willaume elected Solicitor.
Mr. Gowlland, Surgeon, resigned.
Mr. Louis Stromeyer Little elected Assistant Surgeon.

1863. Decided to pension all Nurses after twenty years' service—12s. a week.
Mr. George Critchett, Surgeon, resigned.
Mr. Jonathan Hutchinson elected Surgeon.
Mr. Walter Rivington elected Assistant Surgeon.
Dr. William John Little resigned.
Dr. Ramsbotham resigned office of Obstetric Physician.
Dr. Nicholas Parker elected Physician.
Dr. Robert Barnes elected Obstetric Physician, and at his request an Assistant Obstetric Physician was not appointed in his place.
Dr. Hughlings Jackson elected Assistant Physician.

1864. Foundation of Alexandra Wing laid.

1865. Dr. Robert Barnes resigned post of Obstetric Physician.
Dr. Edward Head appointed Obstetric Physician.
Dr. James Palfrey appointed Assistant Obstetric Physician.

1866. Alexandra Wing opened. Cholera year.
Mr. W. J. Nixon appointed House Governor as well as Secretary.
Dr. Nicholas Parker resigned.
Dr. Andrew Clark elected Physician.
Dr. Morell Mackenzie (afterwards Sir Morell) elected Assistant Physician.
Dr. Patrick Fraser resigned.
Dr. Jabez Spencer Ramskill appointed Physician.

1867. The Governors sent a special petition to Parliament for special examination from parochial rates, "or for a continuance of that exemption which the Hospital has hitherto enjoyed."
Dr. Henry Sutton elected Assistant Physician.

Mrs. Jane Nelson resigned post of Matron after thirty-four years' service. Matrons in future were to be appointed by House Committee, and not by Quarterly Courts.

Miss A. M. Swift appointed Matron.

1868. Mr. Thomas Fowell Buxton elected Treasurer.

Sir Edmund Hay Currie elected Chairman (now Secretary of the Hospital Sunday Fund).

Committee decided to appoint a fifth Assistant Physician and fifth Assistant Surgeon.

Mr. James E. Adams elected Assistant Surgeon.

Dr. Samuel Fenwick elected Assistant Physician.

Rev. T. A. Purdy elected Chaplain in place of Rev. Thomas Scott.

1869. Medical College enlarged. Committee seriously considered question of making Out-Patients pay something towards expenses of their treatment.

Mr. John Adams resigned post of Surgeon, and was appointed Consulting Surgeon.

Mr. C. F. Maunder elected Surgeon.

Mr. Waren Tay elected Assistant Surgeon.

Mr. Thomas Blizard Curling resigned, and was elected Consulting Surgeon.

Mr. Louis Stromeyer Little resigned post of Assistant Surgeon.

Mr. John Couper elected Surgeon.

Mr. Jeremiah McCarthy and Mr. Henry A. Reeves appointed Assistant Surgeons.

1870. Dr. John Langdon Down elected Physician, and Mr. Walter Rivington elected Surgeon.

Dr. W. Bathurst Woodman elected Assistant Physician.

Mr. Barry resigned post of Surveyor.

1871. Mr. Archibald Hanbury elected Solicitor. Decided to pay the Assistant Staff who see Out-Patients an honorarium of £50 per annum.

1873. The Grocers' Company gave donation of £20,000 towards cost of New Wing to be called the Grocers' Wing. Decided, that in building the Grocers' Wing arrangements be made for a Training Home for Nurses for the benefit of the London Hospital.

Sir Morell Mackenzie elected Physician.

CHRONOLOGY OF LONDON HOSPITAL

1874. Dr. Herbert Davis resigned, and was elected Consulting Physician.
Dr. Hughlings Jackson elected Physician.
Dr. Stephen Mackenzie (afterwards Sir Stephen) elected Assistant Physician.
Sir Morell Mackenzie resigned.
Dr. Arthur Ernest Sansom elected Assistant Physician.
Decided to appoint Medical and Surgical Registrar at a salary of £100 per annum.
Mr. Ashley W. Barrett appointed Surgeon Dentist, on the resignation of Mr. Henry John Barrett.

1875. Dr. Edward Head resigned Obstetric Physicianship.
Dr. James Palfrey elected Obstetric Physician.
Mr. A. Snelgrove appointed Secretary.
Mr. Nixon (late Secretary) appointed House Governor only.

1876. The Grocers' Wing opened.
Dr. G. Ernest Herman elected Assistant Obstetric Physician.
Dr. Henry Sutton elected Physician (fifth Physician now for the first time).
Dr. Charlewood Turner elected Assistant Physician.
Mr. A. Gardiner Brown appointed Aural Surgeon.

1877. Dr. Bathurst Woodman elected Physician, and died same year.
Dr. Thomas Barlow (now Sir Thomas Barlow, Bart., K.C.V.O., Physician to His Majesty the King) elected Assistant Physician.
Mr. John Adams, Surgeon, died.

1878. The Right Hon. Lord Aldenham elected Treasurer.
Mr. John Henry Buxton elected Chairman.
The Committee urged the necessity of a sixth Assistant Physician. Dr. Gilbart Smith elected Assistant Physician.
Death of Rev. T. A. Purdy.

1879. The Rev. J. S. Whichelow elected Chaplain.
Mr. C. F. Maunder, Surgeon, died.
Mr. James E. Adams elected Surgeon.
Mr. Frederick Treves (now Sir Frederick Treves, Bart., G.C.V.O., C.B., Serjeant-Surgeon to His Majesty the King) appointed Assistant Surgeon.

Dr. Ramskill resigned, and was elected Consulting Physician.

Dr. Samuel Fenwick elected Physician.

Dr. Francis Warner elected Assistant Physician.

1880. Dr. Thomas Barlow resigned.

Dr. Charles Henry Ralph elected Assistant Physician.

Mr. Snelgrove resigned Secretaryship.

Mr. Munro Scott appointed Warden of the Medical College.

Miss Swift, Matron, resigned; and Miss Eva Lückes, the present Matron, appointed.

1881. Mr. A. H. Haggard appointed Secretary.

Mr. James Luke, Surgeon, died.

1882. Mr. Jeremiah McCarthy appointed Surgeon.

Mr. C. W. Mansell-Moullin elected Assistant Surgeon.

Mr. Waren Tay elected Surgeon.

Mr. Edward Woakes and Mr. Mark Hovell appointed Aural Surgeons.

Mr. A. G. Brown, Aural Surgeon, died.

Dr. James Palfrey died.

Rev. J. S. Whichelow retired from Chaplaincy, and Rev. Algernon Grenfell elected.

1883. Dr. G. Ernest Herman elected Obstetric Physician.

Mr. Jonathan Hutchinson (now Sir Jonathan Hutchinson) retired from post of Surgeon, and was elected Consulting Surgeon.

Mr. McCarthy elected Surgeon.

Mr. E. Hurry Fenwick elected Assistant Surgeon.

1884. Mr. John Henry Buxton elected Treasurer.

Mr. Francis Culling Carr-Gomm elected Chairman.

The Committee decided to improve the accommodation for Nurses and to build a Nurses' Home.

Mr. James E. Adams resigned post of Surgeon.

Mr. Frederick Treves elected Surgeon.

Mr. Frederick Eve appointed Assistant Surgeon.

Mr. Rowland Plumbe appointed Architect.

1885. Dr. Arthur H. N. Lewers elected Assistant Obstetric Physician.

Rev. A. S. Grenfell resigned.

Rev. A. Tristram Valentine elected Chaplain.

Dr. Herbert Davies died.

CHRONOLOGY OF LONDON HOSPITAL 311

1886. Sir Andrew Clark, Bart., resigned post of Physician, and was elected Consulting Physician.
    Dr. Stephen Mackenzie (afterwards Sir Stephen) elected Physician.
    Dr. James Anderson elected Assistant Physician.
    Dr. F. W. Hewitt appointed Instructor in Anæsthetics.

1887. Mr. Haggard resigned Secretaryship.
    Nurses' Home opened.
    Dr. C. H. Ralph elected Physician.

1888. Mr. G. Q. Roberts appointed Secretary.
    Mr. Thomas Blizard Curling, Surgeon, died.

1889. Rev. Valentine resigned.
    Mr. John Couper resigned post of Surgeon, and was elected Consulting Surgeon.
    Mr. Mansell-Moullin appointed Surgeon.
    Mr. Jonathan Hutchinson, jun., appointed Assistant Surgeon.

1890. Mr. Edward Murray Ind elected Chairman.
    House of Lords Inquiry into management of Hospitals.
    The Rev. J. D. K. Mahomed elected Chaplain.
    Dr. Langdon Down resigned, and was made Consulting Physician.
    Mr. Walter Rivington elected Consulting Surgeon.
    Dr. Arthur Ernest Sansom elected Physician.
    Mr. E. Hurry Fenwick appointed Surgeon.
    Mr. T. H. Openshaw elected Assistant Surgeon.
    Dr. Percy Kidd elected Assistant Physician.

1891. Dr. Henry Sutton died.
    Dr. F. Charlewood Turner elected Physician.
    Dr. F. J. Smith elected Assistant Physician.

1892. The question seriously considered of having ladies on the House Committee.
    Mr. H. A. Reeves, Surgeon, resigned.
    Mr. Henry Percy Dean elected Assistant Surgeon.
    Mr. Nixon (House Governor) resigned.
    Mr. G. Q. Roberts appointed House Governor.

1893. Mr. John Hampton Hale elected Chairman.
    Dr. James Anderson died.
    Dr. W. J. Hadley elected Assistant Physician.
    Sir Andrew Clark, Bart., died.

1894. Second Nurses' Home built.
Dr. Hughlings Jackson elected Consulting Physician.
Dr. Gilbart Smith elected Physician.
Dr. George Schorstein elected Assistant Physician.

1896. The Hon. Sydney Holland elected Chairman.
Mr. Ashley Barrett (Surgeon Dentist) appointed Consulting Dental Surgeon.
Dr. C. H. Ralph elected Consulting Physician, and died same year.
Dr. Bertrand Dawson elected Assistant Physician.
Dr. Samuel Fenwick elected Consulting Physician.
Dr. Francis Warner elected Physician.
Dr. Henry Head elected Assistant Physician.
Dr. Langdon Down died.

1897. The complete rebuilding of the Hospital commenced.
Second Nurses' Home built.
Dr. J. S. Ramskill died.
Dr. Probyn-Williams elected Assistant Instructor in Anæsthetics.
Mr. Walter Rivington, Surgeon, died.

1898. £25,000 given by an anonymous donor for new Out-Patient building. Letters of admission abolished, and payment for medicine and bandages by Out-Patients commenced.
Mr. Jeremiah McCarthy resigned, and was appointed Consulting Surgeon.
Mr. Frederick S. Eve elected Surgeon.
Mr. A. B. Roxburgh elected Assistant Surgeon.
Mr. Frederick Treves (now Sir Frederick) was appointed Consulting Surgeon.
Mr. Jonathan Hutchinson elected Surgeon.

1899. Mr. Edward L. Raphael (the late) gave donation of £10,000 for the endowment of the Jewish Wards. He also gave a similar amount in 1903.
Mr. Percy Furnivall elected Assistant Surgeon.
Dr. Charlewood Turner resigned.
Dr. Percy Kidd elected Physician.

1900. It was decided to have five Assistant Surgeons.
Dr. Charlewood Turner died.
Dr. Robert Hutchison elected Assistant Physician.

CHRONOLOGY OF LONDON HOSPITAL 313

1901. The Isolation Block built at a cost of £32,000.
The Pathological Department built at a cost of £19,143.
Dr. Frederick W. Hewitt appointed Consulting Anæsthetist.
Mr. Harold Barnard elected Assistant Surgeon.
Dr. H. L. Lack appointed Surgeon in charge of the Throat Department, and Mr. Hunter Tod Assistant Surgeon.
Dr. Probyn-Williams elected Instructor in Anæsthetics.
Mr. Edward Woakes, Aural Surgeon, resigned.

1902. New Operating Theatre Floor and five Theatres built at cost of £13,000. His Majesty King Edward VII.'s serious illness and operation just before the day fixed for the Coronation. Sir Frederick Treves operated. Mr. Frederick Hewitt gave the anæsthetic, and Nurse Haines (one of the Hospital Nurses) was engaged.
Mr. Waren Tay appointed Consulting Surgeon.
Mr. A. B. Roxburgh appointed Ophthalmic Surgeon.
Mr. T. H. Openshaw elected Surgeon.
Dr. Sansom elected Consulting Physician.
Dr. F. J. Smith elected Physician.
Mr. H. M. Rigby elected Assistant Surgeon.
Dr. Lewis Smith elected Assistant Physician.
Dr. J. H. Sequeira appointed Assistant Physician to the Skin Department.
Mr. Mark Hovell appointed Consulting Aural Surgeon.
Mr. Hunter Tod elected Surgeon to the Aural Department.
Mr. James Sherren elected Assistant Surgeon.
Dr. Samuel Fenwick died.

1903. His Majesty the King and Her Majesty the Queen opened the Out-Patient Department. The site, building, and equipment cost £83,000.
Mr. G. Q. Roberts resigned Secretaryship, to become Secretary to St. Thomas's Hospital.
Mr. Ernest W. Morris elected Secretary.
Dr. Sequeira appointed Skin Physician.
Dr. Russell Andrews elected Assistant Obstetric Physician.
Dr. Ernest Herman appointed Consulting Obstetric Physician.
Dr. Arthur Lewers elected Obstetric Physician.
Sir Stephen Mackenzie resigned post of Physician to the Skin Department, Dr. Sequeira being appointed in his stead.
Dr. Henry Head elected Physician.

Dr. Morton appointed Medical Officer in charge of the Electrical Department.

Mr. John Henry Buxton resigned Treasurership.

1904. Her Majesty the Queen elected President.
The Earl of Derby (then Lord Stanley) appointed Treasurer.
Dr. Gilbert Smith died.
Dr. W. J. Hadley elected Physician.
Mr. W. T. Lister appointed Ophthalmic Surgeon.
Dr. Cecil Wall elected Assistant Physician.
Mr. James Hora endowed the " Marie Celeste " Wards.
New Laundry built at cost (with site) of £32,000.

1905. The Eva Lückes' Nurses' Home built (the third Nurses' Home), at cost of £47,000.
Mr. Munro Scott, Warden of the Medical College, completed the twenty-fifth year of his Wardenship.
Mr. Hugh Lett appointed Assistant Surgeon.
Sir Stephen Mackenzie appointed Consulting Physician.
Dr. G. Schorstein elected Physician.
Dr. Otto Grünbaum elected Assistant Physician.

1906. Dr. Schorstein died, and Dr. Dawson was elected Physician.

1907. Dr. Theodore Thompson elected Assistant Physician.
Dr. Robert Barnes died.
Dr. Sansom died.

1908. Statue of Her Majesty Queen Alexandra erected in grounds.
Mr. Russell Howard elected Assistant Surgeon.
Mr. Harold Barnard, Surgeon, died.
Dr. Philip Panton elected Clinical Pathologist.

1909. Appointment of Lady Almoners. Anonymous gift of £20,000 for Medical Research. Opening of the Tyrnauer Baths.
Mr. Mansell-Moullin appointed Consulting Surgeon.
Sir Stephen Mackenzie died.
Mr. Henry Percy Dean appointed Surgeon.
Mr. Richard Warren appointed Assistant Surgeon.
Dr. Morton resigned.
Dr. Gilbert Scott appointed in charge of the Radiographic Department.

1910. Mr. E. Hurry Fenwick appointed Consulting Surgeon.

INDEX

Accounts Department, 265
Admission, rules of, 10, 67, 108-10, 178-9
Advertisement, old method of, 67
Alexandra Wing, the, 87, 135, 166
Almoners, 11-12, 264, 282
Anæsthetics, discovery of, 172
  rooms for administering, 21
Andrée, Dr., 26, 46, 61, 291
Apothecary, ancient duties of, 173-5
Arderne, John of, 41-2
Audley, Rev. Matthew, 62-3, 292

Bacon, Francis, influence of, on medicine, 40
Bacteriological Laboratory, 202, 233, 239
Baker, Mr. Fotherley, 26
Baptist Head Tavern, meeting at, 25
Barbers, Guild of, 43, 44
  as surgeons, 37, 41
  unscrupulousness of, 41
Bischoffsheim, Mr. and Mrs., 276
Black Swan Tavern, meeting at, 48
Blizard, William, appeals for funds, 190-3
  birth and education of, 144-5
  death of, 154
  knighthood of, 149
  Medical School founded by, 107, 145-6, 186
  offices held by, 151-2
  personality of, 147-8, 151, 152
  Samaritan Society founded by, 150
  separate wards advocated by, 157-8
  surgical skill, 147

Building Fund, raised by Bishop of Worcester, 78
  plans for employment of, 83-5
Buxton, Mr. John, 53
  Mr. John Henry, 53, 229
  Mr. Thomas Fowell, 53, 169

Charter, Hospital, first obtained, 180-1
Chaucer, quoted, 38
Cholera, epidemics of, 163-8
Clark, Sir Andrew, 232
Cobb, Mr. John, 102, 103, 104
Cole, Mr. Josiah, 26, 48, 55
Convalescent Home at Felixstowe, 232
Creighton, Dr. Charles, 31, 39
  quoted, 32-6

Departments :
  Electrical, 14, 222
  Estate, 255
  Finsen Light, 12, 151, 237
  Nursing, 243-8
  Opsonic, 238
  Orthopædic, 17
  Out-patient, 4, 9, 12-17, 66, 258, 261, 263-5, 284, etc.
  Photographic, 225
  Röntgen ray, 222
  Steward's, 248-52
  Surveyor's, 255-6
  Theatre, 262-3
Derby, Countess of, 22
Diet table, 69, 252-3
Dispensary, 16, 256-62

Economy, reports on, 123-6
Electricity, treatment by, 222
Ellicot, John, F.R.S., 177
Elliston, Miss Marion, quoted, 273-5

315

INDEX

Endowment of Medical Research, 203, 228
   of Finsen Light Department, 233
Estate Department, 255
Examinations, qualifying, started, 139-40

Feathers Tavern, the, meetings at, 24, 25, 33, 44
Featherstone Street, first site of " London Infirmary," 26, 48
Festival, Annual, institution of, 73
   ceremonies of, described, 74-7
" Field," the, 183
Fielden, Mr. J. A., 231
Financial administration, 24, 50, 54
   committee for, 265
   criticism of, 236-7, 240-1
   economy in, 123-4
   mistakes in, 100
   reports in, 65
Finsen Light, 12-13, 151, 230, 233, 237
Foundation of the Hospital in Whitechapel, 87
Fry, Mrs. Elizabeth, 207
Funds, appeals for, 190-3, 224
   great lack of, in 1897, 225
   Prince of Wales's, 226

" Garden of Eden," the, 23, 183
Governors, methods of procedure, 118-21
   quarterly courts of, 96, 98, 116, 189-90, 241-2
   subscribers known as, 49, 96
Grocer's Wing, the, 87, 169, 209

Haberdashers' Hall, meetings at, 53
Hale, Mr. John Hampton, 218, 220, 223
Harrison, John, surgeon, annual festival instituted by, 73
   assistant surgeon appointed to, 59
   charter, raised question of, 180
   complaints against, 60-1
   Infirmary, advises extension of, 64

Harrison, John, progressive policy of, 101
   pupils of, 61, 186
   share of, in founding Hospital, 25, 26, 47, 51, 82
Hatzfeldt, Princess, 15
Herbs, use of, 38
Hoare, Mr. Douro, 203
Holland, Hon. Sydney, 223-4, 226
Hora, Mr. James, 22, 150, 231
House Committee, the, constitution of, 241-2
   elections of, 97, 101
   meetings of, 98-9, 116-17, etc.
House Visitors, appointment of, 101
   reports of, 102-6
Howard, John, 152, 185
   reforms introduced by, 155-7
Hydrophobia, epidemic of, 144
Hygiene, disregard of, 69-70
   reports on, 104

Infectious cases, 23, 68, 164-5
Infirmary, the London, becomes the " London Hospital," 77
   extension of, 64, 69
   opening of, 26, 48
Inoculation Department opened, 233
Isolation Block, 183, 227, 288

Jewish Wards, the, 21, 126, 130-5, 231
" Jews' House," the, 69
Josso, Mr., first chairman, 49

King's Fund, the, 240, 263
Kitchens, the Hospital, 21

Lease of London Hospital, 82-3
Levy, Mr. B. W., 320
Liptrap, Mr., joint founder of Medical School, 107
Lister, Lord, 157, 158, 159, 162, 216
" Lock," the, 65
Lowther, Sir James, 63
Lückes, Miss Eva, 23, 210, 214, 244
Lupus disease, treatment of, 12-13, 230, 233, 237

INDEX

Mainwaring, Mr. Robert, 80, 83-5
Marie Celeste, Maternity Wards, 21, 22, 231
    Samaritan Society, 150
Matron, the, duties of, 243-5, 246-7
    type of, in 1742, 57-8
Mazuza, the, in Jewish wards, 21
Meares, Mr., 63
Medical School, the, 186-203
    departments of, 202-3
    endowment of, 203, 228
    foundation of, 41, 145, 186
    services of, to the Hospital, 200-1
    students of, 187-9, 197, 267-8, 279-80
Medical science, recent advance in, 219
    state of, from sixteenth to eighteenth centuries, 37-46, 51, etc.
    study of, first organized, 40
Medical Staff, present duties of, 266-7, 277-8
Motto, hospital, 148-9
Myre, Mr. William, 63

Neil, Mr. Richard, 49-50
Nightingale, Miss Florence, 208, 213, 244
Northcliffe, Lord, 235
Nurses, accommodation for, 22-3, 58, 245
    in early days, 56-9, 204-6
    Lückes' Home for, 23
    present duties of, 211
    salary of, 212
    training-school for, 210

Operating theatres, 21, 160, 162-3, 176, 216-17, 230, 262-3
Opsonic Department, 233, 238
Orthopædic Department, 17
Out-patient Department, 12-17, 66, 258, 261, 263-5, 284, etc.
    abuse of, 111-12, 130
    extension of, recent, 228-30
    origin of, 52

Pathological Laboratories, 232, 239

Payne, Dr., quoted, 37-8
Pensions, hospital, 208, 212, 245
Pharmacy Department, 16
Photographic Department, 225
Plague, epidemics of, 31-2
Poor Law Infirmaries, 271, 278, 281, 282
Potter, Mr. G., 25
Prescott Street, site of hospital transferred to, 51
Prince of Wales's Fund, 226-7
Provisions, hospital, management of, 248-52

Queen Alexandra, 150, 228-9, 233, 234, 291
    statue of, 82, 233

Raphael, Mr. Edward Louis, 135, 231
    Mr. Louis, 135, 231
Rates of London Hospital, 184
Rebuilding, recent, 227-8
Receiving-room, the, 3, 6, 7, 9, 263-4, 287, 290
Röntgen Ray Department, 14-15, 222
Rothschild Fund, 135
Rudge, Rev. Mr., 126

Sclater, Mr., 25
Scott, Canon the Rev. T., quoted, 166-8, 169-71
    Mr. Munro, 203
Secretary, the, duties of, 242, 268
Serum, treatment by, 220-1
Sisters, Nursing, 206, 207, 212, 246, 254, 260
Snee, Mr. John, senr., 25
Staff, the, advantages of being on, 279
    alterations on, 70-1
    duties of, former, 48
    election of, 241-2
    Medical, 266-7, 277-8
    quarrels among, 112, 136-8, 173, 187
    Surgical, 266-7
St. Bartholomew's Hospital, 26, 27, 28-30, 200, 271
Stern, Baroness J. de, 232
Steward, the, duties of, 248, 252
St. Thomas's Hospital, 26, 30

INDEX

Students, medical, 187-9, 197, 267-8, 279-80
Surgery, barbers, practised by, 37, 41
  pioneers of, 157
  precautions of modern, 159-60
  recent advance in, 219
Surgeons, Company of, 44
  duties of, 266-7
  Guild of, 43
  Royal College of, established, 44
Surveyor, the, duties of, 256
Sydenham, physician, 40

Tredegar House, 210, 211, 220, 244
Treves, Sir Frederick, 19, 230
Tyrnauer Baths, 15

Voluntary hospitals, 270-285
  State aid for, 282

Wards, appearance of, 17
  children's, 20
  Jewish, 21, 126, 130-5, 231
  Maternity, 21-2, 231
  separation of, advocated, 112, 158
Warren, Sir Peter, 87
Webb, Mr. Godfrey, 55
Whitechapel Road, dangers of, 80, 153
  district, 182
  original building in, 87
Worcester, Bishop of, 77-8
Worrall, Mr. Samuel, 80, 81, 82

X rays, use of, 14, 222

THE END

BILLING AND SONS, LTD., PRINTERS, GUILDFORD

SELECTIONS FROM MR. EDWARD ARNOLD'S LIST

KNOWN TO THE POLICE

By THOMAS HOLMES,
SECRETARY TO THE HOWARD ASSOCIATION.

Demy 8vo.   10s. 6d. net.

Daily Telegraph.—"This careful and well-considered utterance of a peculiarly well-situated observer of the seamy side of life and character deserves to be widely read and pondered."

Christian World.—"It is intrinsically of thrilling interest, and it is a most valuable contribution to the materials for study of the seamy side of sociology."

Daily News.—"Whether as a book of humanity, or as a plea for some urgent changes in society, it has a unique interest among the books of the year."

Saturday Review.—"Mr. Holmes is always strong; the book abounds in bold and valuable suggestions."

Liverpool Daily Post.—"Mr. Holmes' wide knowledge and generous outlook on human nature make his book as interesting as it is valuable for all who would understand the psychology of police-court society."

A PARSON IN THE AUSTRALIAN BUSH

By THE REV. C. H. S. MATTHEWS.   Illustrated by the Author.

Third Edition.   Crown 8vo.   3s. 6d. net.

Extract from a letter from the ARCHBISHOP OF CANTERBURY.—"Your breezy and inspiring book . . . will do real good in England, and, I hope, in Australia too. I thank you cordially for writing the book."

Church Times.—"Mr. Matthews deserves well of the Church for giving us a bright, suggestive, illuminating account of work in some back-block districts of Australia."

Daily Express.—"It is a novel, a diary, and a book of travel all rolled into one. It is also something more. It is a common-sense attempt to promote a better understanding between the motherland and one of her youngest children."

LONDON : EDWARD ARNOLD.

MISS LOANE'S BOOKS

THE QUEEN'S POOR
By M. LOANE
Cheaper Edition. 3s. 6d.

Morning Post.—"The author's experiences of district nursing, combined with an aptitude for observing character, have enabled her to produce a book which is instructive, pathetic, or diverting, according to the point of view, and doubtless many of her readers will be alive to all three qualities."

Church Times.—"This is a book which no one can afford to neglect who works among the very poor, or who desires to know the conditions under which they live, and the point of view from which they regard various problems of life. . . . A real and solid, albeit informal, contribution to social and economic knowledge."

NEIGHBOURS AND FRIENDS
By M. LOANE
Second Impression. 6s.

Spectator.—"Miss Loane confirms the teachings of the best thinkers in the science of exchange. Hence the superlative value of her books. But if Miss Loane's books are remarkable from the practical side, they are hardly less remarkable from the literary."

Daily Mail.—"This is a book which should on no account be missed by those interested in social questions. Miss Loane's remarkable books on the life of the poor have attracted widespread attention."

AN ENGLISHMAN'S CASTLE
By M. LOANE
Second Impression. 6s.

Spectator.—"Deserves the most earnest attention of every man who cares for his country, and who is anxious to see her people happy and independent."

Globe.—"A good deal of the interest of Miss Loane's latest volume will be found, at the present juncture, in its bearing on the probable workings of the Old-Age Pension scheme. There can hardly be a chronicler better able than Miss Loane to supply data from which any ordinarily intelligent mind can make its own deductions."

LONDON: EDWARD ARNOLD.

RA   Morris, E   W
988   A history of the London
L8L85   hospital   2d ed.
1910

Biological
& Medical

PLEASE DO NOT REMOVE
CARDS OR SLIPS FROM THIS POCKET

UNIVERSITY OF TORONTO LIBRARY

SD - #0035 - 100521 - C0 - 229/152/20 - PB - 9781334712029 - Gloss Lamination